Cover Letters

FOR

DUMMIES®

3RD EDITION

by Joyce Lain Kennedy

WILEY

Wiley Publishing, Inc.

Cover Letters For Dummies®, 3rd Edition

Published by
Wiley Publishing, Inc.
111 River St.
Hoboken, NJ 07030-5774

www.wiley.com

WILEY

About the Author

Joyce Lain Kennedy is America's first nationally syndicated careers columnist. Her two-times-weekly column, CAREERS NOW, appears in newspapers and on Web sites across the land. In her four decades of advising readers — newbies, prime-timers, and in-between — Joyce has received millions of letters inquiring about career moves and job search and has answered countless numbers of them in print.

Joyce is the author of seven career books, including *Joyce Lain Kennedy's Career Book* (McGraw-Hill), and *Electronic Job Search Revolution, Electronic Resume Revolution,* and *Hook Up, Get Hired! The Internet Job Search Revolution* (the last three published by Wiley Publishing, Inc). *Cover Letters For Dummies* is one of a trio of job market books published under Wiley's wildly popular *For Dummies* branded imprint. The others are *Resumes For Dummies* and *Job Interviews For Dummies.*

Writing from Carlsbad, California, a San Diego suburb, the country's best known careers columnist is a graduate of Washington University in St. Louis. Contact Joyce at jlk@sunfeatures.com.

About the Technical Reviewer

James M. Lemke has earned a reputation as a leader in talent strategies and processes. He is Director of Organizational Development for Opportunity International. Previously, Jim spent 15 years as a human resources consultant. His client list included: Real Networks, Southern California Metropolitan Water District, Northrop Grumman, Southwest Airlines, Jet Propulsion Laboratory, United Arab Emirates University, and the White House. Jim has held executive positions with Wachovia Bank, TRW, UCLA, Walt Disney Imagineering, and Raytheon. He resides in Buckeye, Arizona. Contact Jim at jmlemke@aol.com.

Acknowledgments

Traci Cumbay, tough project editor and easy colleague. If you like the text pages in Part III, thank TC: She made me do them over. And over. Traci's keen, creative mind is a pleasure to know and think along with.

James M. Lemke, technical reviewer of this book. I don't venture out in print without Jim's great oversight on all things job search. Jim travels the globe staffing a major humanitarian organization and, lucky for me and you, he tracks all the new trends and technology.

John S. Gill, editorial associate and computer genie. A computer science major at San Diego State University, he successfully managed a challenging database with many moving parts. Paying tribute to his masterful performance, Traci dubbed John a "God of organization."

Kelly James, administrative assistant. Kelly helped manage the endless details of collecting the job letter samples that inspire this work.

Gail Ross, literary agent–attorney and friend who continues to help me make the right publishing moves.

Lindsay Lefevere, acquisitions editor and savvy professional who makes the glue stick and the pages turn in the publishing experience.

Debbie Ellis, master career management professional who was always ready to help make this book reach for high standards.

Dr. J. Rigby Slight, who helped keep my eyesight within sight as I squinted to the finish line.

A special salute to **55 richly talented professional writers** (see this book's appendix) who contributed ground-breaking sample cover letters and other superb career management documents to this work. More thanks to **Louise Kursmark** and **Ron Krannich** for tutoring me on how to find these gifted writers.

Publisher's Acknowledgments

We're proud of this book; please send us your comments through our Dummies online registration form located at `http://dummies.custhelp.com`. For other comments, please contact our Customer Care Department within the U.S. at 877-762-2974, outside the U.S. at 317-572-3993, or fax 317-572-4002.

Some of the people who helped bring this book to market include the following:

Acquisitions, Editorial, and Media Development

Project Editor: Traci Cumbay

Acquisitions Editor: Lindsay Lefevere

Copy Editor: Traci Cumbay

Assistant Editor: Erin Calligan Mooney

Editorial Program Coordinator: Joe Niesen

Technical Editor: James M. Lemke

Senior Editorial Manager: Jennifer Ehrlich

Editorial Supervisor & Reprint Editor: Carmen Krikorian

Editorial Assistant: David Lutton

Cover Photos: © Ralph Henning / Alamy

Cartoons: Rich Tennant (`www.the5thwave.com`)

Composition Services

Project Coordinator: Katie Key

Layout and Graphics: Christine Williams

Proofreaders: Jessica Kramer, Penny Stuart

Indexer: Potomac Indexing, LLC

Special Help: John S. Gill

Publishing and Editorial for Consumer Dummies

Diane Graves Steele, Vice President and Publisher, Consumer Dummies

Kristin Ferguson-Wagstaffe, Product Development Director, Consumer Dummies

Ensley Eikenburg, Associate Publisher, Travel

Kelly Regan, Editorial Director, Travel

Publishing for Technology Dummies

Andy Cummings, Vice President and Publisher, Dummies Technology/General User

Composition Services

Gerry Fahey, Vice President of Production Services

Debbie Stailey, Director of Composition Services

Contents at a Glance

Table of Contents

Introduction

Welcome to the newly retooled *Cover Letters For Dummies,* 3rd Edition. Compared to its last incarnation a decade ago, this revision is a different creature. Times change. Communications change. Job-clinching techniques change.

Even if you're an experienced job hunter, you'll find in this book a wealth of fresh ideas about how to robustly present yourself online or on paper. And you'll be surprised by the uncommonly wide scope of content that extends far beyond classic cover letters. In a nutshell, you haven't read this book before.

As career management expert and writer Don Orlando commented upon seeing the updated manuscript — "It definitely is not the umpteenth edition of *Miss Penelope Swain's Letter Writing Guide for Young Ladies and Gentlemen,*"

No, it isn't. In the digital era, cover letters that deliver are vigorous and vivacious, assertive in asking for that all-important interview. What's more, the new-style cover letters partner with a strike-up-the-band parade of creative, hard-hitting career management documents that are anything but sleepy letters of transmittal.

Letters that have no higher ambition than merely to serve as wraps for resumes won't move your hopes and dreams where you want to go in today's fast-changing job market, one that seems to evolve with every sunrise.

In the spirit of providing something for everyone, both new-style and traditional letters are represented in the book's 126 documents. This forward-leaning edition is a milestone for cover letter books. I hope you enjoy reading it as much as I enjoyed writing it.

About This Book

The book you are about to read also marks a milestone in the 13 editions of *For Dummies* books that I've written: It's the first one crafted with a wide collaboration by professional writers in the career management industry. The 57 professionals whose work appears here are among the very best in the business. Their names appear beneath their work and in the appendix.

I'm a big believer in the Community of Intelligence, the school of "everyone's better than anyone," and so I'm immensely proud that this work features top cover letter writers whose samples show you how to know a great letter when you see one or write one.

Conventions Used in This Book

To help you navigate this book, I've established the following conventions:

- ✔ *Italic* is used for emphasis and to highlight new words or terms that are defined.
- ✔ `Monofont` is used for Web addresses.
- ✔ Sidebars, which are shaded boxes of text, consist of information that's interesting and, while not necessarily critical to your understanding of the topic, add to your learning rewards in the book.

Further, in the sample documents throughout the book, I substitute a reminder to add the relevant dates in your document with the word *date* or *dates* enclosed in editorial brackets — [dates] — instead of actual years to keep your attention focused on key career marketing concepts. Similarly, I sometimes substitute such terms as *inside address* and *salutation* to conserve page space for the heart of the message.

Also in the interest of space, I left out handwritten signatures in the letters, but including a handwritten signature on paper or a cursive signature online is an important and highly recommended practice.

Foolish Assumptions

I assume you picked up this book for at least one of the following reasons:

- ✔ You've never written a cover letter — or any type of career management document — and you'd like to see how the pros do it. You're thinking: "If they can do it, why not me? How hard can it be to string sentences together and sound smart?"
- ✔ You have written a cover letter, but it must not have lit up the sky (or else your resume was a goose) because you're still waiting to hear back — four months later.

✔ You're happily employed but worried about the economy. If you're forced to pack up and leave on short notice, you want to be ready. You discovered that your resume is a teardown, and so you're rebuilding it from the ground up but have the nagging feeling that your cover letter is a few tactics short of a strategy. You ask yourself: What is an action close? Why is a postscript a killer sales tactic? When should I be as subtle as an infomercial?

✔ You're ready to move up in rank, and you've heard buzz about some new-style letters you can write to network for leads, or to follow up after an interview to make sure an employer comes back to you with an offer. And you heard that *gasp!* some audacious soul actually wrote a letter asking for a promotion.

✔ You've aware of blazing-fast, technology-based changes in the way people and jobs hook up, and how they post their profiles on social networking Web sites. You want to be sure your career marketing messages are working with you — not against you — in the newest technology sense. You don't want the world to pass you by.

How This Book Is Organized

Being tapped for an interview or series of interviews — and being hired after that — depends on more than merely being qualified for the position you seek. Many talented people have figured that out and are improving their odds with robust cover letters and other career marketing documents. The following five parts give you an arsenal of written ammunition you can use to your advantage.

Part 1: Cover Letters and So Much More!

This part reviews the role cover letters play in a successful job search and introduces a dramatic and rich variety of other career marketing documents that may be unfamiliar to you. You also discover or refresh your memory about the impact of online social networking in communicating career-charging messages. More adventures: Almost a dozen uncommon documents, including six samples, help you make the margin of difference in a highly competitive contest for a great job.

Part II: Creating Compelling Communications

These four chapters help you jump through the writing hoops to come up with Stand Out work. This part shows how your cover letters should look and read, with suggestions on image, content, and language. You get ideas on writing great opening lines and closes that keep your hands on the wheel. You also find tips on identifying and selling your marketable skills.

Part III: Job Letters: Sample the Best

Here's the proof in the power-pudding: A collection of 86 samples — written by the best of America's and Canada's professional career management document writers — show you how to apply the strategies I describe in this book. You see job ad replies and letters for prospecting, networking, and following up after interviews. I bet you'll never look at job letters the same way again.

Part IV: Online Messages: Sample the Best

This part contains 34 more outstanding samples. These messages show you how to impress with branding statements, online profiles, and online cover notes.

Part V: The Part of Tens

In these short chapters, I give you quick bits about job letters. I offer guidance on avoiding unnecessary mistakes and tips on how to score at the top of the class when you're writing online profiles.

Appendix

Here you find a directory of the professional writers whose work appears in this book. Following the directory, I explain what the initials after their names mean, as well as recognize the five professional cover letter and resume writers' organizations whose members contributed to this work.

Icons Used in This Book

For Dummies signature icons are the little round pictures you see in the margins of the book. I use them to laser-guide your attention to key bits of information. Here's a list of the icons you find in this book and what they mean.

This icon directs your full attention to compelling messages that make you stand out from the crowd.

Advice and information that can spark a difference in the outcome of your career message are flagged with this icon.

Some points in these pages are so useful that I hope you keep them in mind as you read. I make a big deal out of these ideas with this icon.

No move or technique achieves the job letter-interview connection every single time. This icon reminds you to think through an issue and try to make the best choice for your situation.

Watch out for deep waters filled with things that bite. This icon signals there could be trouble ahead if you don't make a good decision.

Where to Go from Here

Every author wishes you would start at the beginning and savor every word in lock step until you reach the end of the book. In real life, where you start depends upon your current needs:

- When you've just spotted an advertised job opening you want, immediately read Chapters 1, 4, 5, 6, and 8.

- When you want to do most of your searching online, hit your bull's eye with Chapters 1, 2, 13, 14, and 16.

- When you're at the starting gate and have a couple of weeks to learn your way around career management documents, grant the author's wishes and read this book cover to cover. As I said in *Job Interviews For Dummies,* 3rd Edition, practice recommended strategies, tactics, and techniques. "After you master the information in these pages, you own a special kind of insurance policy that pays off for as long as you want to work."

Part I
Cover Letters and So Much More!

The 5th Wave   By Rich Tennant

"The magazine didn't hire me, but they are paying me $50 to print my cover letter on their joke page."

In this part . . .

Are your cover letters puny pages that do nothing but sit atop your resume or are they bringing full-force strength to a well-crafted marketing message? In this part, you find out how a cover letter can bring the right kind of attention your way. And there isn't just one way to go about it, so this part runs down the many kinds of messages that fit the cover letter bill, including the all-important online communiqué.

Chapter 1

News Flash: Cover Letters Are Grown Up and Have Kids

In This Chapter

▶ Busting unemployment with revolutionary letter power

▶ Surveying the robust family of career management documents

▶ Using cover letters to accomplish specific purposes

▶ Customizing compelling messages for each job you want

▶ Staying clear of spam filters

*O*nce upon a job-hunting time long ago, the term *cover letters* brought to mind drab documents like this one:

> *Dear Sir/Madam,*
>
> *Please accept this letter and resume for the Payroll Manager position as referenced in the Louisiana Times, Nov. 5. My work history and educational background make me an outstanding candidate. I am available for an interview at your earliest convenience. Thank you.*

That style of transmittal letter has become a museum piece.

In this century's brave new world of hypercompetitive job searches, cover letters have not only been reinvented, they've spawned a family of *career management documents* like these:

✔ Intrigue-inducing e-mail cover notes

✔ Deal-closing thank-you letters

✔ Interest-reviving follow-up messages

✔ Star-power bios and branding statements

✔ Image-brightening reference blurbs

✔ Qualifications-matching candidate checklists

  ✔ Humanizing audio and video bites in profiles
  ✔ Eye-popping accomplishment sheets

And there's much more in the new cover letter family. All together, today's family of career management documents — which I also call *job letters* — delivers a spectacular array of self-marketing tools for people who want to be seen, noticed, and hired for the best jobs. That's you, isn't it?

A New Age of Self-Promotion Is Here!

Looking for and landing the job you want is always a challenge, especially in uncertain times. But — lucky you — in one important way, your timing hits the jackpot!

You're in the right century at the right time with the right tools to better manage your career than any generation before.

By seizing the opportunity to capitalize on 21st-century opportunities, you can

  ✔ Change to creative and high-impact letters that bring interviews
  ✔ Switch to gutsy but polite letters that generate hires
  ✔ Shift to persuasive and content-rich letters that position you to win career rewards that matter to you

You live in nothing less than a *revolutionary age for career self-promotion*. How did you get so lucky? This empowering new age is upon us for two main reasons:

  ✔ **Society's changing expectations in message style.** In this era of mass-marketing and media overload, people are so accustomed to vivid, sparkling advertising and creative, clever marketing in every corner of their lives that they no longer pay much attention to feeble, uninteresting messages from job seekers who merely go through the motions. The family of new-style letters is hard to ignore in an atmosphere where HDTV gets attention, but black-and-white TV is ho-hum.

    The new-style letters vary in approach from elegant to elementary, but their missions are the same — picking up the cue from contemporary advertising and marketing, all the best ones are *sales letters*.

  ✔ **Emergence of a technology-rich environment.** In previous centuries, cover letters were joined at the hip with the post office. In this century, the Internet's vast and powerful e-mail and social networking services supply unprecedentedly wide vistas to carry new-style messages.

For clarity, I pause to emphasize that despite the loosening of collars in the new wave of job letters, conservatively styled cover letters aren't dead. They continue to be preferred in certain buttoned-down industries, such as banking, medicine, and government service. Why? Because they're persuasively and expertly written to satisfy the tastes of executives in those industries. (See for yourself the conservatively styled cover letters that appear in Parts 3 and 4.)

As creativity and technology turn new pages in recruiting circles, the cover letter has morphed into an extended family of hard-hitting messages that influence how the working world sees you and treats you.

Cover Letters Are Alive and Sell

Considering our digital world in which millions of people send their resumes off to online boarding schools without cover letter guardians, you may ask whether the cover letter model (new- or old-style) continues to lead the parade of written job docs. More bluntly, are cover letters still valuable?

The answer is a resounding *yes!* These resume sidekicks pack far too much firepower to be left on the sideline, according to two 2008 surveys:

✓ You leave interviews on the table when you skip cover letters: so concluded a survey I developed with talent selection expert Alise Cortez, PhD. Three-fifths (60 percent) of a cross-section of 83 American employers, human resource specialists, and recruiters sampled say they read cover letters always, often, or sometimes. Two-fifths (40 percent) read resumes rarely or never. Dr. Cortez is a founding partner of ImprovedExperience. com, a third-party research firm headquartered in Ft. Lauderdale, Florida, that specializes in surveys for the human resource industry.

✓ Big company managers overwhelmingly prefer their resumes with cover letters. A poll of 150 executives in major U.S. companies reveals that a whopping 86 percent rate cover letters as valuable, with only 14 percent calling cover letters not valuable. Moreover, 80 percent of polled executives say cover letters accompany resumes they receive electronically. The poll was developed by OfficeTeam, a leading staffing company headquartered in Menlo Park, California.

In summing up widely held opinion among people in the employment business, OfficeTeam executive director Dave Willmer explains why your resume should never leave home without a cover letter at its side:

Submitting a resume without a cover letter is like not shaking hands when meeting someone for the first time. Those who aren't including cover letters with their resumes are missing an opportunity to make a good first impression and set themselves apart from other job applicants.

Will your cover letter save the day?

When a rookie recruiter, who hasn't yet been taught the finer points of analyzing data-packed resumes, doesn't know what to make of yours but doesn't want the boss to know that he or she doesn't know, your resume's new address can be the reject pile.

A cover letter treatment is the recommended therapy to save your resume from certain candidate death merely because a rookie can't measure its value. Why? Letters are easier to analyze than resumes. The rookie reads the letter and immediately knows what you bring to the table. Wanting to look like a savvy judge of talent, the rookie recruiter is now likely to pass your package of letter and resume up the line to a senior recruiter who does know how to evaluate resumes and who can extend interview invitations.

The takeaway: Attaching a cover letter that zings with your qualifications for the job can keep your resume (and job hopes) alive.

A Stand Out cover letter does much more than keep your resume warm during its long trip to a hiring manager. Cover letters done right can step up and accomplish a number of important getting-you-noticed purposes, which the following sections outline.

Looking good at first light

Use a cover letter to immediately position yourself as a most valuable person. First impressions are very hard to change. And your cover letter often is an employer's first inkling that you're on the planet and for hire. You can use your cover letter to show yourself to be alert and attentive by editing out all the typo goofs for which your high school English teacher would have given you a big fat F.

Targeting the employer's needs

The resume focuses on you and the past. The cover letter focuses on the employer and the future. Tell the hiring professional what you can do to benefit the organization in the future.

Failure to understand this simple principle is a critical mistake, advises career grand master John Lucht, CEO of RiteSite.com, a respected Web site for professionals seeking jobs at six figures and up. Lucht explains:

Lots of people figure that the cover letter is about them and what they want. Wrong! It should be about what the employer wants that they provide. Dump the 'I'm looking for' — both the attitude and the words. Instead say, 'Do you need?' And make the 'need' one that you — as your attached resume clearly spells out — are the ideal person to fill.

Showcasing your attractive personality

Your cover letter is a chance to bring more personality to your application than a resume can carry. It suggests, even subliminally, whether you're open to new ideas, results driven, energetic, a people person, cheerful, agreeable, and cooperative, to name but a few premium employer-pleasing qualities.

Most chief executives say that employee turnover is one of their biggest headaches. Personality is a key ingredient (along with knowledge and skill) in being a good fit for a job, which is why some employers give personality tests to candidates. Your cover letter offers early clues to your personality fit for the job.

Closing gaps in your work record

Your cover letter is the ideal vehicle to explain — on your terms — any disruption in your work history. The basic strategy explains the gap as a positive achievement: You studied further, gained business-related transferrable skills while raising children, served in the military, undertook volunteer activities, moved to a new location for a good reason, or resolved a non-recurring health problem.

When your resume has time holes in it and you don't explain how you productively filled the time and kept your skills current, yoking your past and your future is very difficult. In that case, entry-level offers are the most likely outcome. (Followed closely by no offers.)

Highlighting your skills and accomplishments

Your cover letter is the perfect place to emphasize the high-interest factors that whet a hiring authority's interest in knowing more.

This is your chance to connect the dots for hiring authorities and recruiters, counsels Lynne Sarikas, director of the MBA career center at Northeastern University's College of Business Administration:

> *Most likely you have not done this exact job in this exact industry before and don't assume they will figure out how your experience is transferable. Show them how you meet their specific needs and the unique value you bring to the table.*

By the way, don't sabotage this purpose by merely repeating your resume using different words and mixing them up a bit. That's a time waster, and you don't want to be thought of as one of those.

Demonstrating your communication skills

Every survey of employers' most-wanted skills seems to include the ability to communicate well. By a strange coincidence, almost every professional-level job seeker claims the ability to communicate well — without offering proof.

An impeccable and robust cover letter provides that proof. It's your chance to show that you have the chops to communicate clearly, that you're downright articulate.

Taking the wheel

An action close on a Stand Out cover letter tells the recipient that you'll proactively call to set up an interview. It establishes that you have initiative and aren't one to sit around and wait for interview manna to fall in your lap.

Of course, an action close isn't always possible in a digital exchange when you don't know to whom you're applying. Or when you don't know who's in charge of a task force selection committee. In situations where you can't take the interview initiative, maintain your image of a "person of action" by encouraging the hiring authority to quickly contact you.

Meet the Letters Family

Like all the best families, the job letter clan has its share of first and second cousins and an occasional odd uncle. The following sections show you how the relatives line up.

Job ad reply letter

The head of the letters family is the category of cover letters written in reaction to a published job opening in print or online. Responding to published job openings is the most common job search letter activity. Pay the job ad reply letter the courtesy of customizing it to point out how you match the requirements of the position it addresses.

You find everything you want to know about writing job ad reply letters in Chapter 8.

Prospecting letter

Sent selectively to a relatively small number of potential employers with whom you have some sort of connection (same industry, personal meeting, affinity group), these self-marketing, direct-mail messages are similar to broadcast letters and may overlap with networking letters. Call them prospecting, broadcast, or networking letters: Whatever you call them, you need them. I dissect and illustrate prospecting letters in Chapter 9.

Broadcast letter

A type of self-marketing direct mail, the biggest differences between broadcast and prospecting letters are scale and relationships. You send broadcast letters to big numbers of potential employers with whom the sender has virtually no connection. In fact, job seekers often use commercial mailing lists to develop their broadcast letter address book. True believers in the pay-off for broadcast letters insist that their secret to success is the distribution by postal mail or online of large numbers of enticing letters ("a numbers game"), with persistent follow-up by phone or e-mail. Find out more in Chapter 9.

Networking letter

Most networking letters ask for job leads, not for job interviews. They're addressed to human networks, requesting that members respond by phone, e-mail or Twitter. (Twitter is a Web site and service that lets users send short text messages from their cell phones to a group of individuals.) Networking letters typically reach out to those with whom you have some kind of affinity — fellow alumni, members of your church, civic organization, or buddy group, and so on. Additionally, you may send a networking letter for other reasons — to a hiring authority with whom you've recently met, for example; in such situations, you *do* ask for a job interview. Find networking letters in Chapter 10.

Resume letter

An odd uncle in the letters family, this direct postal or online mail document doesn't contain a separate resume per se. (However, you may attach a separate accomplishment sheet.) A storytelling approach weaves the facts of your work history into a narrative describing your objective. A resume letter is a good choice when your fundamental qualifications are sound but you need to gloss over gaps or other problems. When interestingly written, the letter pulls in readers because everyone likes a good story well told. A resume letter can be categorized as a subset of a broadcast or prospecting letter. Find samples in Chapter 11.

Job fair cover letter

Deciding in advance which companies you want to target at a job fair enables you to write attention-getting cover letters to leave with your resume at the land booth or send online to a virtual job fair. View a job fair sample letter in Chapter 9.

Try a twist by pairing a cover letter with an accomplishment sheet instead of a resume; see Chapter 11.

The vast majority of fair visitors don't make the extra research effort and instead just hand over generic documents, which gives you a huge opportunity to Stand Out from the crowd.

Thank-you letter

Think of a letter written ostensively to thank a hiring authority for an interview as what it really should be: another turn at bat to drive home your winning run, not merely an extension of your mother's etiquette lessons to show your good manners. Focus on facts and comments that advance your candidacy for selection. Chapter 12 contains chapter and verse on thank-you letters and includes great samples, as well.

Follow-up letter

Also an after-interview communication, a follow-up letter is designed to spur decision action or even serve as a comeback effort to revive your candidacy after a period of thundering silence from the employer. Chapter 12 hosts super follow-up letters.

Professional branding statement

How will prospective employers, clients, and customers perceive you professionally — as Sam Slacker or Sam Superstar? As Betty Boob or Betty Best? That's what personal branding is all about — your image and your reputation. What you deliver for the money, you expect to be paid. Chapter 13 is home base for crafting professional branding statements based on accomplishments and specializations that make you memorable in the job chase or on the consulting scene.

You can use a professional branding statement in letters, online profiles, accomplishment sheets, resumes, interviews, blog biographies, and elevator speeches. Even if you never get around to weaving a branding statement into a document, the mere act of writing one is a great way to concentrate your mind on what you're selling.

Online profile

Growing more popular by the minute, this second cousin in the job letters family ranges from short and sweet (executive bio, described in Chapter 13) to a Yao-Ming-tall Web portfolio stuffed with links — photos, blogs, vlogs (video blogs), lists of publications, certifications, licenses, audio or video sound bites, and more. You name it, online profiles have it! Chapter 13 is your destination for online profiles.

How important are the quality of your online profile and other mentions of concern about you on social networking sites? *Very!* To cite a single but typical late 2008 survey of 3,169 hiring managers by online job site CareerBuilder.com, 22 percent screened potential staff members by using social networking profiles. This figure was up from 11 percent just two years earlier. An additional 9 percent said they plan to start using online profiles. In sum, almost a third of recruiting and staffing professionals are using or plan to use social networking sites to check up on potential hires.

About a third of hiring managers said that they had dismissed a candidate after what they discovered on social networking sites. Biggest offenses: information posted about drinking or using drugs, provocative subjects, or inappropriate photographs. More turnoffs: poor communication skills, lying about qualifications, candidates using discriminatory remarks related to race, gender or religion, and an unprofessional screen name.

The good news is that the survey found that 24 percent of hiring managers said that they found content on social network pages helped seal their decisions to hire candidates.

E-mail cover note

Cover notes, which you find aplenty in Chapter 14, are kid brothers and sisters to cover letters. They're short and to the point. Typically, you send them in text in the body of an e-mail to introduce your attached resume, which usually is presented as an MS Word or PDF document.

Pulling Out the Stops with Special Marketing Messages

One of America's iconic comedians, the late George Burns, told audiences how he defined happiness. "Happiness," Burns said, "is having a large, loving, caring, close-knit family in another city."

That quip works as a metaphor for an elite branch of career management documents. The documents in this group, described in Chapter 3, may as well be in another city because they come out only for special occasions, which are:

- ✔ When the job you want is master of the universe and you're thinking "fat chance that will happen"
- ✔ When the job is exactly what you hope to find, and you can't bear the thought of it slipping through your hands
- ✔ When the job is madly desired by so many competitors that you need to do something really special that makes you Stand Out

Special marketing messages generally are extra, load-bearing documents you take along to interviews, leaving them behind to remind decision-makers of your worthiness. Turn to Chapter 3 to find out what I'm talking about.

Sing, Cover Letter, Sing

Call upon your inner muse before desperately resorting to sending out a skimpy, generic cover letter that brings you neither glory nor notice. Pledge to write cover letters that employers actually read; inspire intrigue by creatively using the right words and sending the right facts. Although Part II contains this book's mother lode of writing advice, here's a digest of tips to paste on your copyholder.

Customize and use names

Is your job search stalling after you submit a cover letter and resume package but before you're offered an interview? If that's your experience, why keep repeating failure?

Realize that, like the dearly departed all-purpose resume, the era of the generic cover letter is gone. Switch to a best practice of customizing each cover letter you send — not only in content, but addressed to the specific hiring manager instead of the threadbare approach of "Dear Employer " or "Dear Sir/Madam."

When you can't discover the hiring manager's name (by calling the company or through research), you're stuck with using a generalized introduction that's better than nothing but not as effective as "Dear Ms. Carmel," or "Dear Mr. Alvarez."

Speak the right language

Consider the recipient of your information. If the organization is conservative and traditional, keep the presentation of your information conservative and traditional. By contrast, when the targeted organization is creative and entrepreneurial, the addition of a splash of gifted words or a flourish in design tempts the doorkeeper to let you in.

I explain in Chapter 6 that the opening of your letter has to hook the reader, selling him or her on your abilities. One of many devices employed to hook readers is the use of a quotation. But here's the danger: Don't risk being perceived as a poet without a point by leading off with a nice but unrelated quotation that goes nowhere. Connect inspirational quotations with your strengths, or skip the quotation.

You can take more chances in approach and language when you really know your audience. To illustrate that principal, career coach Don Orlando in Montgomery, Alabama, passed along a high-risk real letter he wrote some years ago for a client who wanted to become chief of staff to a U.S. senator. She used her network to gain understanding of the senator's personality and preferred standard operating procedures. Discovering that he was known for giving curt answers, had a short fuse, and preferred take-charge staffers, here's the letter Orlando wrote for her:

Your job search for a chief of staff is over. Please tell your secretary to expect my call at 10:30 EDT, Monday, 28 July, to arrange an interview. I will need twelve minutes of your time on the day that is best for you.

During that short meeting, if I cannot convince you that I can arm you with bulletproof information that moves your agendas forward among all your constituencies, I will leave your office at once.

But if I can, I will start work the following Monday.

She was hired.

State the reason you're writing

Always tell the reader why you're writing, but be tactical about it. To reply to an advertised job, name the position title and where you saw the ad, but don't squander valuable real estate doing so in the opening paragraph. Instead, accomplish the same thing by positioning that information in the upper right-hand corner in the subject line "regarding" space. Other ways to handle the reason you're writing are presented in samples throughout this work.

Explain why you're a top candidate

Your basic message should be: "Here are examples of work I've done and accomplishments I've achieved that match what you're looking for." Because you research the company online, you're able to show why your skills and competencies are right for the job and can benefit the company. You explain any gaps in a positive way.

Accomplishments are job-offer magnets. Employers hire for results, not responsibilities. And they like numbers — percentages, dollar amounts, or other key measures wherever possible to quantify achievements and accomplishments.

Tell them why you admire them

You needn't gush with insincere praise when explaining why you'd like to work for a company, but intelligent compliments are a staple of effective cover letters. You won't be believable unless you get a line on the company before writing your letter. Why bother? Because your appreciation of the workplace where he or she toils makes the hiring manager feel important.

Declare what's next

In closing your letter, reprise your enthusiasm, confirm your desire for an interview, and state what the next step will be. Preferably, you use an action close, telling the recipient that you will follow up and when that will happen. In some instances, you will have to wait for them to contact you. Find out all about the action close in Chapter 6.

Read and reread

Go beyond using your computer's spell checker tool to review your job letters for typos and grammatical errors. Ask a friend or mentor to look over your letters as a backstop. Your words are going out into the hiring world as your only representative. If they don't go out in first-rate order, you never get to show off your stuff in person. Chapters 4 and 5 give you writing tips that enable you to write with the skills of a grammar snoot without actually having to be one.

Be a savvy submitter

When you plan to send your application package of cover letter and resume online, bear in mind the advice I received from Susan P. Joyce, editor and Webmaster of Job-Hunt.Org.

Spam filters have been called into service seemingly everywhere because spam messages now comprise an estimated 78 percent of all e-mail received. That means that up to 10 percent of your messages won't make it through to the intended recipient. Susan Joyce explains how to up your odds:

- ✔ **Be very careful with the message subject.** Be precise and concise, while avoiding the "unsafe" words below. When you're responding to a specific posting, the job title is the safest, clearest, and most helpful subject for the recipient.

  Stay away from words like *free, testing, money, urgent, payment,* and *investing.* Look at the spam messages you get and avoid their terminology and methods. Find synonyms or use a completely different approach to the subject.

  Avoid using all caps and punctuation, particularly exclamation points and dollar signs.

- ✔ **Watch the words you use in the body of your message.** Spam filters check the bodies of messages as well the subjects, so similar problems apply.

- ✔ **Know that you are usually safest using unformatted text, rather than rich text or HTML.** If you do use formatted text, be wary of using colored text and backgrounds, and avoid including fancy technology (Flash or other animation) unless the technology is related to a job requirement.

- ✔ **For a really important message, you can add a line that requests confirmation of receipt.** When confirmation doesn't come through, you can follow up. This can be a good excuse to call.

A Different Kind of Cover Letter Book

As this first chapter explains, career management docs are becoming important success drivers in a digital era. Cover letters now head up an entire family of new-style job letters, online profiles, and amazing self-marketing creations you can't afford to ignore. Visit the family reunion in the following pages, illustrated by 126 great new samples from professional cover letter writers.

Keeping everything straight

When you send resumes and cover letters in an MS Word document, send them to yourself first to be sure that they survive their electronic journey formatted the way they left home. You may find that some portions of the text slip and slide around, winding up in the strangest places. Here's an easy solution: Send each Word doc as a PDF (portable document format) attachment. PDFs arrive looking identical to the way you send them. You can quickly convert any document into a PDF for free at www.pdf95.com.

Chapter 2

Creating Images Online for Now and Tomorrow

Ru open 2 nu ideas? If so, pay attention to this whack-upside-the-head jolt: Your online image is becoming as important as the customized cover letters and resumes you send in more familiar kinds of employment explorations.

Just as computers changed the rules of job search 15 years ago, Web 2.0 services are becoming job-pantry staples for finding employment and managing careers. And — good news! — many of the letters and other career management documents you see in this book lend themselves perfectly to dealing with your online image and job moves.

Hop onto news of the specifics at a glance.

Web 2.0: A New Online Jobscape

In the new Web 2.0 world of interactive Internet, you may not be certain who's who and what's what in the new social tools. (*Social* in this usage means collaboration with others to achieve a goal.) Here's a brief rundown to help you make sense of a fast-forward competitive job market:

✔ **Blog:** Originally created as Web-based journals written by one or more writers. Today's sophisticated versions read like mainstream media stories and columns. You can just read blogs and move on or you can post your comments for others to see. Frequencies of a blog's publication vary from daily to weekly to occasional.

Recruiters sometimes write blogs that job seekers can follow to pick up employment-opportunity intelligence. Additionally, recruiters may canvass blog writers for names of potential candidates who are tops in a field. Blog writers themselves may be experts in a field and become the object of a recruiter's professional affections.

A *vlog* is a blog that contains video content. A small but growing section of the *blogosphere* devoted to vlogs is called the *vlogosphere*.

✔ **Instant messaging (IM):** Real-time communication between two or more people. Job seekers IM for leads and company research with people on their buddy lists, and sometimes with recruiters. You can also receive new job postings by IM.

✔ **Podcast:** An audio message (file) sent over the Internet. Podcasts can be downloaded and played on portable media devices (iPhone or BlackBerry) anytime in any place. Typically, a podcast is sent from employer to candidate, not the other way around.

✔ **RSS (Real Simple Syndication):** Subscribers to these services, which are usually free in employment uses, receive content updates when available from selected Web sites. The RSS job agent feature is especially useful to job seekers wanting to discover new job openings that match the job seekers' criteria.

✔ **Search engine:** Retrieves information — including company research and personnel — sought by specific search terms. A few general search engine examples are Google, Yahoo! And Ask.com.

Job search engine (also called *vertical job search engine* or *aggregator*): Collects millions of job listings from thousands of job boards, newspapers, company Web sites, and other resources, making the search for jobs much easier for job hunters. A few job search engine examples are Indeed.com, SimplyHired.com, and GetTheJob.com.

✔ **SEO (Search Engine Optimization):** Technical and strategic maneuvers that increase the traffic driven by search engines to a Web site. Recruiters and employers use SEO to deliver job seekers to their Web sites. And technology-wise job seekers call upon SEO to drive traffic to their own Web sites, hoping to bring favorable mentions of themselves to page 1 or high on page 2.

Additionally, job seekers use SEO techniques as a tool to clean up stains on their digital dignity. In stain removal, the core SEO idea is the crowding out bad news with good news, a process described in books and online articles. Find details on how to repair a stained online image by searching the Web for "Internet defamation."

✔ **Social media:** An umbrella term for Web-based technology where the media can be easily shared by affinity groups; covers such technology as blogs, podcasts, video, RSS, and photo-sharing. Illustrations of those with varying degrees of career management significance include LinkedIn, YouTube, MySpace, Facebook, Ning, and Technorati.

✔ **Social network services:** Web-based services that give users a way to find people with similar interests. The services connect users by enabling them to join online communities and interact directly with each other. Some of the interactivity focuses on job search and recruiting. The services provide different methods for interaction, including discussion groups, messaging, e-mail, and commentary on blogs. The social media noted in the previous bullet point also are examples of social network services.

The difference between social media and social networking is *observation* and *interaction*. Social media enables social networking. That is, social media can exist without social networking, but social networking can't exist without social media. Example: When a recruiter views an online profile posted on a professional social media Web site such as LinkedIn, the recruiter is *observing*. But when the recruiter is motivated to contact a person who is observed, the recruiter is *interacting*.

While all the tools described above may play a role in your travels to employment, social networks are the focal point of this chapter.

The Great Connecting: Online Networking Services

Connect. Communicate. Collaborate. Find jobs. Hire employees. All these good things are ascribed to the rising phenomenon of online professional social networking services, which some very smart people say is well on its way to changing the face of recruiting in the United States and other developed nations.

As an example of what experts are saying, globally recognized human capital guru Kevin Wheeler recently advised recruiters on the recruiting Web site www. ere.net that both a personal and a corporate presence on a social network (such as Facebook or MySpace) is a top tool for success. Wheeler also ranks the participation in *professional* online networks (such as LinkedIn) as being right up at the top of essential tools that link business people and careerists who know each other together in a Web of interconnections.

First, a little background: Social networking services originally became popular in 2002 as fun things to do among teenagers and those in their 20s and 30s. MySpace and Facebook were the big winners. With LinkedIn's 2005 entry into the marketplace, the social networking services became business things to do. Facebook and MySpace now encourage professionals in business, as well as fun seekers in their original base, to post online profiles. But LinkedIn has captured the prestige and numbers in the professional and business market.

Valued at more than $1 billion, LinkedIn continues to expand its purpose-driven franchise. In 2008, CNBC and LinkedIn sealed an alliance, in effect combining their business audiences. The deal followed an alliance months earlier between LinkedIn and *The New York Times*. Other newspapers such as the *Chicago Sun-Times* are using social networking to offer reader forums, blogs, and communities.

Why the race to pair up old and new media? Traditional content owners intend to hang on to their audiences and advertisers as they move to new media environments. Online social firms need to keep their sites compelling with relevant content. It looks as though the alliance between old and new media will continue to grow like Jack's Beanstalk.

Downsides to social networking

Online networking clearly is too gigantic a sea change to be ignored in an increasingly hypercompetitive market for the economy's best jobs, but I'm not saying that everything is peachy in online networking land. Here are some of the concerns that I see and hear expressed by networkers and critics:

- **Networking fatigue.** Some networkers have grown tired of what once was novel. The essential problem may be that they sign up for every new networking site in sight, and then find they're spending too much time keeping up with their sign-ups.

- **User frustration.** *Aggregating* means combining and forming a whole; Web sites as Indeed.com and SimplyHired.com aggregate content to make it easy for job hunters to search for specific advertised jobs. Although a host of start-ups are aggregating social networking profiles, online videos, and more, no dominant aggregator has yet appeared for social networking.

  As countless social networks continue to pop up — especially those with a niche focus — the environment has become splintered and its bounty hard to harvest.

  To illustrate, an anonymous but obviously veteran networker on a reader forum laments the usage dilemma: "I have 225 first-degree connections, 17,200 second-degree connections, and 1.7 million third-degree connections. By the numbers, this is a healthy network. But what do I do with it?"

Reconnoitering resources

Shameless disclosure: Why do I mention only the biggies in this chapter? I do so to keep my sanity, as the virtual vendor world seems to grow by the minute. In the past 15 years I've observed virtual recruiting firms launch, hype, merge, acquire, fail, rebrand, and switch focus faster than most of us can track. That's why I stick with the main online players, who are less likely than start-ups to bite the dust, or to quickly revamp their mission the day after this book is published. I do list a number of leading social networking services in Chapter 13, and I daily wish each of them good health and long life.

But I feel your pain and understand that you need more specifics to tackle social networking in all its glory — but that's a different book. So try the following suggestions:

✔ If the history and the current composition of the social networking industry are important to you, jump on Wikipedia to search for Social Networking Services and List of Social Networking Websites.

✔ To review a list of current recruiting vendors with succinct descriptions of the services each offers, visit `directory.ere.net`.

✔ For an easy guide to whistling while you're working your way through social networking know-how, refer to a how-to book, *Seven Days to Online Networking* by Ellen Sautter and Diane Crompton (2008, JIST Works).

✔ Grab a copy of Alison Doyle's *Internet Your Way to a New Job: How to Really Find a Job Online* (2008, HappyAbout.com).

✔ Find many niche social networks with a search engine, such as FindASocialNetwork, `www.findasocialnetwork.com`. For search terms, use your industry, career field, geographic location, or just the word *jobs*.

✔ **Eternal digital billboards.** Like resumes, online profiles (See Chapters 13 and 16) can be like the guest who came to dinner and stayed and stayed and stayed. Documents love it out there in cyberspace.

Enshrined in time, resumes and profiles can pigeonhole a job seeker, putting the seeker into a particular category that may be too rigid. Examples: If a profile pigeonholes Josh as a photographer, he risks being overlooked for his work as a sculptor and painter. If a resume pigeonholes Jeanine as a public accountant, she risks being overlooked as a candidate for a senior internal accountant position. Candidates can't be sure that sophisticated online research does not reveal chameleon-like presentations.

So why not just try to say you're a one-person-band in your online profile or resume? Except for micro-sized companies, employers usually prefer to hire a specialist, not a jack of all trades.

Three ways to win in social networking

As job seekers migrate to online profiles, how can you be sure that your wild party or frat days don't put your online professional person in the dumpster? By bearing these tips in mind.

✔ **Check yourself out.** Google yourself periodically to see what's being said about you on the Internet. If there's a problem, see SEO tips earlier in this chapter.

✔ **Make circumspect comments.** Don't let it all hang out about what you did last night or make statements such as "My boss is a boob" or "We should call in sick tomorrow and hit the beach."

✔ **Skip snippy talk.** You take your reputation in your hands when you blog barbed or negative observations about employers and specific people, unless you are in the blogging business as a political commentator or entertainment critic. Otherwise, put an online smile on your face.

✔ **Employers' legal risks.** Employers fear legal exposure if, prior to meeting a candidate in person, they uncover information about the candidate's characteristics that can lead to discrimination in hiring — such as gender, age, sexual orientation, or religious beliefs. Even when a hiring decision is made without bias, the employer may have to defend the non-hiring choice to the Equal Employment Opportunity Commission, or in a court of law.

✔ **Recruiters' time management woes.** Recruiters may source (find) candidates themselves or subcontract the work to professional sourcers. Scouring social networking sites, blogs, and other Web 2.0 resources eats up enormous amounts of time.

A secret garden of informal references

Although your online presence — including an online profile — increases your visibility to headhunters out shopping, it can also squash your chances of getting the job.

Formal reference checks are made just before or just after a job offer. But a kind of pre-reference check that can be called "informal reference checking" appears to be a growing practice.

Here's what happens: Recruiters and hiring managers turn to Google or another search engine to get a heads-up on potential candidates and then move to such social networking sites as LinkedIn, Facebook, and VisualCV. When they like what they see, the headhunters decide whether an individual is worth talking to.

Even if the writings and photos you posted when you were young and foolish are beyond professional criticism, remember the popularly held beliefs that "birds of a feather flock together" or "a man is known by the company he keeps." Because your network is a reflection of you, be selective in keeping your network filled with individuals you'd be proud to stand next to. Use good judgment in "friending" others and the groups you join. In a time of informal references, you want your online presence to be empowering, not handicapping.

Start Spinning Your Web

No one method of search has a lock on finding attractive employment. Yes, you can still find a good job without turning on a computer, or wearing out your thumb texting or twittering on wireless phones with nano-sized keys that you can barely read. At least for now you can, and if you're 60 or older, you probably can outrun the relentless shift to technology-driven recruiting and job search.

But otherwise, if you're over 40 but younger than 60, think twice before putting on your Andy Rooney mask and welding yourself to a metaphorical manual typewriter. In challenging economic times, merely being good at your job may not be enough.

Management seems always to be on the lookout for ways to cut costs, including labor costs. If the budget-whacking agenda doesn't take hiring for your job beyond your borders, it may take it domestically to younger workers who'll toil for less pay than older-and-wiser individuals.

 Get an edge by making sure you know how to use social networking technology — even if you have to take a class in it — and practice writing Stand Out career management messages that show you can make or save money for an employer.

P.S. As we stand between technologies and generations in these changing times, this book's technical reviewer, Jim Lemke, wants me to remind you not to forget to integrate multiple approaches to produce a truly effective job-search strategy. Use everything from newspapers and job boards to traditional networking and job fairs, to headhunters and social networking sites. Consider yourself reminded.

Audio sound bites in your profile

A Stand Out online profile never sleeps.

A routine online profile sleeps with the fishes.

Help your profile stay wide awake and totally dry by including an audio bite. Keep it short — perhaps 15 to 20 seconds. For a topic, you can give your branding statement — who you are and what you bring to an employer's table. (See sample branding statements in Chapter 13.)

You can also insert a video bite into your profile, but an audio bite is easier to do well and is likely to be more acceptable to employers for several reasons, including these two:

✔ Employers are reluctant to accept video resumes for fear of bias claims from job seekers based on such visuals as age, ethnicity, or disability. Their reluctance presumably extends to short online profile video bites. With the exception of performing arts and other jobs where looks matter for business reasons, cautious employers don't want to see what you look like in a video or even in a photo until you've walked in the door for your interview. The law isn't settled yet about how visuals on social networking sites will be evaluated for potential bias.

✔ Most people aren't great at public speaking, and being in front of a camera is even harder. You may do yourself more harm than good if you're not an accomplished presenter.

But if you'd like to enliven your online video with a dash of audio or video but are a little shaky on the technical side, here's the step-by-step drill, according to reviewer Jim Lemke:

1. **Determine the type of audio or video file you must upload to the host site.**

   The host site, not you, decides what it will accept. LinkedIn, for example, allows you to import to your profile only a JPG, BMP, or PNC file. But other profile hosting sites allow you to upload a WMV or Mac format video, or a WMA or MP3 or MP4 audio file. Huh?

   If you insist on knowing more — or anything at all — about the above files, look them up in Webopedia (www.webopedia.com).

2. **To find the type of file the host site will accept, look on the site's profile edit page, or a subsequent page.**

   When you're not sure what's acceptable, you can enter *audio* or *video* in the host's content search box or help screen.

3. **Still puzzled? Befriend a geek.**

Chapter 3

Special Marketing Messages Outrun Rivals

....

In This Chapter

▶ Discovering new-style career marketing documents

▶ Discovering how to put special docs to work for you

▶ Sampling distinctive messages to remember and build on

....

As an adequate candidate, you get balcony privileges to watch the game. As a good candidate, you earn a chair at the interview table. As a Stand Out candidate, you deal a winning hand and collect the pot.

Are you interested in going all out to become a Stand Out winner? Don't miss a word of this chapter even if your answer is filled with clap your hands enthusiasm — "Yes, I'll do whatever it takes, even slave all day over a hot keyboard." This information's for ambitious you, especially if you're in a professional or managerial career or hope to be in one before long.

In return for your commitment to take on extra career management work, this chapter rewards you with a round-up of extra good ideas you can use to deal a winning hand. Six ideas are illustrated with samples, and five others are noted in a sidebar. With the exception of the I-want-to-be-promoted letter (the second sample), the six sample documents can be used in a multitude of ways:

✔ **Before an interview:** Use them as a cheat sheet to prepare for interviews — as if you're studying for a test. (Actually, you are.)

✔ **During an interview:** When shared with an interviewer, your marketing documents are a talking-point guide to focus conversation on the important agenda of why you're the winning candidate.

✔ **After an interview:** As an interview leave-behind, these documents are a concrete reminder of why you are the ultimate choice.

✔ **Way after an interview:** Send a powerful memo (along with a letter; see Chapter 12) of your interest in the position — especially if you sense that, metaphorically, you're stuck on a desert island and you need to amp up interest in your candidacy.

Running Through Extra-Credit Job Search Documents

As you get serious about developing one of the following documents, you'll be going the extra mile. Don't worry; it won't be crowded. Going the extra mile means that you do more than most competitors are willing to do and that you position yourself to win the prized job.

Most of these six document samples probably work best on paper, but they can be e-mailed as a MS Word or PDF attachment.

The first three documents were written by cover letter professionals. Their names appear beneath their samples and their contact information appears in the appendix. My associate, John S. Gill, and I wrote the last three.

Next up: My observations about each career marketing document illustrated by a sample.

Accomplishment sheet

Also called an *accomplishment statement, proof of performance,* and *capability statement,* the *accomplishment sheet* commonly takes a full page to detail the particulars of a candidate's impressive qualifications. An accomplishment sheet can be packaged with a resume, handed out at job fairs or in networking groups, or left behind after an interview.

This sample is built on an eye-catching design to lasso attention. It puts together branding statements, qualifications, skills, achievements, a quote from the candidate's performance review, and honors.

Request-for-promotion letter

Surprise! This is a different kind of new-style career marketing tool, one by an internal candidate — a truck driver who believes he is ripe for a promotion and hoping to spur management to step up to the plate and give him one. But self-selecting yourself for a promotion is a difficult task.

Rather than ask verbally and risk a pat on the back before being sent on his way by a boss who may forget the conversation within ten minutes, the truck driver wants to go on record that he's qualified to move up. Solution: A letter.

This kind of letter is not easy to write. The sample makes the candidate's case by being respectful and not overly pushy but yet persuasive in requesting that the company recognize that he is a promotable candidate.

Leadership addendum

Career marketing letters have always been balancing acts. The busy reader wants information fast. The accomplished job seeker wants credit for all she's done. The leadership addendum, which professional Don Orlando masterminded, solves this dilemma. The force behind the addendum, and the force behind a great resume, is the same: compelling proof that you can solve your target company's problems.

In the resume, those proofs are concise. In the addendum, your skills come alive in story form — specifically a story about your value. The multiple headlines capture the reader's interest. Your description of the problem you solved, the actions you took, and the payoffs you got make the reader think: "I need someone like that!"

Checklist comparison

Pow! No document more directly links a candidate's desirability for a position than a thorough comparison of requirements and qualifications. Make your case by deconstructing a position statement, line by line, and then detailing how you fill the bill, again line by line. Some checklist comparisons can run many pages, but this sample is only two pages, plus a cover to add gravitas and identify its mission.

This sample and the next two document samples describe the same candidate, Amanda Duvall, and the nonprofit agency job she seeks.

First 90 days forecast

This sample is especially relevant for upper level management candidates but can be adapted for professionals and mid-level managers who have the authority to make important policy decisions.

The critical period in a career move often is said to be the first 90 days, a honeymoon period that allows the new person to get a good start. Entire books have been written about how to forecast the first 90 days in a job, but the actual document tends to run between 5 and 25 pages, headed by an executive summary, such as the one shown here.

The purpose of preparing a projected early achievements paper is to show hiring decision-makers that the candidate truly understands the requirements of the job and the level of performance expected.

Reference commentary

Reference dossiers are classic collections of full-length reference letters, each of which is customarily presented on the writer's or company letterhead. With companies being merged, shuttered, and relocated faster than ever, former bosses and coworkers may be scattered to the four corners just when you need to reach them for references. That's why you should collect a reference letter whenever you, a boss, or a coworker leaves a company.

By contrast, the reference commentary, a new format, is a two- to three-page — plus cover — document of short testimonials, each only one to five sentences. It is similar in style to signed blurbs that appear on book jackets.

You can present a reference commentary in an interview, using it as an ice-breaker to kick off conversation and set up a favorable impression right from the start. Say something like this:

> *I'm assuming that at some point you may want to check my references. In the meantime, this commentary reflects a quick glance at the endorsements of people who know my work as it relates to this position.*

The reference commentary is produced on a home computer, using standard PC or Mac software. A half-dozen blurbs — each of which focuses on a different selling point about you — are scattered across pages that maximize white space for a clean, speed-reading design.

Speaking of speed, an efficient way to construct your reference commentary is to draft blurbs that produce a diversity of favorable comments. If you know the reference givers well, you can ask whether they'd like you to save their time by drafting the statement for them; busy people often are happy to praise you but appreciate your doing the writing for them. When you don't know the reference giver all that well, tactfully ask if you can suggest a focus and offer examples of the short blurbs others have provided.

The reference commentary is a first-impression marketing tool; it supplements but does not replace full letters of reference from former employers and associates that you may need when hiring is imminent.

The sample, the last one in this chapter, illustrates a cover and the first page of a reference commentary.

Now — it's sample time!

More documents to make you Stand Out

In this revolutionary age of self-marketing, strong qualifications and smart communications are a job-winning combination; milk it for all its worth. Along with the six career marketing document samples shown in this chapter, consider these other creative documents that your competition may not know about.

Reference sheet

Usually a one-page document, sometimes two pages, a reference sheet is delivered upon an employer's request, and lists references and their contact information. It includes a summary of your relationship with each reference and the trait or qualifications the individual reference will address.

Specialty profile

Typically a one-page document that is fastened to your resume and details a strength related to the position you seek. Examples of subject areas: technology, leadership, training, presentations, client lists, projects, and mini-case studies.

Expert report

Suggested as a networking tool by career coach Jack Chapman, this four- to ten-page report describes how to do a simple but essential task relevant to the job being sought. Example: "10 Proven Tips to Reduce Costly Employee Errors."

Blog biography

If you write or contribute to a blog, consider your biography as a career management tool. Fuss over it until you come across as someone you'd like to hire to save the world. Example: Scot Herrick on www.cuberules.com. Other than blogs, you can also use a biographical sketch for speaking engagements and industry announcements.

Case history sketch

This interesting but rare document is intended to spark a free-flowing conversation between a candidate and an interviewer; several case history sketches may be shared with an interviewer. The sketches, printed on good quality, white 8.5" x 11" paper should be in 12-point type with ample white space and short paragraphs. Each case history sketch is small — one to two pages. The sketch recounts an engaging true accomplishment experience of the candidate, familiar or exotic.

As an example of the familiar, Chitra, an office products sales representative, was soaked in a sudden shower burst before an important presentation. Looking like a wet mop, Chitra joked about her experience and made the sale.

As an example of the exotic, Brad, a salesman of expensive private aircraft, was called to an interview with a private equity company executive. The company sought a special kind of sales rep who could handle the challenge of dealing with powerful customers around the globe. Brad described the time when he sold a multimillion-dollar jet to a South American chief of state. A few months later, Brad's customer called to thank him because the jet was critical in his escape from rebels who were trying to kill him. "Brad," the chief of state said, "If you hadn't persuaded me to buy that jet, I wouldn't be alive today."

Sketches can also be delivered verbally, of course — if the right conversational opening occurs. But it's easy to slide a few papers across the desk and casually comment, "Here are a couple of true stories to give you a glimpse of how I operate." And, of course, the case history sketch package is a good marketing reminder to leave behind at the interview.

Douglas S. Ames

"Looking forward to relocating."

34 Sun Way ▪ King City ON ▪ 705-555-0111 ▪ Cell: 416-555-0112

Senior I.T. Professional

▪ ▪ ▪

~ delivers award-winning I.T. solutions ~

- Over 20 years' I.T. experience from systems technician through several management roles, culminating in current role as Director, Information Technology.
- All experience has been in a 24.7.365 real-time environment that developed calm crisis management skills and ability to accurately and quickly diagnose problems.
- Strong technical background ensures thorough project knowledge; further, interest in sales and marketing developed appropriate I.T. business solutions strategies.

Proven Record of Delivering:

· Capital Projects Management	· Budget Management	· Customer-centric Solutions
· Leadership & Team Building	· Multi-site Operations	· Performance Management
· Executive Presentations	· Outsourcing Strategies	· Efficiency Improvement
· Strategic Planning	· E-Commerce	· Consensus Building

· **Also:** MCSE Certification and Award-winning employee

"It is rare to have an I.T. leader so customer focused . . . you view the departments you serve as customers." - comments from Performance Review, (date)

Career Notables:

- Inaugural winner of President's Achievement Award, The Written Press.

- Groomed for role as Director, I.T. while in position of Manager; in addition to in-house management courses, completed manager's course with Schulich School of Business.

- Launched revenue-generating platforms: the self-serve news release portal generates 5% of the organization's annual revenue; ABC project generates a further 10%.

- Slashed escalated trouble tickets by 75% and improved staff morale by redistributing staff responsibilities: help desk staff now contribute to understaffed operations issues.

- Launched annual performance review, with a "twist": requested staff to submit informal self assessment; strategy led to succession planning and improved workplace morale.

Stephanie Clark, BA, CRS, CIS — Kitchener Ontario, Canada

JOHN GORDON

405 Hopewell Avenue   (724) 555-0111
Findley, Pennsylvania 16345   Fax: (724) 555-0111

[Date]

Dear Mr. Marsh:

At this time, I would like to take the opportunity to express my goals and aspirations to be considered for a position with more responsibility. I am confident in my ability to perform capably at a higher level. Let me share the reasons why I feel this way.

Five years ago, I came onboard at Health and Medical Care Solutions with a strong work history, a desire to succeed, and the confidence that I could make positive contributions to the Health and Medical Care Solutions team. Over the years, I demonstrated dedication to my work and consistently took on additional responsibilities. For example, I took the initiative to acquire my commercial driver's license (CDL), not only for my personal benefit, but also for the success of the company, as I fill in for drivers when needed. Co-workers recognize my skills and aptitude for solution-finding and demonstrate their confidence in my knowledge by coming to me for advice. Three years ago, my dependability, reliability, and knowledge were rewarded by advancement from level one pay scale to level two after only two years on the job.

I feel ready for the next step, confident that I can handle more responsibility, and respectfully request a promotion and/or to be considered as a candidate for supervisor, should a position become available.

Thank you,

John Gordon
Bio-Technician/CDL Driver

Jane Roqueplot, CPBA, CWDP, CECC — Sharon, Pa.

Carla L. Johnson 4140 Carter Lane Kansas City, MO 64101 ◻clj2006@knology.net ☎ 816.555.0111

To: Mr. John Markwell, CEO, BizJet

Leadership Addendum

Please don't look for any generalized list of "qualifications" here. I thought you deserved to see documented proof of performance, aligned closely with the values I laid out in my letter to you. I hope these condensed examples encourage you to explore how I might serve BizJet.

Refocusing an established corporate culture by capitalizing on best technology and leadership practices:

The problem: I inherited a business that had slowly changed its self-image from "successful" to "comfortable." Our team thought we were in the business of just selling products and services. They saw each new sale as a discreet event, a number they hoped would grow. I just couldn't stand seeing our good people not getting satisfaction from what they did. No wonder we couldn't keep a stable sales staff. It bothered me that our customers often saw us as "order takers." In short, doing business at arm's length was shortchanging everyone. I knew our team and our customers deserved a lot more.

The actions: First, I made sure every employee knew we sold *productivity*, not product. Then I reached out to our customers with the same message, but packaged in a way I knew would appeal to them: We wanted to be their success partners. Soon my staff was seeking out our customers to find *all* their wants and their needs. Our people became masters at what drove our customers' businesses.

We automated what we learned, instituted data mining, optimized inventory order points automatically—in short, I gave our people and our customers everything they needed to build mutual success.

The results: Soon our sales force's commissions were 300 percent greater than before. Market share doubled in just 18 months. Sales employee turnover dropped from 20 percent a year to less than 5 percent. Most of all, employees wanted to come to work, our competitor's top performers wanted to work for us, customers wanted to see our reps, and I couldn't wait to reward excellence all through our firm.

Getting ahead of customer perceptions to beat the competition:

The problem: We almost became the victim of our own success. We convinced our customers that we sold productivity they had to have. But when our products needed service, most customers accepted the established industry standard that dictated an eight-hour delay before they were up and running well again. That may have been the *industry* standard, but it sure wasn't mine.

More indicators of return on investment **DayJet** *can use…*

Carla L. Johnson _____

The actions: I had all the expertise right in house: our service engineers. I asked them how we could cut the eight-hour down time in half. It might have been the first time management recognized them for their expertise.

The results: Soon we were returning our customers to full operation in half the time. But by then, the relationship I built with our engineers, and they with our customers, had taken on a momentum all its own. Eventually, the time to return to service dropped from 8 hours to less than 90 minutes. We rarely lost a customer to service concerns from then on.

Motivating customers to help our cash flow:

The problem: Over time, we allowed our customers to take a casual view of our payment terms. We were telling people we wanted to be paid in 30 days, but we were accepting most payments 45 days or more after we delivered our products. That's why we could rarely forecast our cash flow well. That's why our ability to invest in growth was crippled.

The action: I knew our administrative staff felt somewhat underappreciated. Could I transform collections—a job most people disliked—into a motivator for this group? I found the key: having them share in the rewards through a bonus system based on the amount they collected.

The results: Collection times soon fell to less than 30 days. I made sure everybody knew how our administrative staff had positioned us for better and faster growth.

Expanding into an unknown market to meet very aggressive growth targets:

The problem: The company that bought my firm demanded uncompromising growth: 25 percent a year! They asked me to help them expand into a new market, some 250 miles to the south, an area we knew very little about.

The actions: We soon identified two likely acquisition targets: one barely making a profit and another in the red. Of course, we went beyond the usual, rigorous due diligence to find what our new customers would want. We not only uncovered their wants, they helped us identify the local sales "stars." That's all we needed to apply the best practices we had learned on our home ground to our new market.

The results: We were up and running in just under 18 months. Revenue in this new growth market escalated from $1.8M to $6.0M in 9 years.

Don Orlando, MBA, CPRW, JCTC, CCM, CCMC, Montgomery, Ala.

KEY REQUIREMENTS: CANDIDATE'S QUALIFICATIONS

CHECKLIST COMPARISON

Workforce Partnership of Austin
Exec Director/President and CEO

Amanda Duvall
Cell (936) 555-0111

You Require	Amanda Duvall Delivers
◆ Overall administrative leadership, supervision, and control of large entity that provides variety of job training/employment services	✓ Am currently serving as Mayor of Crystal Valley, Texas, and Managing Director of StarPower Staffing Inc. Leadership, supervision, and control of large departments that have provided information technology services to large companies. Included in this responsibility was the creation of individual training programs. Have led numerous seminars on job search for a number of public companies and for local trade associations.
◆ Budgets, fundraising, grant writing	✓ To finance the Local Train, made numerous trips to Washington to persuade staff of key members of congress and senate. Met with U.S. Transportation Secretary Robert Saxtra to secure federal dollars, as well as Crystal Valley congressional delegation (I meet with them yearly on transportation projects). As Workforce Partnership CEO and chief fundraiser, I will show you the money.
◆ Direct preparation, review, presentation, and control of annual operating, system and support, and program policy budgets for the Policy Board	✓ Created budgets and completed detail reviews of budgets at StarPower Staffing Inc., Security Midwest, and City of Crystal Valley.
◆ Establish and maintain lines of communication with a wide range of community, contractor, and employer-based organizations	✓ As a government official and businessperson, have worked with a wide range of the public. At StarPower Staffing Inc. and, earlier at Technology Finder, have worked with over 75 companies negotiating contracts with employers and providing over 500 contract employees.
◆ Effectively communicate orally and in writing	✓ Have created myriad reports, statistical and analytical, throughout career; frequently speak and make presentations in boardrooms and auditoriums.
◆ Establish effective working relationship with management, employees, and the public, representing the diverse cultures and backgrounds	✓ Public service, including being popularly elected three times as Mayor of Crystal Valley, speaks to my history of establishing effective working relationships with a wide range of people, from administrative assistants and letter carriers, to managers and high-ranking government officials. References will validate my unblemished track record in diversity hiring and respectful treatment of all.

Amanda Duvall, Cell (936) 555-0111

You Require	Amanda Duvall Delivers
◆ Prepare and give public presentations on Workforce Partnership initiatives	✔ Given well-received presentations for StarPower Staffing Inc., City of Crystal Valley and at many other organizations. Understand use of PowerPoint presentations and video technology.
◆ Treat employees, representatives of outside agencies, and members of the public with courtesy and respect	✔ As references indicate, my interpersonal relationships are in good shape. Behavioral courtesy toward and respect for all is embedded in my personality and always has been.
◆ A graduate degree is desirable	✔ Hold master's degree in counseling with emphasis in organizational behavior and group dynamics (University of Texas at Austin).
◆ Ten years of executive level experience working with senior level executives within government and private sector organizations as well as governing boards, councils, and committees	✔ Over twenty years as an executive in seven organizations. Twelve years as an elected official.
◆ The individual appointed must have a reputation that reflects the highest public ethics and personal integrity, as well as flexibility and creativity in meeting the needs of customers	✔ References document my reputation for the highest public ethics and personal integrity.
◆ Possess knowledge of current and future workforce needs	✔ First-hand experience "in the trenches" with a number of high tech, biotech, and general business entities, determining staffing requirements. And am abreast of national and regional job trends and statistical sources of data.
◆ Possess knowledge of State and Federal employment and job training programs, contract administration, and grants management	✔ Created and negotiated three-blanket service contracts with the General Services Administration (GSA). Have passed a thorough audit of services provided to a federal agency. Have participated in federal training programs on GSA contracts. Have followed state and federal job training programs from the original CETA jobs program.
◆ Possess knowledge of public and private sector management practices and systems	✔ Maintain knowledge and awareness of managerial practices, systems, and trends through reading of journals (such as *Business Week*, *Austin Business Journal*), reading of various books, attendance at seminars from Software Industry Council. Spot check Web site news and blogs as well.

Amanda Duvall, Cell (936) 555-0111

[Date]

TO: Workforce Partnership of Austin; Task Force Selection Committee
Attention: Joanna Ramirez and Perry Johansen, Co-Chairs

FROM: Amanda Duvall, 936-555-0111

This report outlines the focus I will give to your major areas of concern and expectations for the first three months if you select me to serve as your new Executive Director/President and CEO for the Workforce Partnership of Austin. This plan, subject to revision after hire, is based on the information now available to me.

Action Plan for the First 90 Days

Executive Overview

- ◆ Resolve office-lease chokehold now draining agency funds.
- ◆ Establish strong rapport with staff at all facilities.
- ◆ Analyze effectiveness of grant-writing function.
- ◆ Review entire funding system and auditing protections.
- ◆ Visit OneStops; review job- and labor-market reporting systems; review operating contracts; meet with contractors.
- ◆ Appoint task force to assess quality of training and job-search services to clients, including use of Web 2.0 interactive services to speed hiring rates. Review mechanism for assurance of ongoing implementation of up-to-date best practices.
- ◆ Consider appointment of volunteer ambassadors to aid staff in promoting employers' participation in Workforce Partnership activities.
- ◆ Revisit mechanism for incoming reports from headquarters staff and OneStop managers.
- ◆ Issue concise weekly progress report to Policy Board.
- ◆ Make contact with managements of other workforce agencies.

(Note: 10-page report follows the executive summary)

C O N F I D E N T I A L

REFERENCE COMMENTARY

C A N D I D A T E : A M A N D A D U V A L L

21 Austin leaders have
their own reasons to
applaud Amanda Duvall
Cell (936) 555-0111

"An outstanding community leader, Amanda was born knowing how to get different groups of people to put aside their differences and work together for the good of all."
Jim Page Rogers
Austin City Council

"Amanda is a rising star!" **Jose Alvarez, CEO, Pactory Presh Inc.**

"Amanda is a very competent individual who continues to do a bang up job on every task she takes on."
The Rev. Morton Jay
Austin, Texas

> ## "Amanda Duvall is a natural leader who keeps chasing her mission until she brings home the prize."
> **Betty Jean Morris, Membership Chair**
> **Crystal Valley Chamber of Commerce**

"She's personable and you can't help but admire Amanda's ability to get things done on time and done right."
Tim Barcelona
Little League Coach
Broward County, Texas

"I've known Amanda Duvall for 20 years and her ethics are the highest. I've never seen her do anything questionable. Her word is her bond. Sign me up as a supporter."
Calle Coho, HR Specialist
Louisiana Corp.

"A first-rate executive, Amanda Duvall never lets projects slide. She understands every part of the word 'deadline'. People like working for her because she's fair."
Summer Rose
Administrative Assistant to City Manager
Crystal Valley, Texas

Part II
Creating Compelling Communications

The 5th Wave   By Rich Tennant

"Well kid, if your resume's as good as your cover letter, you've got a place with this gang."

In this part . . .

Content is cover letter king. The chapters in this part of the book guide you toward crafting bulls-eye messages. You find suggestions for adding zing to your words, starting your letters strong, and closing with a line that puts you in command and in demand. You get writing guidelines that make sure your first impression is faultless and great tips for representing your skills at their attention-garnering best.

Chapter 4

Writing Your Way to a Job

*W*hen should a resume risk its reputation by going unescorted into the mean streets of the job search? Almost never. The exception is when your resume is parked on a job site database where you hope it'll be the reason for a recruiter's *aha* moment.

But when your resume is vigorously making the rounds of prospective employers, do yourself a favor and send along a bodyguard — a cover letter. As I explain in Chapter 1, a cover letter adds another pleasing dimension to your presentation by allowing an employer to glimpse your personality and notice your use of language. Done with flair, a cover letter adds spice to the somewhat impersonal record that is your resume.

A cover letter usually arrives on computer but occasionally on paper. However you send it, a cover letter — and its extended family of self-promotional materials — is a vital tool to grow your future.

Not so fast, you say. You can barely write your name, much less a letter that'll snatch an employer's racing eye. I'm betting you can do better than you think. The following pages show you the nuts and bolts of how to communicate effectively. At the very least, this guide will coach you to recognize a Stand Out communication when you see one.

Still feeling uncomfortable at the thought of putting pen to pixels? Maybe you can find a word-wealthy friend with whom to trade a few home-cooked meals or tickets to a hot event in exchange for well-chosen verbs and nouns.

IF U R interested, plz . . .

Text-speak is a *no* on cover letters. Y? The texting made popular by cellphone-accessorized thumb jockeys is a different language, one not appropriate for business writing. The brevity of language demanded of text messaging doesn't meet writing standards, as in "I'm applying for your GR8 job." Yes, there are still standards, and they are enforced by people who read cover letters and resumes. Text-talk and they won't CU later.

Advantages of Stand Out Cover Letters

When your cover letter attracts interest, employers read your resume to confirm a positive first impression. (Alternatively, other employers turn first to your resume and, when they like what they see, page back to your cover letter to glean other bright gems about you.) The trick is to make your letter qualify for the short stack of keepers, not the big pile that gets passed over. So what's the trick?

Five hallmarks define a Stand Out cover letter, separating it from a one- or two-sentence yawner attached merely to restate the obvious — that your resume is attached. These hallmarks are

- ✔ Strong personalization
- ✔ High energy
- ✔ Relevant information
- ✔ Moderately informal
- ✔ Interesting to read

Admittedly, creating these works of job-hunting art takes time. But there are at least ten good reasons why a Stand Out cover letter is worth every minute you spend working it up.

- ✔ **Making a good first impression:** As your first knock on the door, a Stand Out letter grabs the attention of a hiring professional: "Hey honcho, stop, look at me! I have the qualifications that you need to make money for you or to save money for you. Here's what I can do for you!"

- ✔ **Putting focus on an employer:** Psychologists are right — we all like to think about ourselves. That goes double for employers. The Stand Out letter focuses on the employer, in contrast to the resume, which focuses on you.

- ✔ **Selling your benefits, not features:** As sales aces know, customers buy benefits, not features. They buy the sizzle, not the steak. Your letter is a great chance to personalize your qualifications in terms of benefits. By correlating an employer's requirements with your top competencies and skills, your knowledge, your work experience, and your achievements, you can believably claim that a specific organization is a perfect place for you to make a valuable contribution.

✓ **Showing savvy without boasting:** A Stand Out letter demonstrates your ability to understand and fulfill a company's specific needs. It shows that you are smart enough — and committed enough — to scout the company's products, services, markets, and employment needs.

✓ **Warming up your audience:** Somewhat like the built-in acceptance that occurs when a studio announcer warms up the audience before a TV star appears, a Stand Out cover letter presells your attractiveness as a candidate. It predisposes the hiring professional to like you, forming an image of you as qualified, personable, and superior among competitors in a high stack of applications.

✓ **Keeping a measure of control:** A Stand Out cover letter puts a degree of control in your hands. It sets up a reason for you to call an employer, if an employer doesn't beat you to the phone. By promising to call within a given time frame, when you do call you can truthfully get past a gate-keeper by saying that your call is expected. And when you're blocked by voicemail, a good tactic is to leave another message saying when you will call again. And do it, showing that you are a candidate of your word.

✓ **Indicating that you do good work:** A Stand Out cover letter is evidence that you're able, knowledgeable, talented, and that you take pride in your work. By contrast, a poor and boring letter suggests that your work will be poor and boring.

✓ **Confirming critical thinking skills:** A Stand Out cover letter shows the employer how your mind works — how you formulate ideas and pull them together into a rationale that makes sense. Moreover, your cover letter proves that you can communicate your thoughts in writing — a useful requirement for sales letters, memos, and reports.

✓ **Taking years off your image:** If you're a job hunter more than 15 years out of school, make a point of showing that you don't believe the way you worked yesterday is necessarily the best way to work today and tomorrow. Mention major changes a target industry is undergoing and explain what you've done to keep pace. A cover letter is an ideal place to convey that you're on the curve as new business worlds stir.

✓ **Knocking on new doors:** When your most recent work experience is different from the career field you want to enter, use your cover letter to accent your skills that best match the new field. Should you mention why you want to switch? Generally, I wouldn't; doing so just calls attention to your less-than-perfect match for the job. At times, though, it may be necessary. Suppose that you worked for four companies, each of which was sold. You might conclude your letter by saying

> *I am well qualified for a small company where wearing many hats is useful. I gained broad experience in different environments during [dates] at four companies: A, B, C, and D. Each company was acquired, resulting in changes of management. Despite departures of key personnel, excellent references about my successful performance at each are available.*

Disadvantages of Stand Out Cover Letters

There aren't any.

Many Job Hunters Have Writer's Block

When you find yourself struggling with writing a cover letter, the biggest reason may be that you haven't thought through your career goals. You really can't do your best writing about where you want to go until you know where that is.

Even when you're certain of your direction, you may still be stuck at square one. This phenomenon is called writer's block.

One cure writers use to break through writer's block is called freewriting. Writing becomes a problem for some people when they try to start at the beginning. When you freewrite, take about 15 minutes to randomly scratch out your thoughts on paper or pound away at your computer keyboard. Do not slow down to organize or edit. After you've pushed your pen for the full 15 minutes, read over your work. Mark ideas, words, and phrases that you can use in your letter. You may wish to freewrite several times until your thinking ink warms up.

Another technique to stop staring at a blank page is to answer the following questions. Find a friend to help you brainstorm, and make notes as you go.

✔ Whom do you picture reading your letter? What is that person wearing? In what environment is that person reading your letter — a well-ordered office or a room that looks like a teenager's landfill?

✔ Which qualities do you want to emphasize in your letter?

✔ Why will your letter be interesting and important to the reader?

✔ What benefits do you bring to the reader's company?

✔ What special skills or talents set you apart from the competition?

- ✔ Why do you think your employability (person-specific) skills will help you fit into a new company?

- ✔ How are your previous jobs similar to those you now seek? If the jobs are different, what skills are the same and transferable?

- ✔ What do you like about the company to which you are applying?

Here's a tip for people who speak better than they write. Recruit a friend to engage in a recorded discussion about the target job. Tell the friend why you are a hot prospect to fill it. From that recording may come sound bites that lift your letter out of humdrum status.

Keep in mind as you embark on the process of learning to write Stand Out cover letters that your first draft is probably going to be shredder food, but your editing and refining can fix *almost* anything.

Ugly Typos, Ugly Letters, Fewer Offers

No self-respecting guide to job letters would dare omit a finger-wagging warning against sloppy word work. So here's a stern but true lecture.

In my contacts over the years with thousands of people who hire people, never have I known even one hiring authority to preach the virtue of goofy grammar, bizarre punctuation, typing errors, wayward lowercase, texting abbreviations, or other crimes against accepted language usage. Everyone who reads jobs letters and resumes is against that sort of thing.

Watch out for these familiar missteps:

- ✔ **UnAcxeptable spelling.** No large academic studies have confirmed it, but anecdotally, it's no surprise that spelling shockers are responsible for big numbers of rejections for blundering job seekers. My assessment comes from nearly constant reports of such blunders as managers who attempted to describe their previous "rolls" (they meant "roles") and applicants who cannot even spell the word "error" correctly.

   If you're writing too fast to be accurate, remember that simple mistakes can put your brand at risk. Fast is good but accurate sells.

- ✔ **Grammar gaffes.** Spell checkers can't help letters that say things like "would of" known instead of "would have" known. For a crash course in good grammar, see handbooks published for administrative assistants and secretaries; otherwise, retake English 101.

- ✔ **Poisoned proper nouns.** Addressing a letter to "Mr. Michael R. Forest" when his name is correctly spelled "Mr. Michael R. Forrest" won't win over an employer; it just convinces him that you have a short attention span.

The moral to this warning: Proofread until your eyes fall out of your head. Many hiring professionals blow off even a qualified candidate if even one typo appears in a cover letter or resume. Hiring is in the details.

Overcoming What-If Worries

What-if questions are legitimate worries when writing cover letters whose solutions may not be obvious. Here are answers to some of these common concerns:

- **What if I'm responding to a recruitment ad? To whom should my cover letter be addressed?**

  Send your Stand Out cover letter with a resume (See my book *Resumes For Dummies,* 5th Edition.) to the individual named in the ad. Follow instructions.

- **What if the ad's instructions say to send the letter and resume to the human resources department?**

  Do it. The resume will likely be put into an electronic database and stored for a long time; you may be considered for a number of open positions. In addition to following instructions, send a Stand Out cover letter to the name of the department hiring manager (your prospective boss). Say that your resume is on file with HR. Get the hiring manager's name by anonymously calling or use the social networking connections I describe in Chapter 2.

- **What if I don't know enough about the position to write a Stand Out letter?**

  Look up job descriptions for similar positions and read recruitment ads. Try to make online contact with people in the target career field or industry. You can also go after a long shot: Try to get through on the telephone to a person who does similar work for a competitor.

- **What if I'm responding to an executive recruiter? Do I send the same materials?**

  Yes, but mention that while you're very interested in this position, you would like to be considered for other jobs if this one doesn't pan out.

- **What if I'm initiating a possible opening at a company that hasn't advertised one?**

  Research to determine who has the authority to hire you. Send your self-marketing materials to that person. Even more effective is to meet your target at a professional meeting or find a third party whose name you can use as an introduction.

The Anatomy of a Cover Letter

Every cover letter contains the same bones beneath its unique skin of qualifications and experience. The upcoming sections take you from head to toe of a cover letter.

Contact information

Your mailing address, cell and home telephone numbers, e-mail address, and blog address (if you have a business-related blog, not a party blog) appear first on a job letter.

When you're applying for an international position, spell out your state followed by a comma and USA (Mesa, Arizona, USA). Further, include a Skype address on the last line of the contact information (Skype: darrylroberts).

For contact information layout ideas, look at the sample letters in Part III and Part IV.

Date line and inside address

Place the date two lines below your contact information and place the inside address two lines below the date. Aligned with the left margin of the page, enter the name of the person to whom you're writing (with the correct prefix, such as Mr. or Mrs., Dr. or Rev.), followed on the next line by the company name, and followed on the next lines by the address. If you know the job title of the addressee, include that information on the same line as the addressee's name or on the following line.

On the right side of the page, aligned with the inside address information, you can include a subject line labeled RE: (which is an abbreviation for Regarding) to highlight the reason for correspondence.

Salutation

Your salutation is like the eye contact that establishes a connection and begins the dialogue. Do your best to identify the person who will read your letter and address that person directly. Not only does your reader appreciate being addressed by name, but this personal bit separates your letter from the ones written by people who didn't take the time to do a little research into the company.

If you absolutely can't uncover the name of the hiring manager, write *Good Morning.* It's a cheerful way to begin. Because no one enjoys reading mail addressed to a generic person (remember all the junk mail you've trashed addressed to *Dear Resident?*), never address your letter to *Dear Sir or Madam,* or *To Whom It May Concern.*

Try, try, try to discover the name of your reader. It's courteous, it takes initiative, and it indicates genuine interest in the company and, most importantly, in the job.

Introduction

Your introduction should grab your reader's attention immediately. (See Chapters 5 and 6.) As the "head" of your letter, it appeals to the head of your reader, sparking interest that will compel a hiring authority to keep reading as it states the purpose of the letter.

All sorts of rules are given for ways to start your cover letter. Some say, don't start with "I." Others advise shock value and creativity, a risky approach unless you're a skilled writer. Still others suggest you begin with the name of a mutual acquaintance. The most important rule is to engage the reader's interest. Period.

Body

The body of your letter provides essential information that the employer should know about you — competencies, skills, accomplishments, and quantified statements describing your past achievements. *Remember to focus on the benefits you bring to the employer's table.* Work in a branding statement if you have one. (See Chapter 13.)

The body should include a very brief background summary of your relevant experience. This is information that the reader can get from your resume, so don't spend too much space on it in your letter. But don't be tempted to leave it out. Without this key selling point, your reader may never get to your resume.

Conclusion

The last segment of your letter expresses appreciation and explains what happens next. It says when you will call to set a time for an interview, or it motivates the hiring authority to call you before anyone else does.

Closing, signature, and enclosure line

The closing section is the handshake before parting, sincere and warm. *Sincerely, Sincerely yours,* and *Very truly yours* are the most popular, but other choices include *Best regards* and *All the best* or just *All best.* Don't forget to put a comma after your closing line.

If your name doesn't appear in your contact information at the top of your letter, type your name below your signature (four lines below the closing) so that there will be no confusion about spelling.

When your penmanship runs to chicken-scratch, try to make your signature legible. Any employer prefers to be able to read what someone handwrites instead of having to interpret it.

After you've motivated your reader, the enclosure line provides a direction. Indicate the item that you've sent with your cover letter, such as a resume or portfolio. This line directly follows your typed name or signature.

Get Ready to Write

When you want your career to take off, make your cover letters terrific! Take more risks, offer more surprises, and find fresh ways to sell your benefits and skills. Pledge to never send out a run-of-the-mill letter again. From now on, you're in Stand Out mode!

Chapter 5

Language That Snap-Crackle-Pops

As you work to get the right razzle dazzle into your cover letter, here's a writing tip from the pros: Visualize your reader and write specifically for that reader. Speaking directly to your reader may seem obvious, but this tenet is said to be one of the most overlooked aspects of effective writing. Writing to a real person makes your letter more personable and interesting to read. It shows you have considered your reader and want that person to understand what you have to say.

If your blank sheet of paper is beginning to look like the place where you'll spend eternity, rip a page from a magazine featuring a picture of someone who could be reading your letter, tape the picture to your computer, and write to that specific person. Who cares if you select a picture of a conservative middle-aged man with gray hair when in reality the reader of your letter is a vivacious, young woman with bouncing red curls? No matter. The process — the visualization allowing you to target a particular human being — is what counts.

Refreshing Your Language

I once asked a friend who writes and publishes career books whether he genuinely likes to write. "Well, no," he responded, "I like *to have* written."

That sentiment sums everything up for many who do almost anything to avoid writing but who know that they can't escape this lifetime without learning to write certain things — self-promotional job letters are some of those things.

Make this task easier for yourself not only by reviewing a few rules of grammar, but also by reminding yourself to answer the big "So why?" and "So what?" questions in every letter.

So why are you writing?

Never assume the purpose of your letter is obvious to your reader. You are writing a cover letter — or another type of job letter — ultimately aimed at employment.

If you're writing a cover letter, you want to land an interview. Say so. Try to maintain control by saying that you will be in touch at a specified time to see whether an interview is possible. When this approach seems impractical, like when you respond to a blind recruitment ad, close with a benefit you offer — "My former boss describes me as the best multimedia designer in the state. Can we talk?"

If you are writing another type of job letter, tell your reader exactly what you want. Leave no room for guessing.

So what? How does it matter?

For each sentence you write, ask yourself, "So what? What does this information mean to my reader — a benefit gained, a loss avoided, a promise of good things to come — what?" Don't, for instance, merely list a bunch of skills and achievements — what good will those skills do for the person who reads your letter?

Must you always interpret for the reader the benefit of your skills and achievements?

- ✔ Yes, if a ghost of an outside chance exists that the benefits of your skills and achievements will not be evident to the reader.
- ✔ No, if the listing of your skills and achievements is so strong that an eighth grader will get the message.

For more illustrations of when you must interpret your benefits, look over the sample cover letters in Part III.

Getting in the habit of asking yourself "So why?" and "So what?" boosts the power of your job letters by 100 percent.

Technical versus nontechnical language

Tailor your language to your reader. If you're an engineer writing to another engineer, use technical language. If you're an engineer writing to a director of human resources, your reader may not understand technical engineering language; explain any technical terms in simple, everyday language.

Concise but thorough

Because your reader may be pressed for time, aim to write a concise but thorough cover letter. Tell your reader as much about yourself as you can, but don't make your reader wade through extra words and unnecessary details. Consider the following example:

> *I am a person who believes that the values of fervent dedication, cooperative teamwork, dynamic leadership, and adaptive creativity really make up the cornerstones and are the crucial components of any totally successful sales venture.*

Revised using concise but thorough language, the same sentence now reads:

> *Dedication, teamwork, leadership, and creativity are essential to successful sales.*

Use short words, sentences, and paragraphs. Avoid cramming too many ideas into each paragraph. Logically break long paragraphs into several short ones.

Write in specific terms; avoid vague descriptions. Use numbers, measures, and facts — detailed information rather than unquantified generalities. Consider the following example:

> *I saved the company a fortune when I instituted a new system for scheduling.*

Now read the same example revised for specifics:

> *I saved the company more than one million dollars in production when I instituted a new system for production scheduling.*

Table 5-1 provides a list of word baggage to avoid and Stand Out words to replace them.

Table 5-1	Stand Out Replacements
Instead of	*Write*
able	can
about	approximately (be precise)
above	this/that
absolutely	(eliminate)
according to	said
ad	advertisement

(continued)

Table 5-1 *(continued)*

Instead of	Write
advanced planning	planning
advise	write/perform
aforementioned	this/that
ahold	reach/get hold of/obtain
alright	all right
along the lines of	like
alot	a lot
a lot of	many/much
arrived at the conclusion	concluded
as per	according to
as to whether	whether
at a later date	later
at the present writing	now
at the present time	now
attached hereto	attached/enclosed
attached herein	attached/enclosed
bachelor's degree	bachelor's
bad	poor/inappropriate
beneficial success	success
better than	more than
between each	between every/beside each
between you and I	between you and me
bit	(eliminate)
but however	but or however
but that	that
cannot but	(eliminate)
can't hardly	can hardly
city of San Francisco	San Francisco
close proximity	close or proximity
close scrutiny	scrutiny
close to the point of	close to
cohese	cohere
concerning the matter of	concerning/about

Instead of	Write
concerning	about
continue on	continue
disregardless	regardless
due to the fact that	because
each and every	each or every
end result	result
entirely completed	completed
equally as	as or equally
estimated at about	estimated at
every other	every (second) day
ex-	former
fewer in number	fewer
file away	file
for the purpose of	for
for the reason that	because
for your information	(eliminate)
gather together	gather or together
good success	success
he is a man who . . .	he . . .
he or she	he
idea	belief/theory/plan
i.e./e.g.	that is/for example
if and when	if or when
important essentials	essentials
in accordance with a request	as you requested
inasmuch as	since/because
in connection with	about/concerning
in excess of	over/more than
in order to	to
in respect to the matter of	about/regarding
in spite of	despite
in the amount of	for
in the area of	about
in the field of medicine	in medicine

(continued)

Table 5-1 *(continued)*

Instead of	Write
in this day and age	now/today
irregardless	regardless
join together	join or together
keep continuing	continue
kindly	please/very much
kind of	rather/somewhat
known to be	is/are
know-how	knowledge/understanding
large portion/number of	most of/many
last but not least	(eliminate)
like for	like
like to have	(eliminate)
lot/lots	(eliminate)
love	(eliminate)
magnitude	importance/significance
master's degree	master's
more essential	essential
more perfect	perfect
more specially	specially
more unique	unique
most carefully	(eliminate)
most certainly	(eliminate)
mutual cooperation	cooperation
mutual teamwork	teamwork
near future	soon
needless to say	(eliminate)
new innovation	innovation
new record	record
now pending	pending
of between/of from	of
optimize	increase efficiency
outline in detail	outline or detail
overall	comprehensive/final

Instead of	*Write*
per	(eliminate)
per diem	daily
per annum	yearly
period of	for
plan ahead	plan
please be advised	(eliminate)
point in time	now
presently	now/soon
qualified expert	qualified or expert
rather unique	unique
reason is because	because
reason why	because
regarding	about
represent	composed/made up of
respecting	about
revert back	revert
scrutinize closely	scrutinize
seem	(be more specific)
seriously consider	consider
several	many/numerous
should/would/must of	should/would/must have
spell out in detail	spell out or detail
subject	(be more specific)
subject matter	subject
subsequent to	after
sufficient enough	sufficient or enough
take for example	for example
take into consideration	consider
target	goal/objective/quota
thank you in advance	(eliminate)
that	(eliminate if possible)
there is/are/was/were	(eliminate)
true facts	facts
try and	try to

(continued)

Table 5-1 *(continued)*	
Instead of	*Write*
unknown	unidentified/undisclosed
unthinkable	unlikely/impossible
very unique	unique
was a former	was/is a former
way in which	way
whatsoever at all	whatsoever
with the exception of	except/except for
yet	(eliminate if possible)
you know	(eliminate)

Active voice versus passive voice

Passive voice indicates a state of existence with words like *be, is, was, were, are, seem, has,* and *been* — the 90-pound weaklings of verbs.

Rather than mucking up your cover letter with wimpy passive-voice verbs ("Production processes were reformed by my innovation and $12,000 per month was saved by the company."), choose active-voice verbs to show off your accomplishments: "My innovation reformed production processes and saved the company $12,000 per month."

Active voice does the heavy lifting you need in your cover letter; it's strong, vibrant, and vigorous — qualities you want to show off to hiring managers yourself.

Past/present tense

For the most part, use present tense as you're writing. After all, your letter is something you're creating now. When you refer to accomplishments or achievements, use past tense.

When your resume says you are currently employed (20XX–Present), remember to use present tense if you refer to your current job in a cover letter. If you slip and use past tense, the reader may assume you've left the job and are pretending to be currently employed.

Fundamentals of Grammar and Punctuation

Grammar slips sink jobs. Many employers see language skills as an important aspect of potential job performance, and nothing says language skills like attention to grammar and punctuation. To help you over some areas that many job letter writers find tricky, here is a brief overview of frequently made mistakes and how to correct them.

Sentence fragments

Sentence fragments signal incomplete thoughts. They neglect essential components. For example,

> *Although I work in Detroit, making $200 an hour.*

This fragment is missing the subsequent subject and verb needed to finish the "Although I work . . ."

> *Although I work in Detroit, making $200 an hour, I would prefer to work in Atlanta to be near my family.*

To test your sentences, speak each one aloud, out of context. Imagine walking up to someone and saying that sentence. Would the sentence make sense, or is something missing? If so, add the missing information.

Run-on sentences

Run-on sentences are two complete sentences written as one. For example,

> *I finished writing my cover letter, it's great!*

This run-on should read:

> *I finished writing my cover letter. It's great!*

Each sentence contains a complete thought and should stand on its own.

Run-on sentences stand out as grammatical errors.

Dangling participles

Dangling participles are words ending in *-ing* that modify the wrong subject. For example,

Running across the water, we saw a huge water beetle.

This sentence literally means that we saw a water beetle while we were running across the water — a Guinness Book of Records feat! Try this instead:

We saw a huge water beetle running across the water.

Dangling participles are good for laughs, but they indicate imprecision or lack of care.

Misplaced modifiers

Like dangling participles, misplaced modifiers modify the wrong subject, often resulting in hilarious miscommunications. For example,

Ben taught the dog, an inveterate womanizer, to bark at all blonde women.

The dog is an inveterate womanizer? Probably not. Revised, this sentence makes more sense:

Ben, an inveterate womanizer, taught the dog to bark at all blonde women.

Semicolons

Semicolons can be tricky, and so you should probably avoid them if you don't feel comfortable using them. In essence, semicolons are weak periods; they indicate a separation between two complete sentences that are so closely related they shouldn't be separated by a period.

As you can see, this definition is not specific. You may simply use periods between every sentence. You won't break any rules, and you'll avoid using semicolons incorrectly.

The only rule for semicolons is as follows: When you introduce a list of complete sentences by using a colon, separate each sentence with a semicolon. For example:

*I accomplished the following: I networked all the computers,
company-wide; I designed a new system for scheduling; and I broke
the world's record in typing speed.*

Again, you can avoid this use of semicolons in your cover letter by placing each item on a separate line set off by bullets. No punctuation is necessary at the end of each line. For example,

I accomplished the following:

- *I networked all the computers, company-wide*

- *I designed a new system for scheduling*

- *I broke the world's record in typing speed*

Punctuation in parenthetical expressions

If a parenthetical expression occurs in the middle or at the end of a sentence, place the punctuation outside the parentheses. Some examples include the following:

Cover letters are essential (see Chapter 5).

Cover letters (and resumes) are essential.

Cover letters (and resumes), essential to the job search, are important.

Question marks and exclamation points, when part of a parenthetical expression occurring in the middle of a sentence, are the exception to this rule. Some examples include the following:

The interview (or was it an inquisition?) was a disaster.

My cover letter (a masterpiece!) took four hours to write.

If a parenthetical expression stands alone as a sentence, place the punctuation inside the parentheses. For example,

(I will discuss these skills in a moment.)

Hyphenating words for clarity

When you use two words together as a description of another word, use a hyphen. Examples include

next-to-last job

long-range plan

To test whether you should use a hyphen, take out one of the descriptive terms and see if the description still makes sense. For example,

> *next-to-last job*

without one descriptive term, becomes

> *to last job*

Doesn't make sense, does it? Because the three words "next to last" cannot be used individually as a description and still make sense, you need hyphens between them.

The same rule applies for two nouns used together to express a single idea. Examples include

> *light-year*
>
> *life-cycle*

For greatest accuracy, check a dictionary, such as www.Dictionary.com.

Abbreviations

Use abbreviations only if you have previously written out what the abbreviation stands for. For example, do not write *UCSD* if you have not previously written *University of California, San Diego (UCSD)*. Never assume that your reader knows or will be able to figure out what an abbreviation stands for.

Abbreviations such as *AIDS* and *DNA* are so well known that they do not have to be defined. Also, some technical jargons commonly use abbreviations. In that case, write to your reader. If your reader will understand the abbreviation, use it.

Consecutive numbers

When you use two numbers in a row, avoid confusion by writing out the shorter of the two numbers:

> *six 9-person teams*

Or revise your sentence to separate the numbers:

> *six teams of nine people*

A number at the beginning of a sentence

Whenever a sentence begins with a number, write out the number rather than using numerals. Better yet, revise the sentence so that the number does not appear at the beginning.

Commas

In general, use commas anywhere you would pause if you read the sentence aloud. If you're a person who pauses often while speaking, this suggestion probably won't work for you. My advice is to ask several people to read your letter for punctuation and grammar and follow their suggestions. Or get a good punctuation guide and follow it.

Commas in a series

Whenever you have a series of terms separated by commas, use a comma after the next-to-last term for clarity. Some examples include the following:

Cover letters, resumes, and interviews make up part of the job search process.

Dear Mr. Barnes, Ms. Collins, and Ms. Schultz:

This technique is called the *serial comma.* Newspapers don't use serial commas because they slow down reading. Be consistent in your use of commas. Don't use a serial comma in one paragraph and no serial comma in another that calls for one.

Capitalization

Capitalize trade names, like Band-Aid, Kleenex, and Xerox. Avoid using these trade names to refer to a class of things or to an action. For example,

I need a Band-Aid.

Use *bandage* unless you specifically want the brand-name product.

I need to Xerox some papers

is also technically incorrect. Write

I need to photocopy some papers.

Resist the urge to Capitalize words to make them Stand out as Important. Doing so is not only wrong, it looks Contrived and Juvenile.

Capitalize titles of departments, companies, and agencies

Any official name of a company, department, agency, division, or organization should be capitalized. Examples include

> *U.S. Department of Labor*
>
> *Department of Safety*

Don't capitalize words such as *department, company,* or *organization* when used as a general word rather than as part of a specific title. For example,

> *I work for a division of Toyota.*

Table 5-2 provides a handy chart to guide you through grammatical thickets.

Table 5-2	Stand Out Grammar Guide		
Error Term	*Definition of Term*	*Don't Do This*	*Do This*
Subject-verb disagreement	Subject and verb don't agree, resulting in a grammatically incorrect sentence.	Our team, as well as the company, *value* ambition.	Our team, as well as the company, *values* ambition.
Active voice vs. passive voice	Active voice relates an action (good); passive voice relates a state of existence (bad).	I *was trained* in all aspects of public relations.	U.C.I. *trained* me in all aspects of public relations.
Sentence fragment	Phrase lacks a subject and/or verb, revealing an incomplete thought.	*Unlike some applicants.*	Unlike some applicants, *I bring* talent and diversity.
Run-on sentence	Contains more than one complete thought; may lack punctuation.	Every writer knows how important grammar *is, I* know you really value marketing, and sales skills, in your business correspondence.	Every writer knows the importance of *grammar. I* also understand you value marketing and sales skills in your business correspondence.

Error Term	Definition of Term	Don't Do This	Do This
Subject-pronoun disagreement	Pronouns don't agree with subject, resulting in a confusing or easily misunderstood sentence.	When *someone* reads, *they* should pay attention to details.	When *someone* reads, *he (or she)* should pay attention to details. Or, When *people* read, *they* should pay attention to details.
Misplaced modifiers	Incorrect placement of a description of one subject in a sentence with two subjects; result is confusion.	Falling more than 500 feet, we watched the daredevil bungee jump off a cliff.	We watched the daredevil bungee jump, falling more than 500 feet off a cliff.

Formats for Organization

Following are several formats to suggest how your letter can be organized. You can use any organizational format with any occupation.

- **Problem/solution:** The problem/solution format starts with "Here's the problem" and ends with "Here's how I solved it." Case histories and success stories blossom in this favorite format for cover letters and resumes.

- **Inverted pyramid:** News stories use this format. You start with a lead paragraph summarizing the story, with the following paragraphs presenting facts in order of decreasing importance. In your cover letter, you state a comprehensive goal, career desire, or position at the beginning and then provide specific examples in the following paragraphs to support your aim.

- **Deductive order:** Much like the inverted pyramid, the deductive order format starts with a generalization and ends with specific examples supporting the generalization. For example, you can start by making a general statement about a skill, and then support that statement with facts.

- **Inductive order:** Begin your letter with a story or anecdote and then lead the reader to the conclusion you want him or her to draw from the story or anecdote. Explain how that story or anecdote supports your ability to succeed at the job you've targeted.

> ✔ **List:** Separate your letter into distinct points and set off the points with headings, bullets, or numbers. Put the most important point first. This format is especially effective for enumerating skills or achievements. Combine it with another format (such as the requirements-qualifications match letter that leads off Chapter 8) for extra punch.

Read for Smoothness

When you finish writing your letter, read it over just to check its organization. When you read it, each line should fit into the other. You shouldn't really notice that a new sentence has begun. You should feel "prepared" for everything that you're about to read.

To avoid jarring the reader with an abrupt change of subject, ask yourself, "Why did I place this sentence or paragraph after the one before it?" If the answer isn't obvious in your letter, the flow of your text is probably choppy and unclear to the reader. Analyze what's not working and rewrite until the letter reads smoothly.

Three simple tips to improve your letters

✔ Highlight short sentences and lists with bullets, asterisks, or em dashes. For example,

• Won Orchid award for building

* Won Orchid award for building

— Won Orchid award for building

✔ Start with a short quote that reflects the employer's policies or values.

✔ Reword portions of the employer's mission statement or other documents, and work these phrases into your letter as you describe your skills, work ethic, and values.

Chapter 6

Great Lines for Success

. . . .

In This Chapter

▶ 27 Knockout opening statements

▶ 35 Powerhouse mix-and-match phrases

▶ 16 Action closing statements

▶ A last line that's impossible to ignore

. . . .

Suppose you receive a letter that begins

Time flies when you're having fun.

That oldie probably won't entice your reading interest.

But suppose you receive a letter that begins

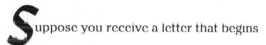

As Muppet Kermit the Frog says, "Time's fun when you're having flies."

That line is different. That line is funny. That line lassoes your attention, roping you into reading further to find out what message is being communicated with such a goofy statement. (What's *your* guess?)

I'm not suggesting that you start job letters with frog quotes or other whimsical statements. Instead, I am pointing out that you must work to grab immediate reader attention and then hold it tightly throughout the complete text of job search correspondence.

This chapter outlines strategies and words designed to do exactly that. You can use a variety of approaches, ranging from riding on the coattails of a personal connection, to responding to the requirements of a job ad, to creating drama with words that intrigue, words that excite, words that *zing!*

Starting Your Letter

The best information to pop in your opening line is a known name. A personal referral works wonders. In this approach, you begin with the name of a mutual connection. Someone whom the letter's recipient likes or respects or, at least, has heard of. Name dropping virtually guarantees that your letter will be read. Additionally, you can score points by identifying yourself as a member of an affinity group, such as the alumni of a college or member of a civic organization. Name is the game!

In addition to names, here's another high-octane approach: Launch your letter with a clear statement of what you want, quickly followed by the qualifying benefits you offer that directly relate to the requirements the hiring company seeks. Or turn it around — lead with the skills and benefits you offer before saying what you want.

Still another way to energize your opening: Create a narrative hook *(Time's fun when you're having flies)*. In the broadest sense, a narrative hook is a literary technique in the opening of a story that "hooks" the reader's attention to keep eyes scooting down the page. A cover letter hook often is a thematic statement, followed by a flashback to the history the reader needs to understand it.

Here's an example of a thematic opening hook that was successfully used by a woman who, after a two-year absence, wanted to return to her original career in the automotive industry:

> *Any claim that the grass is greener outside the auto-industry fence is a myth! At least it is for me. After 20 years of rock-solid experience in our industry, a series of outside opportunities briefly tempted me to cast eyes elsewhere. But not for long.*
>
> *My inner voice keeps shouting loud and clear that the auto side is where I belong, and that's why I'm selectively contacting you. I hope you will see how adding me to your quality operation will be a big win for Standford Motors.*

Don't waste valuable opening-line real estate by focusing on the source of a job post — *I saw your ad in the KoKoMo Express last Sunday.* Handle sourcing head-on in the regarding ("RE:") line in the upper, right-hand quadrant (cruise the sample cover letters in Part III). Example: *RE: Your job ad in the KoKoMo Express, June 14.*

Sell, don't tell! As I mention in Chapter 1, cover letters in today's marketplace are really sales letters. Rather than whispering through an old-school letter of transmission — *Please find my resume attached, Your Royal Honor.* — open with a strategic bang!

A Sampling of Grand Openers

So what do contemporary openers look like? Review the following 27 Stand Out opening line examples that are sure to make a job letter jump out of the pack right from the start. Read and grow creative.

- I recently met with James Smith from your firm, and he strongly recommended that I send you my resume. Knowing the requirements of your open position for a financial analyst, he concludes that I am the ideal candidate. Your opening does seem to be tailor-made for my experience at CityWide Financial Services.

- During your visit to UCSB last fall, I had the pleasure of hearing you address the issue of FuelCO oil rigs off the coast of Santa Barbara. As a UCSB June graduate, I . . .

- My computer skills developed from childhood, plus my well-honed interest in technology advances, and my recently completed education in computer science make me a strong candidate for a position as an entry-level software engineer at your highly regarded company.

- I recently graduated with a 3.75 GPA from the University of California, where I was a research assistant to Dr. Joe Famous, engineering department chair.

- Since you will soon be working on photo sessions for the spring catalog, I enclose my portfolio showing how ideal my background in photography and design is for your marketing strategies.

- Juliette Nagy mentioned your company has opened a division of sporting goods and suggested that I contact you. As a former high school coach for several sports, I believe I have the mix of skills and knowledge you're looking for.

- Your speech was inspiring, Ms. Luna-Mendez. Soon I will have completed my master's in physical therapy, just in time for your entry-level openings in the PT ward.

- The breakthrough research being conducted at Hughes Medical Labs is too exciting to miss out on! I'm looking forward to following up our phone conversation with a sit-down meeting to explore how I can make a contribution as a member of the early warning symptoms task force. I provide a link to relevant information about exactly what I can add as a biology researcher who has managed several challenging projects.

- I enjoyed our meeting at the Rancho Santa Fe Garden Club and, as you suggested, am sending you this additional information to review before we get together.

✔ Chaim Isenberg of the Grenwich and Co. accounting firm suggested I contact you regarding opportunities in your warehouse division in Champagne. My background documents considerable success in the areas of loss prevention and asset recovery, which I understand are high on your list of requirements.

✔ Noting your posting for a civil engineer with environmental experience, here's my question: Will your environmental services department reach its Green Acres corporate goal of providing a "turnkey" approach to environmental investigation and remediation, or will it always struggle with solving complicated projects, from engineering and design issues through remedial construction? You'll never know without the best person for the job to follow through for you. Arguably, that's me and here's why: (bulleted highlights of achievements, experience, education, awards, and quotations from satisfied clients).

✔ I thrive on challenge. When I read your posting for a corporate fitness trainer, I thought lightning had struck and that you wrote about that opportunity hoping to find me. I have three years' experience in freelance fitness training following my military service, and, IMHO, an opinion confirmed by clients, I'm fired up and ready to go!

✔ You mention several things in your posting for a reality show screener that make me think you're looking for someone with my proven assets. Let me briefly explain.

✔ Terry Ann Torre, who supervised my work as an intern with your company, recommends that I apply to you for the position of assistant customer service manager. Here are some of the reasons Ms. Torre is recommending me: (bulleted list of reasons).

✔ Serendipity! As a graduating senior, I am delighted to learn that *Wonderful Merchandising Magazine* has just named Better Bargains Inc., a company I've long admired, one of the top ten best places to launch a career!

After developing good skills in fashion merchandising, personnel practices, and salesmanship in my cooperative education program, I have begun to search for a position in retail marketing. I will graduate June 2 and am crossing my fingers that you'll be one of my first interviews.

✔ After working four years on The Hill as a legislative assistant on the House Rules Committee, I understand the inner workings of the political system and could prove to be a valuable asset to a firm such as yours. A few of my areas of expertise: (no more than six bulleted items).

✔ Are you in the market for a sales pro who has set sales records for four different companies and trained dozens of high-performance sales reps?

✔ Congratulations on the opening of your new insurance branch. Watching your progress over several years, I've seen that A-123 Insurance Company has earned "street cred." That leads me to believe that you and I see the insurance business through the same lens: excellent customer service!

✔ I have a successful and reliable work history dealing with the public that would make me an excellent employee for your new store. Interested? My resume would like to meet you, and so would I. Here's why:

✔ Velia Acevedo has suggested I forward my resume to you for consideration for a current administrative assistant opening in the escrow department. Through conversations with Velia at a continuing education class, I learned what it takes to be a successful support professional at your firm. I am confident that I have the head for numbers and word processing skills to make the grade.

✔ Road-tested but not battle-scarred, I offer the necessary qualifications and experience to deliver real revenue results during my first 30 days as a senior sales representative. Please allow me to document my abilities when we sit down and talk about my becoming part of your team.

✔ Preparing to respond to your ad in today's Chicago Tribune, I did some research and discovered that we're both Northwestern grads. Is this serendipity or what? I hope our mutual alma mater is a harbinger of good things to come and that we'll be cheering on the same side in the workplace as well. As this letter very briefly outlines, my qualifications and your requirements for an industrial engineer are joined at the hip.

✔ Chances are excellent that I'm the multi-talented graphic designer you seek in your "multi-talented graphic designer" post on Job-Hunt.org. With extensive experience in multimedia, marketing, and print design, I work within budget to deliver world-class catalogs and brochures, logos, Web site design, Flash, video photomontages, and DVD cover design.

✔ As a new USC graduate, I've been hoping to find the kind of position you're staffing because I have exactly the background you're asking for. Specifically, the following columns match item for item: (The company's requirements are listed in the left column, and in the right, your matching qualifications.)

✔ I understand that your firm is in search of individuals with (skills) and (qualifications). I think I've hit the jackpot, and maybe you have as well. Don't you love finding the perfect match?

✔ In reviewing my resume, you will find that I possess all the attributes of a perfect match, from (skills) to (experience or attributes). I am excited to learn of your job opening because I have been searching for a company just like yours to make real use of my experience.

✔ (Mutual contact) thought my resume measures such achievement in the function you supervise that he assured me he would pass it on to you; in the event it hasn't yet reached your desk, here's a copy.

What makes these opening lines work?

✔ Some drop names.

✔ Some connect to a common experience.

✔ Some reveal knowledge of the company involved.

✔ Some use a narrative hook.

✔ Some aim at alumni of a graduate's college.

✔ Some ask a question.

✔ Some refer to the content of an employer's ad.

All show that the person writing the letter is someone who goes an extra mile to do a superior job. A person who has just the kind of motivation that employers hope to hire.

But not everyone gets it.

Avoid Leadoff Losers

This section shows you how *not* to open your letters. These leadoff losers are snatched from real correspondence supplied by recruiters and HR specialists. Comments in italics that follow each line colorfully express the employer's silent point of view. Read and be warned!

✔ I was recently let go due to a reduction in force, which is why I wish to apply for your position in merchandising.

Nothing like starting on an upbeat note.

✔ Having recently completed an assignment in the Commonwealth of Independent States (the former Soviet Union), I am interested in pursuing and advancing my career opportunities into this arena.

Arena? What arena? Here. . . . There. . . . Where?

✔ In most organizations, job performance, whether excellent or inept, doesn't count, as long as you conform and play politics. I believe that performance does count! I have recently been notified by Dunnie Pharmaceuticals that my R&D position will be eliminated in the near future.

Does this translate to: I wasn't much of a team player? Is that why the job seeker's position is being eliminated?

✔ I am currently in search of a job; I have no particular preference for any area, for as you can see from my included resume, my experience includes a broad range.

One who will take anything masters nothing. As movie pioneer Sam Goldwyn once said, "Include me out."

✔ I am writing in response to the advertised position for a production coordinator. I am very interested in advancing in my field and making a transition into the aspects of the communications profession described in your ad.

Do you want to advance in your field (which is what?), or do you want to make a transition, or do you want to do the work I need done?

✔ If you or someone you know could use a graphic designer, please pass my resume on to interested parties, or call me as soon as possible.

If you're asking me to be your agent, remember, agents get 15% off the top.

✔ My partner and I are dissolving our business after 15 years of working together. I am interested in a position at Fred & Associates and have enclosed a resume for your review.

A business divorce is rarely just one person's fault: Are you a pain in the back country? And what is it you want to do for me?

✔ When a customer calls for a quote, your firm's future is in the hands of the sales staff. I have big hands.

Huh? Close but no cigar. And keep your hands to yourself.

✔ To maintain solid growth, a company must have marketing and sales professionals who can jump on a market before the competition does. My background proves I can do that.

Tell me something I don't know. I've been in this business for 30 years.

Learn from your false starts. As the Japanese proverb has it: "Fall seven times, stand up eight."

Skip Salutation Snoozers

Although not the dead-letter-walking mistakes of the leadoff losers in the preceding section, these salutation snoozers do have sedating effects:

✔ In response to your recent job posting for a hospital clown, please accept the enclosed copy of my credentials.

Earth to bozo: The sick kids in this hospital need cheering up by an imaginative, funny clown who colors outside the lines. Next!

✔ In a recent edition of Craigslist, your ad for a television producer piqued my interest and I have therefore enclosed a copy of my resume.

Yawn.

✔ Please accept this letter and resume for the product marketing manager position as referenced on your company's Web site. I am sure that my work history and educational background will benefit the future endeavors of your company.

Your letter is boring; you're probably boring, too. About 500 people answered our ad, and most are just as mediocre as you seem to be.

JUDGMENT CALL

Should you use a template?

Has this frustration happened to you? Short on time, you scout the Web for one of those free cover letter templates, fill in the blanks, send it off to an employer with your resume, and watch your hair turn gray waiting to hear back? What went wrong?

Among many things that may have doomed your candidacy is the cover letter itself. When that happens, the cover letter you sent did not adequately distinguish you from the crowd as being worthy of the time and cost of interviewing you in the flesh.

Interview-generating cover letters are customized and persuasive, not perfunctory and canned. The communications that open interviewing doors in competitive job markets are really sales letters disguised as cover letters.

The winning ones take time to add zest, energy, and marketing muscle.

No advocate of wheel-spinning, I can't recommend the use of the free cover letter templates that are widely available online. They simply don't pack the wallop you need to stand out like the only red tulip in a field of yellow tulips.

Nonetheless, some job seekers just can't get started on cover letters without a support system. If you're raising your hand on that one, check out Susan Ireland's *Ready-Made Cover Letters,* (www.susanireland.com). Her package of downloadable software is available for a fee, offering customizable cover letters for a wide range of job seekers. Ireland, a talented writer and author of several job search books, is a leading cover letter authority.

> ✔ I am very interested in opportunities within your company. Enclosed please find my resume for your review.
>
> *Sure you are. You and hundreds of other unfocused job hunters who will take whatever jobs they can get.*

Cover letters and resumes begin to blur after skimming a dozen or so of them. Just imagine the glazed-over eyes after a hiring professional reads hundreds of cover letters! Some letters jump out of the stack, enticing the reader to tackle the resume; in other words, they make the cut. Others may as well be stamped with invisible ink: *Ignore me.*

As your mom probably told you: You really don't get a second chance to make a good first impression. Openers count!

Power Phrases to Use Anywhere

After you've punched out your openers, keep your cover-letter mojo going as you flesh out the middle with paragraphs and lines that strongly emphasize your belief in yourself and your strengths.

Don't be shy about listing qualifications, skills, competencies, accomplishments, and achievements. Use numbers wherever you can. If you spot a concept you like in the 35 following examples, think of a way to adapt it to your situation. Or mix and match the ideas expressed.

- ✔ I am particularly well-qualified for your (job title) position, as the following highlights illustrate. I would enjoy the opportunity to meet with you to explore how I can contribute to your organization.

- ✔ For your convenience, I will keep this letter especially brief. The job you're trying to fill (job title) seems to have my name on it, thanks to my qualifications in (skills) and (experience).

- ✔ Your position for (job title) strongly appeals to me because (tell why).

- ✔ If our meeting confirms my understanding of your open position for (job title), I am confident that with my skills in (name skills), I can make an immediate and valuable contribution to (name of employer).

- ✔ My successful background demonstrates the skills you require in (name of position). Briefly, I offer (bulleted lists of accomplishments and achievements).

- ✔ As my resume shows, I have substantial and successful experience in (field/position/skill).

- ✔ As we discussed earlier, my extensive professional experience can benefit virtually any employer. However, (company name) is of special interest to me because (explain why).

- ✔ (Name of employer's company) ranks Number One in companies I prefer to join.

- ✔ I look forward to meeting with you to further discuss my background and to show you some of the (skills or competencies) that I have developed.

- ✔ I'm working to be a part of a company that wants to be recognized as a leader in both ___ and ___. When I have the opportunity to meet with you, I believe you will agree that you want to use my skills and competencies on your watch.

- ✔ What you're asking for and what I can deliver sound like a match!

- ✔ As one of six siblings, I was born in a team environment and understand the payoff of pulling together in an endeavor.

- ✔ During my three years in purchasing with Tidewater Productions, I've been credited with yearly savings in the $50,000 to $75,000 range. This resulted from a combination of skillful negotiation and replacing underperforming vendors. Wouldn't you like me to save money for your company?

- ✔ My experience with women's health issues, coupled with demonstrated successful performance in the offices of medical school clinics, suggests that I could make a significant contribution to your practice. Perhaps we could meet to more thoroughly explore this possibility.

✔ Because I haven't yet notified my current employer of my intent to leave, I count on your treating this response to your posting with appropriate sensitivity. *(Employers often prefer to hire employed candidates, rather than unemployed candidates.)*

✔ I am happy with my job and am considered to be a high performer by my current employer. Unfortunately, I do not see a path to advancement in the foreseeable future. That is why I am contacting you about future openings in the (career field or functional area) at (name of organization).

✔ One of my friends, Salvador Rondavi, works for your company. He recommends that I contact you about a position as a management trainee. He is more than satisfied with his work and from what he says, I am sure I would like it as well and will do my utmost to win your professional praise.

✔ Please allow me to highlight some of my accomplishments that are relevant to your requirements.

✔ Staying current with new technologies and products, and applying those that offer improved profit results, is a point of pride for me.

✔ As a versatile IT trainer, I bring significant experience and fast-moving flexibility as new products are introduced to your workforce. Additionally, my BA in psychology has given me a useful depth of knowledge in successful motivation practices.

✔ I am long on effort and enthusiasm, although short on experience. Examples of my passion for doing the job well are in references I gained as a student from my employers and customers, such as the following achievements: (list references).

✔ I completed a number of successful projects for the physics department in my capacity as student administrative monitor. I believe the knowledge I acquired there would transfer extremely well to your engineering department.

✔ Jason Luo, my former manager, now retired, complimented me for being the hardest working and most reliable assistant he'd had in his 40 years in the casino business. He was especially impressed with my (name top achievement).

✔ As a member of The World Tomorrow Society's Green Futures Committee, I focused on the impact of reusing and recycling waste on various industries, including ours. I'd be delighted to share that data with you when we meet to explore ways I could be useful to Command Construction.

✔ When my last fundraising goal went over the top, I was credited with a big slice of its success because I encouraged everyone's input and buy-in. My talent for inclusiveness brings in record contributions.

✔ I'm proud of a track record that's tops with managers, clients, and coworkers, as this single example from Shelly Kornfield, my former supervisor illustrates: "Give the assignment to Pam and you won't have to think about it anymore."

- In my last position, managing an assisted-living facility, I saved 8% of the annual budget without compromising care; I would welcome sharing the details with you in a meeting to discuss the possibility of my joining your well-respected organization.

- After completing two baccalaureate degrees in just four years, I believe that my education, student employment experience, and dedication to hard work and problem-solving make me an A-list candidate to join your workforce.

- My senior year's academic result: A 3.7 GPA with President's Honors, despite my student job requiring 30 hours a week, illustrates that I know how to dig in and get the job done.

- Given my global supply chain experience, I'm confident that we may have mutual interests.

- My recent earnings reflect gains I brought to my employer; with your firm's reputation for paying fair market rate, I'm wide open to discussing compensation when we sit down to talk.

- With my technical skills and understanding of your market, I can step into the position and be immediately productive.

- At my previous position on the East Coast, within two years I received praise for playing a key role in raising my branch's basement ranking for customer service (#57 out of 60 stores) to top ranking customer service (#3 out of 60 stores) in the nationwide organization.

- Accustomed to doing more with fewer resources, I can help your firm ride out a financial storm in a tight economy. After meeting with me and assessing my ability to run a tight ship that sails upright, you may decide you can't afford not to hire me.

- While I was the fundraising chair for my PTA organization, I planned the campaign, wrote the appeal to potential donors, and organized an e-mail solicitation tree. The result: We raised $27,000, a 130% increase over the previous year.

The power phrases in the preceding list are anchored with accomplishments, achievements, skills, the promise of a benefit, or personal characteristics that suggest you will be a likeable model of efficiency, making money or saving money for your lucky future employer.

For the record, I've always had trouble separating accomplishments from achievements. After looking it up for the zillionth time, I can report that *accomplishments* are extended events — for example, the act of John's climbing a mountain. *Achievements* are culminating, instantaneous events — the act of John's reaching the top of the mountain. That's the long and short of it. Go forth and craft statements alive with accomplishments and achievements and gain that interview.

Words that stick when you're stuck

When you're struggling to capture the exact verb that expresses the vigor of your background, glance at this mini-list to jog your wordsmith talents.

Do you need more ways to say what you've done? Try this quick free fix: Type "list action verbs" on Google or another browser. Stand back for an avalanche of words.

accomplished	formulated	played a key role
achieved	headed up	produced
actively participated	investigated	profitably
administered	led	project managed
co-developed	leveraged	restructured
dealt effectively	managed	scoped out
decreased costs	marketed	solved
delivered	negotiated	supervised
established	orchestrated	took the lead in
exceeded target	persuaded	turned around
facilitated	planned	upgraded

Keep Control with an Action Close

After you write a great letter extolling your major match-up for the job you're chasing, maintain momentum with a close that brings you closer to your goal: an interview. You have three basic choices: an action close, an action close plus, and a no-action close.

Action close

Close your letter by telling the reader when you will call for an interview. By setting the agenda, you assure your reader that you will follow up with an action step that brings together a competent candidate with a lucky employer. An action close says that you're on the scene to help and will contact the employer at a specified time:

I'm ready to make money for you and look forward to speaking with you personally. I will call you early next week.

Action close plus

Pump up an action close with a suggestion for action sooner rather than later — "I'll call you, but if you're ready to roll, you can call me right away."

An action close plus is the best choice for many situations. Your enthusiasm suggests that you're organized and vigorous, but adding a note of urgency by inviting an employer to call you may motivate the employer to prioritize the interview and move up the timetable for a meeting.

Turning an action close into an action close plus is simple, requiring merely one line at the end of the close. The line is "If you would like to meet with me sooner, you can reach me at (phone number)."

I'm eager to sit down with you to discuss the contribution I can make to ABC Organization as it works to create a regional planning group. I'll follow up with a call next Wednesday. Or, you can reach me immediately on my mobile phone at 888-888-8888. Thank you for your time and consideration.

No-action close

A no-action close hands control of the interviewing process over to the reader. It essentially says that you'll sit tight and wait by the phone for an employer to call. This is the weakest way to close your cover letter.

A copy of my resume is enclosed for your review and consideration. If you have an interest in my background, I would be pleased to hear from you.

Letting the employer chase you

A-list job seekers with high-demand skills — a rare bunch — can make a case for using a no-action close to avoid looking too eager. The strategic merit of presenting yourself as so attractive a candidate that employers will bust their chops to hire you was straightforwardly expressed by master yogi Baba Hari Dass: *If you chase the world, it runs from you. If you run from the world, it chases you.*

Everybody else: Resume cover letters are a form of marketing. Hang onto control of your interviewing process by using an action close.

Examples of the Action Closes

You need a competitive edge to get ahead in a competitive market today. Here are 16 solid closes to help you score that interview.

✔ I look forward to our conversation. I'll e-mail you in a few days to coordinate a time that's convenient for you.

✔ Because e-mail can't replace face-to-face discussion, I'll call soon to set up an interview.

✔ Thank you in advance for reviewing my resume. I enthusiastically anticipate discussing my qualifications in an interview. I'll e-mail you on Thursday to validate your interest.

✔ I look forward to speaking with you personally to discuss your specific needs and my ability to meet them. I'll call your administrative assistant next week to see what time would be most convenient for you.

✔ I welcome a personal interview to discuss how my qualifications can augment your company's excellent reputation for purchasing acumen. I'll e-mail you on Tuesday to see whether we can meet.

✔ I'm excited about employment opportunities within your agency and hope to explore contributions I can make. I'll e-mail you within the week to see when your calendar is open.

✔ I hope to play an active role in the future prosperity of your organization. I'll contact you next week to talk about this job or other positions where your needs and my talents meet.

✔ As you requested, here's my resume. I'll check back with you next week to flesh out any blank areas. Thanks for your interest.

✔ My resume follows. I'll telephone you next week to answer any questions you may have and, I hope, set up a time convenient to meet in person.

✔ Recognizing that you may be difficult to reach, I'll check with your secretary next week to set a convenient time for us to meet. Flexibility is my middle name, and I'll be glad to meet during or outside normal business hours. Thanks, and I look forward to meeting with you personally.

✔ Thank you for calling me back today. I'm sorry I was not in but will telephone you tomorrow to find a convenient time to speak with you on the phone and meet you in person.

✔ I'll contact you within a few days to determine if and when your schedule will allow us to meet. Meeting you will not only be a pleasure but offers profitable vistas for both of us. My thanks for your time.

✔ As a resume is limited in the information it conveys, why don't we meet in person? If you need additional facts before arranging an interview, call me at 888-888-8888. Otherwise, I'll e-mail you next week to confirm your interest.

When an ad forbids you to call

How can you use an action close in responding to a job ad that says "No phone calls" or "Don't call us; we'll call you if you match a job opening"? Here are a couple of moves to consider in writing your cover letter.

✔ **Substitute e-mail.** You can still use an action close by changing your promise from "I'll call you" to "I'll e-mail you."

✔ **Play the coincidence card.** Send your cover letter (with an action close) and resume to the company president or hiring manager. Don't mention the ad. The employer's assumption will be that your timing is serendipity — you just happened to apply at the same time the company needs someone with your assets. The company president most likely will forward your material to the hiring manager or HR department with a note calling attention to you.

✔ My salary needs are in line with the position's description and what I bring in abilities. I'll e-mail you Tuesday to see when we can explore specifics.

✔ I would like to discuss with you why this position has my name on it, and I'll call you at the beginning of next week to see what your schedule allows. Or if you need to reach me sooner, my number is listed above.

✔ Perhaps we could meet and jointly explore the many ways I could save your organization considerable time and money. I'm flexible on timing during business hours or afterwards. I'll check your availability next week.

The purpose of your cover letter is to sell an employer on reading your resume and being motivated to take your call for an interview or to contact you for an interview. Without an interview, you're unlikely to be offered employment.

P.S. A Final Important Point

Your effort to write a Stand Out letter is time well invested in your future. And now for one last cover letter tip that direct marketing writers have known for light years — add a P.S. after your signature. And not because you're forgetful.

Adding a P.S. (postscript) to your letter is a spotlighting technique that marketers advise. In this usage, the P.S. does not communicate a point that you overlooked; instead, it communicates a point that you want to stand out and be read. What information can you put in your P.S.? You have two basic choices. They are:

Letters that give something to get something

The following illustration of a graduating senior's cover letter to the marketing manager of a large private student loan company is a bit of a tease. The letter's promise of a substantial benefit — two unpublished survey data points and the hint of more later — speaks directly to the marketing manager's need to identify criteria that can attract potential customers to his product. All he has to do to gain this benefit is agree to meet with the job seeker.

Dear Mr.____:

Students on my campus are scrutinizing private education loans with a new intensity following a batch of high-profile bad press in recent years.

After becoming aware of their increased caution while working as an intern in my college's financial aid office, I followed up with a personal research project surveying 300 students about their criteria for choosing a student loan provider. The project was the basis of a term paper required for my degree in marketing.

Among the marketing conclusions I reached as a result of my research project are these two points:

(Use a paragraph to describe each of the two points).

I hope you will find this information useful, Mr. ___, and also will consider me for your next marketing associate position. To make that decision, you'll need to know more about my background and abilities; my resume is attached. I'll call you Thursday morning to set up an interview. Many thanks.

- ✔ Communicate the single most important thing you want an employer to remember about you. Dangle a benefit. Here's an example of dangling a benefit:

    P.S. I'm anxious to tell you how I increased the net profit by 12% for my employer in 2008. Let's talk soon.

- ✔ After your action close *(note: not an action close plus)* and signature, say something to drive the employer to call you first. Here's an example of urging an employer to pick up the phone and check you out:

    P.S. I would work my heart out to be your best hire of the year. As mentioned, I will call you next week, but if you want to visit sooner, my cell phone is 999-999-9000.

Great Lines Woo Reluctant Readers

If your cover letter and resume duo fall in a noisy and crowded marketplace and no one is paying attention, will it make a sound? Make your words clear, concise, and interesting to read, and your message will wake up the neighborhood!

Chapter 7

Job Seeker's Skills Finder

Are skills central to driving your workplace wins? Short answer: Don't let your cover letters (and resumes) leave home without them. As you read this chapter, forget about being a grammar snoot; instead, laser your attention like a sci-fi ray gun on your developed abilities.

No matter which niche you occupy in the workplace — technician or green-collar worker, professional or manager — mastering skills you can use, and skills that employers are willing to pay you to use, translates to a wonderful employment insurance policy, a giant umbrella to keep you from getting soaked when economic thunderstorms rain on your parade.

Learning how to identify your skills and to believably write and talk about them will be transformative to your job hunt. The payoff is moving from the crowd to the choice. This chapter shows you how to do that, beginning with the way skills are classified.

Decoding the Skills Lineup

I'm the first to admit that the classification of skills, like beauty, is in the eye of the beholder. But we have to start somewhere, so based on government and academic classification systems, here's a no-frills framework that will guide you through the thicket of workplace skills.

One of the noun terms you often find in a discussion of job requirements is *skill set*. If you've wondered what it means, here's a simple definition: A skill set means the skills needed to accomplish a specified task or perform a given function.

Foundation skills

The foundation skills are appropriate for everyone's skill DNA. They are organized into four groups: basic, people, thinking, and personal qualities.

Basic skills

When you have basic skills, you can read, write, perform arithmetic and mathematical operations, listen, and speak.

- **Reading:** You can locate, understand, and interpret written information such as manuals, graphs, and schedules.

- **Writing:** You can communicate thoughts, ideas, information, and messages in writing and create documents such as letters, directions, manuals, reports, graphs, and flow charts.

- **Arithmetic/mathematics:** You can perform basic computations and approach practical problems by choosing appropriately from a variety of mathematical techniques.

- **Listening:** You receive, attend to, interpret, and respond to verbal messages and other cues.

- **Speaking:** You organize ideas and communicate orally.

You have skills because . . .

Here are four springboards for writing and speaking of your skills. You can infer your skills based on history, simply assert your skills, refer to others who identified your skills, or be tested by professional bodies.

- **Inference.** Your prior education and experience suggest your skills.

  With my degree in civil engineering, I am competent to design bridges.

- **Assertion.** You claim you have skills.

  I can design and sell a program of services to the Spanish-speaking market.

- **References.** Others act on your behalf to claim skills.

  My former manager, Carlyle Sangi, says I put together a budget better than anyone she knows.

- **Certification.** Testing and peer evaluation document your skills.

  As a certified industrial ergonomist, I can evaluate your workplace and make required changes to conform to new OSHA rules.

People skills

These are the skills that allow the "wonder of you" to mesh well with others. They include social, negotiation, leadership, teamwork, and cultural diversity.

- ✔ **Social:** You respect the feelings of others, assert yourself when appropriate, and take an interest in what others say and why they think and act as they do.

- ✔ **Negotiation:** You present the facts and arguments of your position and listen to and understand the other party's position, create possible ways to resolve conflict, and make reasonable compromises.

- ✔ **Leadership:** You communicate thoughts and feelings to justify the position you champion, encourage or convince others, and motivate people to believe in and trust you.

- ✔ **Teamwork:** You work cooperatively with others, contribute ideas and effort, and do your share of the work.

- ✔ **Cultural diversity:** You work well with people who have different ethnic, social, or educational backgrounds.

Thinking skills

These skills enable you to think creatively, make decisions, solve problems, visualize, and know how to learn and reason.

- ✔ **Creative thinking:** You generate new ideas.

- ✔ **Decision making:** You have the ability to specify goals and understand reasons not to do something.

- ✔ **Problem solving:** You can recognize a problem and devise a plan of action to deal with it.

- ✔ **Visualizing:** You can picture symbols and organize them in your mind's eye.

- ✔ **Knowing how to learn:** You are able to use efficient learning techniques to acquire and apply new knowledge and skills.

- ✔ **Reasoning:** You concentrate on discovering a rule or principle underlying the relationship between two or more objects and then apply it to solve a problem.

Personal qualities

Classified as skills, these personal qualities include responsibility, self-esteem, sociability, self-management, integrity, and honesty.

✔ **Responsibility:** You put forth a high level of effort and persevere toward reaching your goal.

✔ **Self-esteem:** You believe in your own self-worth and maintain a positive view of yourself.

✔ **Sociability:** You show understanding, friendliness, adaptability, empathy, and politeness in group settings.

✔ **Self-management:** You have a realistic view of your knowledge and skills, set realistic personal goals, and monitor progress toward those goals.

Where There's a Skill, There's a Way

The foundation skills group isn't the end of the story. Other groups of skills are identified by whether they have market value to employers (marketable skills), can be carried around like a mobile phone from one employer to another (crossover skills), or are super-glued to a specific type of work or workplace (job-related skills). Still another term describes skills you're really good at because you love using them (motivated skills).

✔ **Marketable skills:** Simply stated, marketable skills are those that an employer will pay you to use. They're often identified in job ads. By contrast, unmarketable skills are those that no one is likely to pay you to use — the ability to bounce for a mile on a pogo stick, for example. Also unmarketable or barely marketable: obsolete skills.

✔ **Crossover skills:** You may have heard these skills referred to as *transferrable* skills. To my ear, *crossover* is a more modern term. Crossover skills are portable skills that you can use in a wide variety of jobs.

For example, employers value communications skills in positions ranging from apple grower to zookeeper. You can transfer these skills from job to job, industry to industry, or even from one career field to another. I illustrate with a checklist of selected crossover skills in the next section.

✔ **Job-related skills:** Job-related skills are also called *technical* or *professional* skills. Because they're suitable for a particular type of job, they assure an employer that you can actually do the job. You can't always move job-related skills from one employer to another, but sometimes you can. (To gauge mobility, ask yourself: "Who would pay me to use this skill?")

Three examples of job-related skills: The ability to use a certain brand of mold-injection machine; the ability to perform cataract eye surgery; and the ability to spot cheating players in a casino.

✔ **Motivated skills:** "Do something you'd do for nothing" is the theme song of motivated skills. These are the developed abilities that you enjoy doing. Describing a motivated skill in a cover letter is a subtle way of saying you'll excel at a specific assignment: *One of my motivated skills is ____.*

Understanding competencies versus skills

Competencies, which are also sometimes called *success factors, key characteristics,* or *behaviors,* go deeper than skills, according to one definition. A competency is a relatively enduring characteristic that makes possible superior performance in a particular job or role.

In brief, a competency is the X-factor in why of two equally skilled employees in the same company, one hits a home run and another hits a double.

Competency recruiting is an evolving human resource management concept. Study corporate Web sites and determine whether competency recruiting is the policy at your target company. If so, analyze the position you want and develop statements for each competency it requires. If a company is looking for a candidate who has shown "creative leadership," for example, write examples of when you've demonstrated such behavior. Explain how you did it, distinguishing yourself as a top performer.

As I say in my book, *Job Interviews For Dummies,* 3rd Edition, in today's world, "The operative words are *skills* (what you can do) and, increasingly a newer and broader employment concept termed *competencies* (how well you do what you do using natural talents). The competencies concept includes skills and such related characteristics and natural abilities as motivation, industriousness, and attitudes."

The competency program looks at the whole package as it relates to the job the employer wants done. If a company's Web site or recruitment materials mention competencies, you mention competencies in your cover letter. If not, don't refer to competencies but stick to skills.

Speaking Out about Your Skills

Because spelling out your skills adds substance to your claims of being able to put more money in a company's bank account than it will spend to employ you, I've compiled a couple of checklists to help you claim those you own.

Read through the following checklist of foundation skills and the checklist of crossover skills. Mark the words and terms that truthfully apply to you. Include the terms as part of your skills language to use for job search documents and job interviews.

Speaking of interviews, when you claim ownership of a specific skill, be prepared in interviews to give a brief example of how you used that skill and its benefits. If you're asked and all you can come up with on the spot is babble, the interviewer will think you're an inventor, but not the good kind.

While these checklists aren't exhaustive, they're a good start; you may think of other words and terms to use as well.

Foundation skills checklist

A

❑ Ability to learn
❑ Abstract thinking
❑ Accepting consequences
❑ Abstract thinking
❑ Accepting consequences
❑ Accepting criticism
❑ Accepting freedom
❑ Accepting supervision
❑ Accommodating
❑ Active
❑ Adventurous
❑ Affable
❑ Agile
❑ Alert
❑ Ambitious
❑ Amicable
❑ Animated
❑ Appealing
❑ Approachable
❑ Artistic abilities
❑ Aspiring
❑ Assertive
❑ Astute
❑ Athletic
❑ Attendance
❑ Attention to detail
❑ Autonomy
❑ Awareness

B

❑ Benevolent
❑ Benign
❑ Bold
❑ Brave
❑ Bright

C

❑ Careful
❑ Caring
❑ Casual
❑ Cautious
❑ Charismatic
❑ Charitable
❑ Charming
❑ Cheerful
❑ Chivalrous
❑ Clever
❑ Colorful
❑ Commitment
❑ Common sense
❑ Compassion
❑ Compliant
❑ Composure
❑ Comprehension
❑ Concentration
❑ Conceptualization
❑ Concern

❑ Confidence
❑ Congenial
❑ Conscientious
❑ Conservative
❑ Considerate
❑ Consistent
❑ Constant
❑ Contemplative
❑ Cordial
❑ Courageous
❑ Courteous
❑ Creativity
❑ Critical thinking
❑ Cunning
❑ Curiosity

D

❑ Daring
❑ Decisive
❑ Dedicated
❑ Deft
❑ Deliberate
❑ Dependable
❑ Desire
❑ Determined
❑ Devoted
❑ Devout
❑ Dexterity
❑ Dignity

❏ Diligent
❏ Discipline
❏ Dogged
❏ Drive
❏ Dutiful
❏ Dynamic

E

❏ Eager
❏ Earnest
❏ Easy-going
❏ Economical
❏ Efficient
❏ Eloquence
❏ Empathy
❏ Energetic
❏ Engaging
❏ Enjoys challenge
❏ Enterprising
❏ Entertaining
❏ Enthusiasm
❏ Entrepreneurial
❏ Ethical
❏ Exciting
❏ Explorative
❏ Expressive
❏ Extroverted

F

❏ Fair
❏ Faithful
❏ Fast
❏ Firm
❏ Flexibility
❏ Focused
❏ Forceful
❏ Fortitude
❏ Friendly
❏ Funny

G

❏ Generous
❏ Gentle
❏ Genuine
❏ Gifted
❏ Good-natured
❏ Graceful
❏ Gracious

H

❏ Hard-working
❏ Hardy
❏ Honest
❏ Honor
❏ Humble
❏ Humorous
❏ Hustle

I

❏ Imagination
❏ Immaculate
❏ Impetus
❏ Improvisation
❏ Incentive
❏ Independent
❏ Industrious
❏ Informal
❏ Ingenious
❏ Initiative
❏ Innovative
❏ Inquisitive
❏ Integrity
❏ Intelligence
❏ Interest
❏ Intuitive
❏ Inventing

K

❏ Keen
❏ Kind

L

❏ Likable
❏ Lively
❏ Loyal

M

- ❏ Maturity
- ❏ Memory
- ❏ Methodical
- ❏ Meticulous
- ❏ Mindful
- ❏ Modest
- ❏ Motivation

N

- ❏ Neat
- ❏ Nimble

O

- ❏ Obliging
- ❏ Open-minded
- ❏ Opportunistic
- ❏ Optimistic
- ❏ Orderly
- ❏ Original
- ❏ Outgoing

P

- ❏ Patience
- ❏ Perfectionist
- ❏ Persevering
- ❏ Persistence
- ❏ Personable

- ❏ Pioneering
- ❏ Pleasant
- ❏ Poised
- ❏ Polite
- ❏ Positive
- ❏ Powerful
- ❏ Practical
- ❏ Pragmatic
- ❏ Presence
- ❏ Pride in work
- ❏ Progressive
- ❏ Prompt
- ❏ Prudent
- ❏ Punctuality

Q

- ❏ Questioning
- ❏ Quick-thinking

R

- ❏ Rational
- ❏ Realistic
- ❏ Reasonable
- ❏ Receptive
- ❏ Reflective
- ❏ Relentless
- ❏ Reliable
- ❏ Reserved
- ❏ Resolute
- ❏ Respectful

- ❏ Responsible
- ❏ Responsiveness
- ❏ Restraint
- ❏ Retention
- ❏ Reverent
- ❏ Risk taking
- ❏ Robust

S

- ❏ Safety
- ❏ Savvy
- ❏ Scrupulous
- ❏ Self-esteem
- ❏ Self-motivating
- ❏ Self-reliant
- ❏ Self-respect
- ❏ Sense of humor
- ❏ Sensible
- ❏ Sharp
- ❏ Showmanship
- ❏ Shrewd
- ❏ Sincere
- ❏ Smart
- ❏ Sociable
- ❏ Spirited
- ❏ Stalwart
- ❏ Stamina
- ❏ Staunch
- ❏ Steadfast
- ❏ Steady
- ❏ Striving
- ❏ Strong

❏ Studious

❏ Sturdy

❏ Style

T

❏ Tactful

❏ Tasteful

❏ Tenacious

❏ Thinking

❏ Thorough

❏ Thoughtfulness

❏ Trustworthy

U

❏ Unbiased

❏ Understanding

❏ Unprejudiced

❏ Unpretentious

❏ Unselfish

V

❏ Venturing

❏ Versatile

❏ Vigilant

❏ Vigorous

❏ Visualizing

❏ Vivacious

W

❏ Warm

❏ Wary

❏ Watchful

❏ Willingness
to follow rules

❏ Wisdom

❏ Work ethic

❏ Work habits

❏ Working alone

❏ Working under
pressure

Crossover skills checklist

A

❏ Accelerating

❏ Accomplishing

❏ Accounting

❏ Accuracy

❏ Achieving

❏ Activating

❏ Active

❏ Active learning

❏ Active listening

❏ Adapting

❏ Addressing

❏ Adjusting

❏ Administering

❏ Advertising

❏ Advising

❏ Aiding

❏ Allocating

❏ Altering

❏ Amending

❏ Analyzing behavior

❏ Analyzing costs

❏ Announcing

❏ Anticipating

❏ Appearance

❏ Application

❏ Appointing

❏ Appraising

❏ Appreciation

❏ Arbitrating

❏ Argumentation

❏ Arranging

❏ Articulation

❏ Assembling

❏ Assessing cost

❏ Assessing damage

❏ Assigning

❏ Assisting

❏ Attaining

❏ Attending

❏ Auditing

❏ Augmenting
❏ Authoring
❏ Automating

B

❏ Balancing
❏ Bargaining
❏ Blending
❏ Bookkeeping
❏ Boosting
❏ Bridging
❏ Briefing
❏ Budgeting
❏ Building

C

❏ Calculating
❏ Calibrating
❏ Cataloging
❏ Categorizing
❏ Chairing
❏ Charting
❏ Checking
❏ Clarifying
❏ Classifying
❏ Clerical ability
❏ Coaching
❏ Coaxing
❏ Cognizance
❏ Coherence

❏ Collaborative
❏ Combining
❏ Comforting
❏ Commanding
❏ Communicating
❏ Comparing
❏ Competence
❏ Compiling
❏ Complimenting
❏ Composing
❏ Compromising
❏ Computing
❏ Condensing
❏ Conducting
❏ Confidentiality
❏ Conflict resolution
❏ Conforming
❏ Confronting
❏ Consolidating
❏ Constructing
❏ Consulting
❏ Contingency planning
❏ Contracting
❏ Controlling
❏ Converting
❏ Convincing
❏ Cooperation
❏ Coordinating
❏ Copying
❏ Correcting
❏ Correlating
❏ Corresponding
❏ Counseling

❏ Counteracting
❏ Counterbalancing
❏ Counting
❏ Creating
❏ Creative writing
❏ Crisis management

D

❏ Data collecting
❏ Data entry
❏ Debating
❏ Decision-making
❏ Deductive reasoning
❏ Defending
❏ Defining problems
❏ Delegating
❏ Delivering
❏ Demonstrating
❏ Depicting
❏ Describing
❏ Designating
❏ Designing
❏ Detecting
❏ Developing ideas
❏ Devising
❏ Diagnosing
❏ Diagramming
❏ Diplomacy
❏ Directing
❏ Discretion
❏ Discussing
❏ Dispatching

- ❑ Dispensing
- ❑ Displaying
- ❑ Distributing
- ❑ Diversifying
- ❑ Diverting
- ❑ Documenting
- ❑ Drafting
- ❑ Drawing
- ❑ Duplicating

E

- ❑ Editing
- ❑ Educating
- ❑ Effecting change
- ❑ Elevating
- ❑ Eliminating
- ❑ Empowering
- ❑ Enabling
- ❑ Enacting
- ❑ Encouraging
- ❑ Engineering a plan
- ❑ Enhancing
- ❑ Enlarging
- ❑ Enlisting
- ❑ Enlivening
- ❑ Enriching
- ❑ Envisioning
- ❑ Equalizing
- ❑ Escalating
- ❑ Establishing objectives

- ❑ Establishing priorities
- ❑ Estimating
- ❑ Evaluating
- ❑ Examining
- ❑ Exchanging information
- ❑ Executing a plan
- ❑ Exhibiting
- ❑ Expanding
- ❑ Expediting
- ❑ Extracting

F

- ❑ Fabricating
- ❑ Facilitating
- ❑ Figuring
- ❑ Filing
- ❑ Finding
- ❑ Finishing
- ❑ Fixing
- ❑ Fluency
- ❑ Following through
- ❑ Forecasting
- ❑ Foresight
- ❑ Forging
- ❑ Forming
- ❑ Formulating
- ❑ Fostering
- ❑ Founding
- ❑ Framing
- ❑ Fulfilling

- ❑ Fundraising
- ❑ Furthering

G

- ❑ Gauging
- ❑ Generalizing
- ❑ Generating
- ❑ Grammar
- ❑ Graphics
- ❑ Grouping
- ❑ Guessing
- ❑ Guiding

H

- ❑ Handling complaints
- ❑ Harmonizing
- ❑ Heading
- ❑ Healing
- ❑ Helpful
- ❑ Hypothesizing

I

- ❑ Identifying alternatives
- ❑ Identifying causes
- ❑ Identifying downstream consequences
- ❑ Identifying issues
- ❑ Identifying needs

❑ Identifying principles

❑ Identifying problems

❑ Illuminating

❑ Illustrating

❑ Impartial

❑ Implementing

❑ Improving

❑ Incitement

❑ Increasing

❑ Indexing

❑ Indoctrinating

❑ Inductive

❑ Inductive reasoning

❑ Influencing

❑ Information gathering

❑ Information management

❑ Information organization

❑ Information receiving

❑ Informing

❑ Infusing

❑ Insightful

❑ Inspecting

❑ Inspiring

❑ Installation

❑ Instilling

❑ Instituting

❑ Instruction

❑ Integration

❑ Interaction

❑ Interceding

❑ Interpersonal skills

❑ Interpretation

❑ Interrupting

❑ Intervening

❑ Interviewing

❑ Introducing

❑ Investigation

❑ Isolating

❑ Itemizing

J

❑ Joining

❑ Judgment

K

❑ Keeping deadlines

❑ Keyboarding

❑ Knowledge of subject

L

❑ Language

❑ Launching

❑ Laying

❑ Leadership

❑ Learning

❑ Lecturing

❑ Listening for content

❑ Listening for context

❑ Listening for directions

❑ Listening for emotional meaning

❑ Listing

❑ Locating

❑ Logical reasoning

❑ Long-term planning

M

❑ Maintaining confidentiality

❑ Maintenance

❑ Managing

❑ Maneuvering

❑ Manipulation

❑ Mapping

❑ Marketing

❑ Masking

❑ Matching

❑ Mathematics

❑ Measuring

❑ Mechanical ability

❑ Mediating

❑ Meeting

❑ Mending

❑ Mentoring

❑ Merchandising

❑ Minding machines

❑ Minimizing

❑ Modeling

❑ Moderating

❑ Modifying

❑ Modulating

❑ Molding

❑ Money management

- ❏ Monitoring
- ❏ Motivating

N

- ❏ Negotiating
- ❏ Nonpartisan
- ❏ Number skills
- ❏ Nursing
- ❏ Nurturing

O

- ❏ Objectivity
- ❏ Observing
- ❏ Operating vehicles
- ❏ Operations analysis
- ❏ Oral communication
- ❏ Oral comprehension
- ❏ Orchestrating
- ❏ Organizational
- ❏ Organizing
- ❏ Outfitting
- ❏ Outlining
- ❏ Outreach
- ❏ Overhauling
- ❏ Overseeing

P

- ❏ Pacifying
- ❏ Paraphrasing

- ❏ Participating
- ❏ Patterning
- ❏ Perceiving
- ❏ Perfecting
- ❏ Performing
- ❏ Persuasion
- ❏ Photography
- ❏ Picturing
- ❏ Pinpointing
- ❏ Planning
- ❏ Plotting
- ❏ Policy-making
- ❏ Polishing
- ❏ Politicking
- ❏ Popularizing
- ❏ Portraying
- ❏ Precision
- ❏ Prediction
- ❏ Preparation
- ❏ Presentation
- ❏ Printing
- ❏ Prioritizing
- ❏ Probing
- ❏ Problem-solving
- ❏ Processing
- ❏ Producing
- ❏ Professional
- ❏ Prognostication
- ❏ Program design
- ❏ Program developing
- ❏ Program implementation
- ❏ Projection

- ❏ Promoting
- ❏ Proofreading
- ❏ Proposing
- ❏ Protecting
- ❏ Providing
- ❏ Public speaking
- ❏ Publicizing
- ❏ Publishing
- ❏ Purchasing

Q

- ❏ Quality control

R

- ❏ Raising
- ❏ Ranking
- ❏ Readiness
- ❏ Reading comprehension
- ❏ Reasoning
- ❏ Reclaiming
- ❏ Recognition
- ❏ Reconciling
- ❏ Recording
- ❏ Recovering
- ❏ Recruiting
- ❏ Rectifying
- ❏ Reducing
- ❏ Referring
- ❏ Reformative
- ❏ Regulating

❏ Rehabilitating

❏ Reinforcing

❏ Relationship building

❏ Remodeling

❏ Rendering

❏ Reorganizing

❏ Repairing

❏ Repeating

❏ Reporting

❏ Representing

❏ Researching

❏ Resolving

❏ Resource development

❏ Resource management

❏ Response coordination

❏ Restoring

❏ Restructuring

❏ Retrieving

❏ Reversing

❏ Reviewing

❏ Revitalizing

❏ Rhetoric

❏ Rousing

❏ Running

S

❏ Saving

❏ Scanning

❏ Scheduling

❏ Schooling

❏ Science

❏ Scientific reasoning

❏ Screening

❏ Scrutiny

❏ Searching

❏ Selecting

❏ Selling

❏ Sensitivity

❏ Sequencing

❏ Serving

❏ Setting up

❏ Settling

❏ Shaping

❏ Shielding

❏ Situation analysis

❏ Sketching

❏ Social perceptiveness

❏ Solidifying

❏ Solution appraisal

❏ Solving

❏ Sorting

❏ Speaking

❏ Spearheading

❏ Specialization

❏ Specifying

❏ Speculating

❏ Speech

❏ Stabilizing

❏ Stimulating

❏ Stirring

❏ Storing information

❏ Streamlining

❏ Strengthening

❏ Structuring

❏ Styling

❏ Substituting

❏ Summarizing

❏ Supervising

❏ Supplementing

❏ Supporting

❏ Surmising

❏ Surveying

❏ Sustaining

❏ Synthesis

❏ Systematizing

❏ Systems analysis

❏ Systems management

❏ Systems perception

❏ Systems understanding

T

❏ Tabulating

❏ Taking instruction

❏ Talking

❏ Teaching

❏ Teamwork

❏ Technical writing

❏ Tempering

❑ Terminology

❑ Testing

❑ Theorizing

❑ Time management

❑ Training

❑ Translating

❑ Traveling

❑ Treating

❑ Troubleshooting

❑ Tutoring

❑ Typing

u

❑ Unifying

❑ Updating

❑ Upgrading

❑ Using tools

v

❑ Values clarification

❑ Visual communication

w

❑ Word processing

❑ Working with earth

❑ Working with nature

❑ Working with others

❑ Written communication

You can track down more specific skill words in three main ways.

✔ Search job ads in print and online. Pay particular attention to each job's requirements.

✔ Search online for "sample job descriptions." You may have to surf a large number of sites because each typically offers only a half-dozen occupations.

✔ Go to a Department of Labor Web site, O'Net Code Connector, `www.onetcodeconnector.org`, where you see the skills required for an occupation of interest. The skills are called "Detailed Work Activities."

No frills, just skills

Define your skills and what you bring to a new job. When prospecting for your skills, review your last job or college post and think about these issues:

✔ What did you do?

✔ What did you direct others to do?

✔ What did you manage, create, approve, or instigate?

✔ What was the outcome of your actions?

✔ More profits? (How much?)

✔ More revenue? (How much?)

✔ More savings (how much can you claim?)

✔ More accounts (How many? What are they worth?)

Popular Skills that Employers Want

After pinpointing the skills that sell your value, how do you know which of those most help you stand out from the crowd?

A roundup of several surveys suggests skills and qualities that employers often admire. The following list is representative but not comprehensive.

✔ **Effective communication:** Employers seek candidates who can listen to instructions and act on those instructions with minimal guidance. They want employees who speak, write, and listen effectively, organize their thoughts logically, and explain everything clearly.

✔ **Computer and technical literacy:** Almost all jobs now require an understanding, ranging from basic to advanced, of computer software, word processing, e-mail, spreadsheets, and Internet navigation.

✔ **Problem-solving/Creativity:** Employers always want people who can get them out of a pickle. Problem-solving ability can aid you with making transactions, processing data, formulating a vision, and reaching a resolution. Employers need the assurance that you can conquer job challenges by thinking critically and creatively.

✔ **Interpersonal abilities:** Relationship-building and relationship-management are high priorities with many employers. These skills confirm that a candidate can relate well to others, both co-workers and customers.

✔ **Teamwork skills:** The ability to work well with others while pursuing a common goal is a long-running favorite of employers. But so is the ability to work with minor supervision.

✔ **Diversity sensitivity:** In today's world, cultural sensitivity and ability to build rapport with others in a multicultural environment is highly valued by employers.

✔ **Planning and organizing:** Workplace life requires prioritizing and organizing information. Employers value people who, metaphorically, dig a well before they're thirsty.

✔ **Leadership and management:** Leadership consists of a strong sense of self, confidence, and a comprehensive knowledge of company goals. These are qualities that motivate and inspire, providing a solid foundation for teamwork.

Year after year, in survey after survey, employers continue to look for assurances that you can in some way either make money for them or save money for them. If the employer is a nonprofit organization, generally you should substitute the skills you can bring to bear on helping the organization fulfill its mission (unless the mission requires selling products to earn money). Skills useful in saving money are universally desired, including by the nonprofits.

Personal Qualities That Employers Want

In the Great American Skills Sorting, some list-makers mix in personal values, personality traits, and personal characteristics with skills — and that's okay with me. But I've made a second list focusing on a few personal qualities that employers rate highly.

- **Adaptability and flexibility:** Nearly half of employers in a recent survey gave a high rating to "openness to new ideas and concepts." They also like candidates who can work independently or as part of a team, changing gears when required, whether multitasking or adapting working hours and locale.

- **Professionalism and work ethic:** Employers seek productive workers with positive work ethics who stick with challenges until they meet them.

- **Positive attitude and energy:** The last to be picked and promoted are candidates who show gloomy outlooks and emotional immaturity. Exhibit a sunny outlook and energetic, organized behavior.

Everyone wants to hire a paragon of virtue, a model of excellence and perfection. Don't overlook adding your personal qualities — and the behaviors they drive — where appropriate when composing your job-search correspondence.

Give Serious Thought to Certifications

A professional certification can be a kind of passport, identifying you as a citizen of a career field with all its rank and privilege. In other words, professional credentialing is one way to document your ownership of the skills you claim.

Not all credentials are worthy. A credential is worth the effort only if it has industry recognition and respect.

Crash course on certification

Differences in certification exist, but for ease of communication, I include other terms of validation such as *registered, accredited, chartered, qualified,* and *diplomate,* as well as *certified.* Whether the professional designation carries statutory clout or is voluntary, common elements include professional experience, often between two and ten years, sometimes reduced by education. Education standards are included, which may call for minimum levels of both academic and professional education.

Certification examinations are uninviting to many professionals; generally, they require time-consuming study and may include both experience-based knowledge acquired working in the field, and curriculum-based knowledge gained by assigned learning texts.

What's certification worth?

Is certification worth your effort?

Certification has strong appeal in your early career — say, the first 12 to 15 years — as a technique to control your earnings environment. But in business, certifications lose their luster at the vice-presidential level and above. Why? Certifications zero in on specific skills, while top managers are more concerned with the big picture. For consulting, medicine, law, and technology careers, professional certifications never lose their punch, especially for those who hope to work internationally. Continuing education may be required to keep them updated and active.

The credential may be a license awarded by a state board, such as the familiar Certified Public Accountant (CPA), or a voluntary program sponsored by a professional organization, such as the Accredited in Public Relations (APR) designation awarded by the Public Relations Society of America.

Because a given professional certification may not carry stripes for your sleeve, much less stars for your shoulder, investigate first! Clues to look for include the following:

✔ Do recruitment ads call for the professional designation? Do trade publications mention it? What do practitioners in your field advise?

✔ As you change jobs more often, certification can be a kind of passport. It shows that you're a player in your field's global body of knowledge and that you have documented standards and achievements.

✔ Certification can be very helpful if you become sidetracked into too narrow a specialty or stagnate in a company with antiquated technologies or find yourself boxed in by a hostile boss. The boss can still claim that you lack interpersonal abilities, but a professional designation leaves little room to say you're short on job-related technical skills.

✔ You may earn more money by going the certified route. A study of project managers reveals that those with a PMP (Project Management Professional) designation with seven years' experience annually earn $7,000 more than non-certified project managers, a differential that adds up to serious money over the years.

Good Luck on the Great Skills Search

When you're really stumped on naming specific skills that make you stand out and need more help than this chapter or your informal efforts provide, the Internet beckons: Call forth the genie of Google and type "discover your skills." More than 625,000 resources are yours to command.

You can't beg off identifying your skills when writing cover letters and other job search documents. Every employer looks for the skill sets a candidate offers.

Shopping for skills

Small businesses are creating most of the new jobs. But small companies have fewer resources to use in training new hires. That means that for most jobs, you're pretty much on your own to acquire the skills you need.

Large companies, although offering fewer jobs in the aggregate, are still the best places to work to acquire up-to-date skills you can market on future jobs.

Part III

Job Letters: Sample the Best

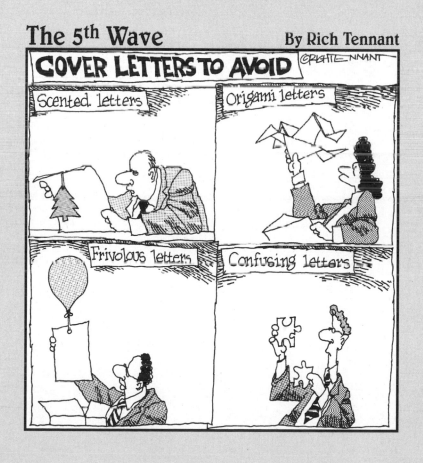

The 5th Wave   By Rich Tennant

COVER LETTERS TO AVOID

Scented letters

Origami letters

Frivolous letters

Confusing letters

In this part . . .

Your main course and the tasty result of ideas set
simmering in Parts I and II, here you find 86 sample
letters cooked up by premium career document writers.
You get a look at job ad reply letters and letters for prospecting and networking. You find choice ways to follow
up after an interview and primo approaches for a bevy of
career situations.

Chapter 8

Job Ad Reply Letters

In This Chapter

▶ Learning from a trove of super sample reply letters

▶ Choosing cool tactical techniques for your specific situation

▶ Viewing interview-magnet approaches anyone can use

Answering a print or online job ad is a nearly universal experience, but the right reply is far from universal. That's why this chapter contains 30 samples — more than any other chapter in this guide. All were written by successful professional cover letter writers who, of course, also write resumes and other outstanding job letter documents; this book's appendix contains contact information for each writer.

These pages hold something for everyone — from new graduate to mid-career professional to seasoned executive.

Read the excellent assortment of occupations and the interesting variety of styles with an eye toward mixing and matching design and marketing elements from one to another. Because the samples range from conservative to forward-leaning, use your judgment in deciding which style best fits your target industry and your personality.

Read all 30 samples and you find a wide range of techniques that snag an employer's interest and hold it all the way to an interview.

Watch for Smooth Moves

The following sections give you the scoop on what's great about the upcoming samples, as well as ideas for putting them to work in your own reply letters.

Magic connectors

Candidates who document point for point their capacity to accomplish what the employer wants done are rewarded with interviews. Several samples illustrate the visual power of directly connecting job requirements with candidate qualifications:

- ✔ A satellite operations manager (Bell) jumps right in with a comment that she's a match. The candidate calls attention to her status of qualified candidate in a vertical treatment. A "You require" list appears on the left side of the page. An "I offer" response appears directly across the page on the right.

- ✔ A diversity development director (Fuller) also uses the left/right design to good effect, concluding with a recommendation from an employer.

- ✔ Alternatively, an innovative quality control manager (Edwards) chose a horizontal requirements-qualifications matching design, using "Your Requirements" immediately followed by "My Supporting Qualifications."

- ✔ A CPA (Kelham) answers an ad for a controller in a nonprofit organization, citing a match between the organization's requirements and his qualifications. He titles each of the six matches with a boldfaced headline and also bolds the position's title in the *Regarding* space.

P.S. winners

Observe the use of a postscript to prod contact by directing attention to a super selling point or a potential benefit to an employer. This old marketing copywriter's trick animates letters and hijacks attention, as you see in the following examples:

- ✔ A candidate who lacks gaming industry experience but is targeting a gaming position in Latin America (Dawson) uses a P.S. to keep him in the running. (Can you guess what it is?)

- ✔ Using a postscript for emphasis, a collections coordinator hopeful (Johnson) offers employers insider knowledge when they call her.

Fast starters

Opening a letter with pizzazz (Chapter 6) contributes enormous value to its successful journey through screening activities.

For example, a Red Cross emergency manager (Horton) opens his cover letter with the intensity of a crime novel — "I don't scare easily." He names his areas of expertise and skills that make interviewing him essential.

Praise starters

Note how some samples presell the candidate by leading off with praise from others at the top of the letter or in a right-hand column. A part-time, temporary instructor candidate (Young) uses quotations from previous performance evaluations to great effect.

To a lesser degree, a potential assistant manager of visual merchandising (Lawrence) praises by saying she hopes to join a "successful, innovative, and best-in-class company." What hiring manager doesn't want to be part of a best-in-class company? What hiring manager doesn't want to interview a person who has such obvious admiration for his team?

We like people who like us. When a candidate sets the stage with sincere expressions of regard and honor, employers are more likely to return the favor with an interview.

Design arts

Some applicant software systems have trouble handling creative formats (see Chapter 11). Even so, some designs are so attractive, they're tough to ignore.

A sales manager (Shields) makes a wise choice of a design that virtually guarantees a stop-what-you're-doing-and-read-this reaction. Using two columns and a vertical rule, the cover letter effectively overviews his value proposition: broad experience, commitment to excellence, excellent communications, and strategic planning.

Looks count in attracting attention in all media, including career management documents.

Chart champs

Notice the high impact of unexpected visual design features, such as charts and graphs:

- A sales professional (Morrison) dramatically uses a graph to illustrate how his sales nearly doubled in one quarter!
- Another sales professional (Botkin) uses a twist: He incorporates the Sales Skills Index, an independent evaluation of skills needed to succeed in the sales environment.

Charts most commonly are used to dramatize sales specialties, but they can be used in any occupation to highlight measurable accomplishments and achievements.

Attention grabbers

Spot the samples' use of bold typefaces, italics, and underscoring to highlight some combination of

- The position sought
- Accomplishments and achievements
- Skills and personal characteristics
- Special benefits, such as security clearances and fluency in more than one language

Calling tasteful graphic attention to factors that cause employers to pay serious attention to you is a trend to consider. Look to the following examples for inspiration:

- An administrative assistant (Lake) uses a boldfaced headline to brand herself — "Nothing great was ever achieved without enthusiasm." — and then successfully ties the quote to her desire to enthusiastically do her very best.

- A senior executive (Connor) literally underscores his interest in becoming a chief operating officer, following with a foxy quiz that asks yes or no questions (each yes answer describes one of the candidate's attractive qualities). He states that he'll consider relocation, an attitude that recruiters like.

- Applying to become the director of instructional technology (Huntington-Woods) for a school district, the candidate chooses boldface type to identify the position she seeks and her qualifying credential, a recently earned master's degree in educational technology.

- A sales executive (Turner) hopes that an emphasis in boldface type sparks subliminal connecting (like coffee and cream) of the name of the company and the title she seeks, melding the two parts into one image describing her as "ABC Coffee Company Senior Account Executive."

- A retail manager (Moran) pops three achievements into a simple ruled box where they can't be missed, an eyes-on move.

- A sales representative (Masters) combines boldfaced type with a ruled box of his favorable ranking in the Sales Skills Index. His opening paragraph also wins hearts and minds of hiring managers.

✔ An accomplished CEO and executive consultant (Luther) makes an end run around the human resources department by pretending not to know of a current search for a new chief executive when he writes directly to the prospective employing firm's board chairman. After suggesting they talk, Luther's letter throws out the bait in boldfaced type, positioning Luther as a visionary who has revolutionized an industry.

✔ A teacher (Richards) used boldfaced type to identify exactly what she seeks — K-8 Teaching Position — in the *Regarding* space so that busy screeners place her paperwork in the right stack to be examined.

✔ An "unretirement" candidate (Simmons) responding to an ad for a maintenance technician adroitly puts his motto in italics: "You can count on me!" as well as his command of systems and equipment. Inspired!

✔ A candidate (Jackson) applying to return to federal service as a civilian Navy employee uses boldface to identify the lodging facility management job and to clearly state that he knows how to operate a luxury brand hotel, which is what the job is about.

✔ A globally minded marketing executive (Smithson) lays out impressive credentials, scoring a direct benefit with boldfaced emphasis on his multilingual skills in Japanese and Italian. Smithson can be irresistible to an internationally focused corporation.

✔ A new graduate hoping to break into a money career as a financial analyst in the investment industry (Nelson) wisely boldfaces his key qualifications. (If the job market worsens in banking, investment, insurance, and financial services, cover letters for these industries are likely to become even more sales-oriented and less conservative.)

Memorable storytellers

Simply being remembered as a qualified individual among faceless hoards of applicants is a big threshold to cross. A memorable story helps employers recall individuals when deciding who to interview. Notice the humanizing touches that bring readers closer to good feelings about unknown candidates:

✔ A new graduate competing for a position as an occupational therapy assistant (Yates) begins her occupational story at the beginning when she was a Candy Striper. The reader thinks "What a nice, thoughtful person."

✔ A competitor for a manufacturing production supervisor position who is relocating to Florida (Jacobs) begins his letter with an unusual tale of an emergency repair of a professional race car. If the interviewer is a NASCAR fan, Jacobs is on track for an interview.

Blue standard-bearers

Job search documents, including cover letters and resumes, are increasingly welcomed by employers of installation, maintenance, repair, construction, and production workers. Plenty of people continue to get jobs without self-marketing documents, but why not get an edge for the best jobs by using every available tool?

An industrial electrician (Macdonald) offers a well-written, no-frills cover letter that cuts to the core of his competencies, skills, and experience for the job he seeks. He also helps the reader by identifying the position title, and where and when the job ad appeared.

Employers of blue-collar workers seek reliable workers, a trait to feature in addition to skills.

Internal achievers

Unless hiring for a position is predetermined (the fix is in), moving up or to a new location within the same organization requires the same level of excellent self-marketing messaging as that of an application to a new firm. Take notice of how a good marketing letter flows to open new doors in the same organization.

A client turned case manager turned candidate for workshop specialist (Jones) explains with clarity and in detail why she qualifies for the new assignment.

Main points

Pay attention to samples that show the wisdom of getting to the heart of the matter. What is the one factor that, if missing, kills interest in the candidate? Look for the following examples:

- ✔ Pharmaceutical sales professional (Marquez) emphasizes in boldface and underscoring the most important element of the position: the candidate's ability to promote drug products by effectively working with physicians.

- ✔ A social worker (Berry) makes a beeline for a program director position by emphasizing how she meets the job's essential requirements: senior social work management experience, family dynamics experience, and a strong clinical and academic background. Spot on!

Always try to pinpoint the make-or-break factor in a hiring decision and nail it.

Classy models and bell-ringing closes

Be aware of traditional samples that speak softly but carry a big carrot. Lacking graphic bells and whistles, such samples depend solely on strong writing and the market value of the candidate's background.

Don't overlook samples that showcase an action close (See Chapter 6). A promise to follow up positions you to pursue the job on your timetable, rather than forcing you to merely bide your time and hope for the call.

Feast Your Eyes

As a last reminder before you read the samples, take note that name is the game in tempting the intended to read your letter. Yes, there are exceptions when you must use a generic title (such as Dear Hiring Manager) because you simply can't uncover the hiring names in a committee structure, or the name of the hiring authority is guarded like a state secret. In the sample letters that follow, I sometimes sacrifice the formal inside address with a name and personal salutation to devote adequate space to making the letter easy to read.

For a pool of some of the zippiest and most enterprising cover letters ever, turn the page and begin reading samples here and continue through Chapter 12. A professional treat awaits you. In my opinion, communications like these promise to change the face of job letters forever, leaving old-school messages behind yesterday's hill.

Maximum message readability is the presentation criterion for each sample cover letter in this chapter. To save space in some superb but lengthier samples, I had to chop the original boilerplate text leading into the letter — most often deleting the recipient's name, title, company and address. So when you see a letter leading off with "[Date, inside address, salutation]," or some variation of that, the generic line is merely a reminder that you can't just say "Hey you, read this!" If you're not sure how to layout your cover letter, turn to Chapter 4.

WANDA L. BELL

✉ 222 Higgins Lane ~ Palo Alto, CA 23354 ~☎ 915-555-0111 ~💻 wanda.bell@comcast.net

[Date]

Dell Advanced Information Systems
Attn: Mr. Dennis Coney, Human Resources Director
12450 Lakeview Circle
Fairfax, VA 22033

SUBJECT: "Satellite Operations Manager" position listed on your company website on [date]

Dear Mr. Coney:

Upon perusal of my resume, you will find that my previous experiences effectively parallel the skill set required for your position.

You Require	I Offer
• Demonstrated experience installing, maintaining, and repairing satellite communications ground terminals, systems, networks, and associated equipment used to support voice, data, and video transfer.	✓ Demonstrated experience installing, maintaining, and repairing satellite communications ground terminals, systems, networks, and associated equipment used to support voice, data, and video transfer.
• BS, Engineering Management with an emphasis in communication systems.	✓ BS, Engineering Management with an emphasis in communication systems.
• 7 years of experience with satellite and radio frequency systems engineering to include managing personnel and projects.	✓ 14 years of experience with satellite and radio frequency systems engineering to include managing personnel and projects.
• Top Secret Single Scope Background Investigation Security Clearance.	✓ Top Secret Single Scope Background Investigation Security Clearance.

I thrive in an atmosphere of challenge and excitement, which I envision accompanies employment with your agency. I welcome the opportunity to meet with you or your designated agency representative to discuss my qualifications and your objectives further. I will follow up with your office early next week to discuss interviewing possibilities. Thank you in advance for both your time and consideration.

Respectfully yours,

Wanda L. Bell

Encl: Resume

Phyllis G. Houston, PARW-CC, NRWA — Upper Marlboro, Md.

DIANNE M. JOHNSON

799 Upper Ridge Road, Pennsburg, PA 18077   (555) 555-0111
E-mail: dsj1953@anyisp.com

[Date, inside address]

Position of Interest: Collections Coordinator

Dear [Name]:

You don't need Tony Soprano to collect what's owed you; there are more socially acceptable ways, and I know most of them.

Please accept this letter of interest and enclosed resume in consideration of the **Collections Coordinator** position, which was recently advertised on Indeed.com. I feel confident that my broad-based experience in ***credit & collections, accounting,*** and ***customer service*** would be a good fit for this position, evident by the following qualifications:

- Proven track record for successfully collecting on past-due accounts for 3 different organizations
- Strong customer relations and rapport-building skills: key elements to negotiating dependable, cost-effective payment arrangements with past-due accounts
- Well-organized and detail oriented: capable of balancing daily tasks and assisting other departments with work overflow, as needed

Because my skills are best explained in person, I would welcome the opportunity to meet with you, to further discuss how I can help mitigate losses and reduce account delinquencies for M&M Commercial Printing. Therefore, I will contact you next week to see when we might be able to arrange a meeting. In the interim, if you need any additional information, feel free to call or e-mail me at your earliest convenience.

Thank you very much in advance for your consideration. I look forward to speaking with you next week.

Sincerely,

Dianne M. Johnson

P.S. If you would like to meet more quickly and learn how I reduced 90+ day delinquencies by 77% for my current employer, call me on my cell phone as soon as you read this: 555-555-0111. Standing by.

Resume enclosed.

Joellyn Wittenstein Schwerdlin, CCMC, JCTC, CPRW — Worcester, Mass.

A N G E L A   D.   L A K E
686 Waterford Road • Waterford, ME 04088 • 207-555-0111 • adlake6@comcast.net

[Date, inside address, salutation]

Nothing great was ever achieved without enthusiasm.

Ralph Waldo Emerson wrote those words more than 150 years ago—yet they certainly ring true even today. And whether it is in the role of an organization's highest official, top operations leader, IT or finance manager, sales associate, customer service rep, or key administrative or support resource, enthusiasm and commitment to excellence are critical to today's successful organizations. In addition to the organizational skills I can bring to GeneTec Systems—detailed below—*you will find me to be a highly qualified administrative professional with an exceptional degree of enthusiasm, energy, and solid work ethic.*

I present myself as a well-qualified candidate for the position of Administrative Assistant III, for which you are presently recruiting. From my performance track record and letters of recommendation, you will see that I can deliver exceptional office management and organizational skills, keen analytical abilities, and a dedicated commitment to exceeding performance expectations. My up-to-date resume and two recommendation letters are enclosed for your review.

As my background indicates, I hold an undergraduate degree in Biology from Boston College and have recently completed several graduate courses in Cell Biology and Genetics at St. Joseph's University. I am very interested in applying my executive assistance skills in a scientific environment that values innovation, hard work, and dedication. You'll find my background reflects achievement in each of my professional positions—along with a reputation for contributing to operations. I am a quick learner able to master new skills, including technological proficiencies. You will also see that I can quickly assess situations and identify ways to optimize business practices. This background is complemented by the following signature strengths:

> Fluent in Spanish and English (written, verbal, reading)
> Excellent follow-through skills
> General accounting and financial analysis skills
> Passion for research—analyzing data and writing reports
> Keen analytical abilities—solid troubleshooting skills

I am confident of my ability to contribute to your organization. I would value the opportunity to speak with you about this opportunity and learn what attributes you are seeking in the selected candidate. Thank you for your consideration.

Sincerely,

Angela D. Lake

Jan Melnik, MRW, CCM, CPRW — Durham, Conn.

Will consider relocation

Martin Conner

1440 Glendale Avenue Scarsdale, New York 10583
✉mconner@gmail.com ☎914.555.0111 (cell) – 908.555.0112 (office)

[Date]

Mr. Sylvester Simmons, CEO
TopLine, Inc.
760 James Parkway
Suite 200
Summit, New Jersey 07900

Dear Mr. Simmons:

If you could design the best <u>Chief Operating Officer</u> for TopLine, would the following meet your toughest specs?

- ❑ A senior executive with a solid track record in industries from multinational advertising and staffing to specialty manufacturing to private equity management

- ❑ A recognized expert in the hard practicalities of harnessing advanced learning to lowered costs *and* better products simultaneously

- ❑ A mentor with a passion for having others think of his convincing suggestions as their own good ideas

- ❑ A leader known for skill in transforming mind-numbing cubicles into prosperous communities

You have just read the "Readers' Digest" version of my resume. You'll find the details on the next pages. That document may not look like others you've seen. I thought you deserved to see, right at the top of the first page, six profit-building capabilities I want to put at TopLine's disposal at once. Backing them up are a dozen examples of companies revitalized, costs cut, profits expanded — all by inspiring people to use abilities they didn't think they had.

My company values my contributions. And I love helping companies of all kinds reach sustainable success. Now, however, I want to make a longer commitment to just one company, free of distractions from other projects.

I thrive when I can listen to CEOs' specific concerns. Perhaps a good next step is to hear about TopLine's special needs in your own words. May I call in a few days to arrange a time to do just that?

Sincerely,

Martin Conner

Encl.: Resume

Don Orlando, MBA, CPRW, JCTC, CCM, CCMC — Montgomery, Ala.

LYNN HUNTINGTON-WOODS

1220 East Hoover, Ann Arbor, MI 48103
734-555-0111 (home) ▪ 734-555-0112 (cell) ▪ lynnhunt@aaps.k12.mi.us

[Date, inside address]

"She is calm and forward-thinking. And clearly she 'knows her stuff.' I would hate to see her leave, but I know she's destined for bigger and better things."
- STEVEN M. TAYLOR, TEACHER, CLAGUE MIDDLE SCHOOL, ANN ARBOR PUBLIC SCHOOLS

"She combines the best technical skills with the sensibilities of a teacher. She is well-known and respected across the district, by teachers, media specialists, and principals. . . .
She is a natural leader. . . ."
- BARBARA G. CREWS, LEAD TECHNICAL SPECIALIST, ANN ARBOR PUBLIC SCHOOLS

Dear Human Resource Professional (when name unavailable):

Please accept my application for the advertised position of **Director, Instructional Technology** with Oakland County Intermediate School District. My resume briefly outlines over 20 years of experience in the field of Education, the most recent of which includes ten years in technical support. I am currently the *Technical Specialist for Ann Arbor Public Schools, and Course Assistant for Eastern Michigan University.*

With a background in teaching, I have always been passionate about the instructional side of technology and recently earned a ***Master of Arts in Educational Technology*** from Eastern Michigan University. I have a reputation as a leader in technology, and as a "big-picture" person. I am known for being highly flexible, team-oriented, and accessible — helping teachers, students, and staff of every level and need.

I offer technical expertise, enthusiasm, commitment, and purpose, and I do this in many ways:

- Model lessons for teachers who might not know how to present technology to students
- Offer teacher training and professional development
- Take a proactive role as communicator, sending e-mail tech tips and giving mini-training sessions
- Successfully assist users of all levels feel comfortable asking questions
- Actively seek training and education to continuously increase my own knowledge base

Thank you for your consideration. I look forward to hearing from you soon to arrange an interview.

Sincerely,

Lynn Huntington-Woods

Vicki Brett-Gach, CPRW — Ann Arbor, Mich.

LANA TURNER

2201 Elm Street • Cleveland, Ohio 44114
lanaturner@yourinternetprovider.com • Home 216.555.0111 • Cell 216.555.0112

[Date]

Mr. Jack Ryan — President
ABC COFFEE COMPANY
8282 Main Street
Cleveland, Ohio 44102

Dear Mr. Ryan:

Leadership — Performance — Results. These are only several of the documented characteristics I offer *ABC Coffee Company* as a **SENIOR ACCOUNT EXECUTIVE.**

With over 15 years of success in managing sales operations in the consumer packaged goods and services industry, I offer the following:

- Keen business acumen with demonstrated success leading cross-functional teams in meeting business development, sales, and operational performance indexes.
- Expert strategist with superior forecasting, profit and loss, market analysis, and competitive positioning qualifications.
- Direct experience with *ABC Coffee Company* product distribution. Converted private label customers to *ABC Coffee's premium brands* in current position.
- Record of creating improved profit margins, vast referrals, and repeat business by maintaining the highest level of customer satisfaction.
- Superior entrepreneurial spirit — accomplished leader recognized by superiors as the "go-to" person capable of delivering successful results under the most difficult management tasks.

In addition to holding a Bachelor of Science Degree in Restaurant and Hotel Management, I have outstanding communication, presentation, and negotiation skills. You will find that I excel in action-oriented roles where meeting the goals of key stakeholders is unwavering.

I am appreciative of the courtesy extended in reviewing this letter and accompanying resume. I look forward to a future conversation where I can demonstrate my enthusiasm in becoming an integral member of your executive team.

Sincerely,

Lana Turner

Attachment

Susan Barens, CPRW, IJCTC — Olmsted Falls, Ohio

Milton W. Shields
479 Niles Road
New Reading, Pennsylvania 90000
shields@hotmail.com

(H) 222-555-0111

(M) 222-555-0112

[Date, inside address]

Re: Field Sales Management

Dear [Name]:

Your job posting for an experienced, top level field sales manager is right on target for my current job search. With years of successful hands-on customer service, sales, and management with a global leader in construction-related products and services, I believe that I can very comfortably meet your requirements as the ideal candidate for this position.

As my accompanying resume clearly indicates, my professional qualifications and personal strengths reveal high-end management qualities, such as commitment, integrity, trust, and insight when dealing with personnel under my supervision. I have motivated my sales staffs to work at earning high commissions and praise for reaching targeted productivity while maintaining customer satisfaction, retaining loyal client base, and expanding new business.

Below is a brief overview of the value I can bring if hired by your firm:

Broad Experience	Fifteen years of competent, reliable, trustworthy service to clients and employees in a highly respected multinational firm that employs over 14,000 in 122 nations.
Commitment to Excellence	High energy leader with a proven record of superior team-building qualities that inspire sales personnel to attain top performance while exhibiting professional standards.
Articulate, Precise, and Confident	Excellent communications abilities that facilitate the work of recruiting, training, coaching, team-building, motivating, and creative problem-solving.
Strategic Planning	Reached profitability target of 9 million dollars through meticulous staffing and in-depth scheduling of 17 Pro Shops.

If you need a strategic sales manager with impressive business acumen and out-of-the-box problem-solving talent blended with proactive team leadership and the ability to execute tactically, then I am your candidate. I would welcome the opportunity to demonstrate how I could benefit your organization. I will call to arrange a meeting convenient to your calendar. Thank you for your time and interest in considering my application for this position.

Sincerely,

Milton W. Shields

Enclosure

Edward Turilli, BS, MA, CPRW — North Kingstown, R.I.

Will consider relocation

Bill Amberly
4140 Wilson Drive – Montgomery, Alabama 36110
✉ wrAmberly1@bellsouth.net – ☎ 334.555.0111 (cell) – 334.555.0112 (home)

[Date]

Mr. Charles W. Moran
District Sales Manager
Arista, Inc.
500 Northridge Parkway
Suite 400
Montgomery, Alabama 36100

Dear Mr. Moran:

> Led our store to be the best of 12.
> Topped 11 tough competitors in single product line revenue.
> The only one to win an Elite Customer Service Award
> every quarter since the award was introduced.

I put the bottom lines at the top of this letter because I think Arista deserves that kind of performance from your next <u>Retail Manager</u>. If you agree, I'd like to explore being that newest member of your team.

To make the hiring decision as easy as possible for you, I've tailored my resume to your needs. Right at the top of the next page you'll find five profit-building capabilities I'd like to put at Arista's disposal at once. Backing them up are 11 contributions I've made to my employers. As you read about them, I hope a central thought stands out: I go beyond just solving problems in my store. I share what I learn with every store in our district.

But any resume, no matter how well customized to your needs, is no substitute for people speaking with people. That's why I'd like to call in a few days to hear about your special retail store management requirements in your own words.

Sincerely,

Bill Amberly
Encl.: Resume

Don Orlando, MBA, CPRW, JCTC, CCM, CCMC — Montgomery, Ala.

MATT R. LUTHER
President, CEO, Executive Consultant
m.luther@worldnet.att.net

2990 Longview Road
Syracuse, NY 10592

Phone: 555.555.0111
Cell: 555.555.0112

[Date, inside address]

RE: Your Search for a President/CEO

Dear [Name]:

I'm looking for the most unique of opportunities — one that requires innovative leadership, decisive action, and impressive results. I am NOT interested in a "status quo" position with a "status quo" organization. Rather, my goal is an executive-level assignment where vision, trend-setting, problem-solving and strategy are key to success. Whether for a start-up, turnaround, international expansion or accelerated growth company, I have the experience, ethics, and the strength of character necessary to build, lead, and win. Here are just a few examples:

- Identified market void, built new company and captured $120 million in annual revenues within first year. Delivered 600% ROI to investor group — 120% over projections.

- Launched another new company to capitalize on emerging market opportunities and created $70 million in annual revenues within just two years.

- Sourced new suppliers and reduced cost of goods 40% for a multinational venture.

- Raised $150 million from VC community to fund acquisition of failing venture.

The list of my career successes is extensive and spans the US, Pacific Rim, Europe and Latin America. I thrive in high-profile, fast-paced, and diverse organizations where I am free to identify opportunities, build relationships, negotiate alliances, and catapult new ventures to unprecedented financial results.

If you are in need of strong and decisive leadership, I would welcome the opportunity to speak to you to better understand your specific needs and more thoroughly detail my experience. As my resume states, I am a *"visionary pioneer who has revolutionized an industry with innovative new products, new marketing strategies, and new distribution channels."* This is the value I bring to you and your organization.

Sincerely,

Matt R. Luther

Enclosure

Wendy Enelow, CCM, MRW, JCTC, CPRW — Coleman Falls, Va.

Joyce Richards

18 Berry Hill Road • East Brunswick, New Jersey 08816

908.555.0111 • joycerichards@anywho.net

[Date]

Mr. David Simmons   **RE: K-8 Teaching Position**
Director of Human Resources
East Brunswick Public Schools
60 Route 537
East Brunswick, New Jersey 08816

Dear Mr. Simmons:

I am a recent graduate of Monmouth University and I am certified to teach Elementary School with a specialization in English for grades 5 through 8.

An educator at heart with a love for children, I worked at a cooperative learning center for special needs children years before entering Monmouth University. It was there that I gained real world experience in teaching each individual child, tweaking and modifying lessons, projects, and classrooms however necessary to reach every student. Most recently, I developed and implemented lesson plans using different learning and behavioral strategies to address all levels of learning readiness for grades first, second, and seventh during my Monmouth University teaching internships. Through this experience, I have developed the skills not only to instruct, but also to motivate.

My most recent position as a Public Safety Dispatcher for the Marlboro Police Department speaks to my character, work ethic, and exceptional ability to communicate. The school district can be assured of my morals and attention to safety and security, and I can be relied upon to handle any crisis in a level-headed, effective manner. Furthermore, I am Red Cross–certified in CPR and first aid.

In addition to my resume, I have enclosed letters of recommendation and a favorite lesson plan. I hope that these documents will give you a sense of what I can offer East Brunswick Public Schools.

I will call your office next week to confirm that I have completed all required application steps and to inquire about the selection and interview processes. I look forward to the opportunity to meet with you to further discuss how I can contribute to East Brunswick schools and the education of your students.

Sincerely,

Joyce Richards

Enclosures: Resume, Letters of Recommendation, Lesson Plan

Joyce Cutler — Colts Neck, N.J.

GERARD KELHAM, CPA

2265 Grove Road, Columbia, MD 21045
(443) 555-0111 ▪ gkelhamcpa@gmail.com

[Date]

National Association of Health & Children (NAHC)   RE: Your Posting on Non-Profit Times
Washington, DC   **NAHC Controller in Washington, DC**
Email: hrjobs@nahcorg.org

Dear Hiring Manager (when name unavailable):

Your need for a Controller to implement NAHC's initiatives regarding aging, behavioral health, children and families, and health hit home with my personal values, as my resume reveals. You will note the match between your requirements and my qualifications. Specifically, they are:

- **Accounting degree.** My Master's courses (Business Law, Business Management, Federal Taxation, and Accounting) are deemed equivalent to an accounting degree. In fact, this is what enabled me to sit for the Certified Public Accountant (CPA) exam and attain my CPA.

- **CPA.** CPA designation current. Member of the American Institute of Certified Public Accountants (AICPA) and the Maryland Society of Certified Public Accountants (MSCPA).

- **8-10 years of experience in an association or non-profit organization.** Nearly 16 years of full-time experience, primarily as a Controller, for an historic international labor union with up to 165,000 members.

- **Experience in an organization with multiple entities.** Financial management and controllership experience for up to 900 local affiliates (US, Canada, and Mexico) and corporate headquarters in Washington, DC.

- **Technologically savvy with knowledge of accounting packages.** My fascination with financial technology has led to a passion for financial and accounting packages and software. You will find a listing of my technology skills on page 2 of my résumé.

- **Expert knowledge of GAAP principles.** In-depth expertise with GAAP, FASB, and SOX, as well as compliance reporting (LM-2, Form 990, and all DOL forms).

With years of controllership experience, combined with my talent for process improvements, high ethical standards, and financial technology know-how, I believe I can meet any and all new challenges in financial management and reporting with your organization. My salary requirements are negotiable; I would be happy to discuss them when interviewed. May we talk soon? I'll call you next week. If you prefer to speak to me sooner, please call me on my cell phone, 443-555-0112. Thank you for your consideration and professional courtesy in reviewing my well-qualified candidacy.

Sincerely,

Gerard Kelham, CPA

Susan Guarneri, MRW, CERW, CPRW, CPBS, NCCC, DCC — Three Lakes, Wis.

Calvin Simmons
300 Burgundy Lane
Turners Falls, MA 98889
Home: (413) 555-0111 • Cell: (413) 555-0112
E-mail: calvinsimmons@aol.com

[Date]

Mr. John Deming
Director of Facility Maintenance
Southwork Manufacturing
Turner Falls, MA 98889

My Motto:
"You can count on me!"

Dear Mr. Deming:

Although I decided to retire at a young age, I have come to realize that I have too much energy and many skills that I still enjoy using. Retirement is definitely not for me. Therefore, your ad for a **maintenance technician** caught my attention, as I offer the key qualifications your company needs.

Specifically, I have an excellent performance record in the operation and maintenance of *building systems and equipment*, including *electrical, HVAC, telecommunications, pneumatic, electro-mechanical,* and *hydraulics.* I am also knowledgeable of *state building codes, safety,* and *other regulatory guidelines.*

My expertise encompasses multi-site facilities oversight, staff supervision, project management, and vendor relations. Examples of relevant accomplishments include reduction in annual maintenance costs and improved functional capabilities while consistently delivering quality service.

Equally important are my planning, organization, and communication strengths. Despite the challenges that can often be encountered, I have completed projects on time and under budget on a consistent basis. I would welcome a personal interview to discuss the value I would add to your company. My resume is enclosed.

Sincerely,

Calvin Simmons

Louise Garver, CPBS, JCTC, CMP, CPRW, CEIP — Broad Brook, Conn.

ROBERT W. JACKSON

4063 Azalea Place ♦ Naples, FL 34109 ♦ 239.555.0111 ♦ email@email.com

[Date]

To: The Selection Committee   **RE: Regional Lodging Operations Manager (NF-1173-05)**
U. S. Navy MWR Organization
Community Support Services Division
610 Dowell Street
Keyport, WA 98345

I bring to the table 25-plus years of exceptional hospitality industry expertise that will serve our sailors and their families well. While on active duty I served in many high-level posts working very closely with senior international diplomats, governmental officials, and senior military officers. I believe that Crew and Family Morale are the cornerstone and backbone of sound military operations.

During the past 10 years I have had the opportunity to manage the personal assets and resources of some of the wealthiest American families. For the past 6 years I have been employed by a Fortune 100 family as their Director of Operations for all of their domestic business affairs. This industry (Domestic Service Management) is a mystery to many, but the intelligence, sophistication, and technical skill needed to be successful in this arena is high. **I meet daily operational demands and standards equivalent to a Luxury Brand Hotel**. I implemented and maintained a Customer Service Program that is world-class and ensured exceptional results.

My full resume package is enclosed for your review and use in selecting the right Executive to build the infrastructure and future blueprint for Regional Lodging Operations for the Commander, Navy Region Northwest (CNRNW), Fleet and Family Readiness Program. This opportunity is truly exciting and well within my professional skill set. Start-up operations are my specialty. My background is long and readily verifiable.

It would be my honor to return to government service. I will bring your organization results and ensure this department is managed with precise, hands-on leadership. You can be assured that I will work with allegiance to guarantee that all CNRNW Lodging facilities and programs are known and judged as world-class.

Sincerely yours,

Lieutenant Robert W. Jackson, U.S. Navy (Ret.)

Enclosures

Judith L. Gillespie, CPCC, CPRW, CEIP — W. Melbourne, Fla.

JAY SMITHSON
187 Madison Avenue #5, Brooklyn, New York 10073
(212) 555-0111 (home) • (212) 555-0112 (cell) • jsmithson@yahoo.com

[Date]

Ms. Shelby Anderson
Vice President of Global Marketing
Allied Technology
One Allied Drive
New York, New York 10021

Dear Ms. Anderson:

In today's economy of domestic and global competition and increasingly innovative technology in manufacturing operations, you need a **Director of Marketing** with the vision and scope to bring multi-site international projects to fruition

With over 10 years' history in marketing and business development in positions of increasing responsibility   beginning with a small, family-owned company and leading to my present position as Director of Marketing and Business Development for Toyota Heavy Industries— I offer that vision and scope.

I pride myself on my ability to become fluent in new technology and industry. I am **multilingual (Japanese and Italian),** and present a strong record of providing decisive team leadership and direction. As a **recipient of the "President's Award" two years running for outstanding contributions company-wide, 2005/2006**, I can bring to Alliant Technology the kind of innovation and leadership that will increase Alliant's market share and global presence as an industry leader.

I am enclosing my resume and will send a copy to Ms. Arden Hotchkiss, Director of Human Resources, as well. Let's meet in person to discuss in greater detail your needs and my qualifications. I will call your office the week of September 4 to determine if an interview may be arranged. If you would like to contact me in the meantime, please call my cell (212) 555-0112, or e-mail me at jsmithson@yahoo.com.

Sincerely,

Jay Smithson

Deborah Barnes, CPRW — Nahant, Mass.

Cara R. Fuller
555 Keller Lane • Columbus, Ohio 43210 • 419-555-0111

[Date]

Attn: Beth Winslow, Administrator
Lois Kane, Chair
Diversity Search Committee
The Ohio State University Extension
003 Agricultural Administration Building
2120 Fyffe Road
Columbus, Ohio 43210

RE: Diversity Development Director

Dear Ms. Winslow:

Throughout my 18+ years of professional employment in the areas of <u>Educational and Organizational Leadership</u>, <u>Multicultural Education</u>, and <u>Human Services and Corrections</u>, I have been recognized as a person who can get the job done. I developed a reputation of being enthusiastic, energetic, creative, a valued team member and team leader who could motivate people to action. The Ohio State University Extension and the College of Food, Agricultural and Environmental Sciences will benefit with me as your next Director of Diversity Development.

As you review my resume I am confident you will determine that my qualifications meet the requirements established by The Ohio State University for this position. Following are highlights of my qualifications:

- Master's Degree or equivalent
  - ✓ Earned Master's degree in Adult Education/Multicultural Education and currently completing Ph.D. in Educational and Organizational Leadership

- Career experience working with diversity issues
  - ✓ As the first Diversity Coordinator at Youngstown State University, 6 new diversity outreach efforts/training initiatives were implemented within 3 months of hire

- Excellent oral and written communication skills
  - ✓ Sought out as public speaker/presenter for large and small audiences on topics such as leadership, cultural diversity, training, etc.

- Management, networking and collaborative skills
  - ✓ Invited media reps to attend Diversity Council meetings to share topics with the community at large. Minutes of meetings are placed in libraries and community centers to bring information to those who are usually disengaged in the community policy process

- Leadership ability in diversity program development and implementation
  - ✓ Motivated and assisted deans in each academic college to form at least one Faculty Diversity Team to work as volunteer groups, developing educational diversity programs

• Willing to work flexible hours	✓ Participate in numerous training workshops, presentations, and collaborative meetings outside "normal" working hours
• Work with minimum supervision	✓ Self-directed and self-motivated to create, implement, assess, and evaluate progress made toward achieving diversity goals
• Able to work with both youth and adults	✓ Take an active part in the college community by serving as advisor for various student organizations
• Effective team player	✓ Collaborate with numerous university units to develop model diversity programs and provide assistance, recommendations, and plans for fostering of faculty, staff and student recruitment, retention, and development activities

Recognizing the need to effectively integrate diversity within the Youngstown State University's daily operations through a notification vehicle, my request to serve as spokesperson for diversity in conjunction with the Director of University Relations was approved by the university president, Leslie H. Cochran, who commended my work by saying,

> *"I am pleased that you have moved forward to answer questions regarding diversity, plan and report campus events, develop a campus diversity Web site, and distribute diversity materials to the community."*

As is evident from the various presentations, workshops, and training I have conducted over the years and the concentrations of my post-graduate education, I am passionate about the issues of diversity and convey this enthusiasm to my colleagues. I welcome the opportunity to share my expertise with the college community at The Ohio State University.

I look forward to meeting with you to answer any questions you may have and to provide you with additional information to supplement what appears on my resume. I happily anticipate your call.

Sincerely,

Cara R. Fuller

Enclosures: résumé, copy of transcripts, professional references, application

Jane Roqueplot, CPBA, CWDP, CECC — Sharon, Pa.

SHIRLEY A. EDWARDS

H. (416) 555-0111 ❖ info@tntresumewriter.com ❖ C. (416) 555-0112
❖ 123 Willowdale Avenue Unit 88 ❖ Toronto ON M3N 5X4 ❖

INNOVATIVE QUALITY CONTROL MANAGER

To quote psychologist and philosopher William James: "It is our attitude at the beginning of a difficult task which, more than anything else, will affect its successful outcome." I couldn't agree more. I hit the floor running — and smiling.

Ms. Jane Smith, Recruitment Manager
ABC Manufacturing
1211 Main Street
Toronto ON M6M 5C7

RE: **Quality Control Manager Posting, Reference # QCM123**

Dear Ms. Smith,

I pride myself on being an innovative, results-oriented, hands-on individual with progressive management experience in quality control and manufacturing. My management style strongly emphasizes teamwork and relationship building founded upon clear communication and expectations.

<u>**Your Requirements:**</u>

1. Minimum five years of progressive management experience.

2. Quality control training and/or certification.

3. Solid hands-on understanding of the requirements of ISO certifications, along with excellent communication, computer, and leadership skills.

<u>**My Supporting Qualifications:**</u>

1. 10+ years of progressive manufacturing experience and growth.

2. Certified ISO 9001 Auditor through York University.

3. Demonstrated leadership capability in driving operations excellence. Strong facilitator with solid computer proficiency and five years' experience implementing ISO certification projects.

In review of my resume, you will note my progressive career growth and experience. What it cannot illustrate, however, is the degree of professionalism, resourcefulness, and dedication that I offer as an employee. A personal conversation will enable us to discuss how I can contribute to the success of ABC Manufacturing. As requested, my salary requirements for this role range from $55k to $65k, depending on the job's complexity. I look forward to exploring this opportunity with you in the near future.

Best regards,

Shirley A. Edwards

Enclosure: Resume

Tanya Taylor, CHRP, MCRS — Toronto, Ontario, Canada

FROM: RYAN DAWSON
TO: BILL JACOBS, CEO & CHIP SMYTHE, COO
ShowDownPokerGames.com

RE: <u>V.P. LATIN AMERICA POSITION</u>

Your request for a multi-lingual, Latin American expert to "build out" Latin America, Central & South America, Mexico, and the Caribbean fits my skill base and expertise perfectly.

It isn't often that that one has the opportunity to take years of sales/marketing/development experience for both Fortune 500 companies and smaller, mid-sized, "family" companies and be offered a position in a well-financed, bold, and growth-oriented company to build a whole new business in a new market.

I speak the language of these regions — not just English, Portuguese, and Spanish, but the terms of their cultures, business dealings, partnering, and collaborating.

I've worked international development/sales/marketing for some big names: Lever Brothers, Sony, and Western Union. I also have built or dramatically expanded South American markets for less-well-known companies: Vigora and Garcia Traders.

We need to talk. You'll see in my attached resume that I meet or exceed virtually all your needs listed in the job opening. I'm here in Miami already and ready to fly south.

Ryan Dawson

8908 Yacht Club Lane # 51C
Aventura, Florida 33181
555-555-0111
ryan_dawson@hotmail.com

P.S. One more plus factor — I'm an online gaming enthusiast!

Gail Frank, NCRW, CPRW, JCTC, CEIP — Tampa, Fla.

sales professional   *Will consider relocation*

Allen P. Morrison
100 Markwell Lane — Montgomery, Alabama 36100
☎ 334.555.0111 — 334.555.0112 (cellular) —✉apmorrison@charter.net

[Date]

Ms. Laura Worth
Sales Manager
TopLine, Inc.
320 Sun Parkway
Suite 17
Montgomery, Alabama 36100

Dear Ms. Worth:

I want you to get the credit for adding ROI to the TopLine sales team. Specifically, I'd like to become your newest sales professional. And, perhaps the best way to link those two ideas is with this graph that shows how I'm performing right now.

Sales Nearly Doubled in One Quarter

What I do isn't magic. I just work harder and smarter than my competition by finding some profitable way to say "yes" to every customer and potential customer.

My focus on your sales needs starts on the next pages. I wanted you to see a resume that offers more than the usual recitations of job titles and responsibilities. That's why you'll find six capabilities I want to put at TopLine's disposal at once. Backing them up are a dozen examples of those capabilities in action.

My company values what I do. And, if I thought our market was growing as fast as yours, I would stay with them. While I cannot control market conditions, I am interested in making even greater contributions to my employer. That's why I'm "testing the waters" with this confidential application.

I do best using the consultative approach to sales. So, as a first step, I'd like to hear about TopLine's sales needs in your own words. May I call in a few days to arrange time to do that?

Sincerely,

Allen P. Morrison

Encl.: Resume

Don Orlando, MBA, CPRW, JCTC, CCM, CCMC — Montgomery, Ala.

DAN J. BOTKIN
9803 Clifton Street ▪ Lubbock, TX 79432
806-555-0111 ▪ danjbotkin@door.com

[Date, inside address, salutation]

It is with great enthusiasm that I apply for your advertised position of Sales Representative. Count me in because my skills are a finely tuned match for your requirements!

In fact, my combination of sales experience and relationship selling skills has given me the opportunity to exceed sales expectations, grow market share, outdistance the competition, and establish a strong foundation for future revenue growth. Two selected accomplishments documenting my qualifications are:

- **Trusting, win-win relationships with customers and suppliers**, including Coca-Cola, Pepsi, McLane, Wal-Mart, Owens-Corning, and other partner companies

- **Consistent, year-over-year pattern of increasing revenues** through robust and downturn economies, from $50,000 to $1.2 million as illustrated below:

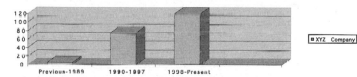

Sales is about making connections — between customer and product, between product and its benefits, and between sales associates and customers. Because I position myself as a consultant to my customers, I am able to gain their trust, make these connections, and pave the way for increased sales as a result.

My resume provides you with specific details of my qualifications, but a personal interview will more fully reveal my positive attitude and potential to assist you in making your numbers — make that *exceeding* your numbers!

You may want to reach me first on my cell phone, 806-555-0112, but I plan to call you on Thursday afternoon to see if we can set a time to sit down and chat. I've done my research on your company, and it's a beacon in the industry. Thank you, Mr. Rockford, for considering adding me to your sales wish team.

Sincerely,

Dan J. Botkin

Enclosure

Dan Dorotik, NCRW — Lubbock, Texas

BENJAMIN R. JACOBS

11 Hillcrest Road ◆ Watkins Glen, NY 14891 ◆ Telephone: 607.555.0111
◆ E-mail: email@email.com

[Date]

Ms. Jayne Harrison   **Manufacturing Production Supervisor**
A-1 Manufacturing, LLC
1326 Adams Road
Daytona Beach, FL 32117

Dear Ms. Harrison:

The other Saturday morning I had an unusual emergency request: Could we make a replacement part for a professional race car? Yes, we could! And we did! From effectively overseeing day-to-day manufacturing operations to enabling that race car to compete that Saturday afternoon, I always derive considerable personal satisfaction ensuring my employer's success.

I'm relocating to Florida and have heard good things about A-1 Manufacturing, LLC. Your advertised opening for a <u>CNC Production Supervisor</u> sounds especially intriguing. Enclosed are my resume and a list of references.

Managing a variety of projects simultaneously is a particular strength of mine. I also handle high-stress situations calmly and efficiently. Other strengths include:

o   25 years experience in a Job Shop
o   Significant production operations and production scheduling knowledge
o   Practiced in the concept of Total Quality Management (TQM)
o   First-rate communication and problem solving skills
o   Cost cognizant, thorough, and efficient

I'd appreciate the opportunity to further discuss how A-1 Manufacturing, LLC, could benefit from my abilities. I will be in your area next week and will plan on giving you a call this Thursday about scheduling an interview.

Thank you for your time in reviewing my resume. I look forward to meeting with you.

Sincerely yours,

Benjamin R. Jacobs

Enclosures

Judith L. Gillespie, CPCC, CPRW, CEIP — Melbourne, Fla.

JULIE E. YATES

2990 Rocky Point Road ♦ W. Melbourne, FL 32904 ♦ 321.555.0111 ♦ email@email.com

[Date]

Mr. Jonathan Burgess, HR Director   <u>**Occupational Therapy Assistant**</u>
Wellness, Inc.
1333 Business Place
Melbourne, FL 32901

Dear Mr. Burgess:

From the time I was a Candy Striper back in high school, I've always been passionate about helping people. Just two years ago, I realized I could best be of service by pursuing a career in occupational therapy.

I was awarded my Occupational Therapist Assistant degree this May at Keiser University where I was an "A" student, and on the honor role and dean's list each quarter.

Additionally, I gained valuable experience while interning at Medical South, LLC, and Health Consultants, Inc.

Working my way through my occupational therapy training, I enjoyed my experiences as a swim instructor, waitress, and teacher. Whether someone is pre-school age, a senior citizen, or somewhere in between, I find I'm easily able to find common ground.

Working with patients, I've learned the special importance of bringing someone out of a shell because "spirit equals outcome."

I'm very excited about starting my new career in occupational therapy and am completely focused on providing the best possible patient service. I'm known for being organized and always eager to learn.

If you believe, like I do, that my qualifications and experiences are of value to Wellness Inc., I would welcome the opportunity to meet with you. I'm enclosing my resume and references for your review.

Thank you very much for your time and consideration. I will follow up next week.

Sincerely yours,

Julie E. Yates
Enclosures: Resume; References

Judith L. Gillespie, CPCC, CPRW, CEIP — W. Melbourne, Fla.

Doreen Jones
45 Valley Road, Nahant, MA 01908
(781) 555-0111 (home) • (781) 555-0112 ext. 555 (work) • djones@creative.org

[Date]

Mr. Bill Evergreen, Director
Careers R Us
5 Franklin Street
Marblehead, MA 05555

Dear Mr. Evergreen:

The position of Workshop Specialist requires consummate skill in thinking on one's feet, facilitating workshops through developing curricula and presenting information in an innovative and professional style, communicating sensitively and diplomatically (and humorously, when appropriate) with diverse populations, and exercising resourceful time-management proficiency.

I have these skills and more. As the Workshop Specialist at Careers R Us of Marblehead, I would bring not only this expertise, but the credibility of a former customer who took advantage of the resources offered—a majority of the workshops, as well as training opportunities—to become one of the career center's success stories.

As a case manager for the past year at Careers R Us in Carver, I have been providing support, guidance, and resources to career center clients. This first-hand experience has given me the in-depth opportunity to understand client needs and challenges, and to view their job search situations holistically. The knowledge and skills I've gained in this position I believe make me an ideal candidate for the Workshop Specialist position.

My background includes:
- Facilitating multiple workshops and counseling customers within a career center setting;
- Designing and copyediting newsletters and books in a deadline-driven environment;
- Counseling adults in a weight-loss clinic setting—a position requiring an abundant amount of tact and sensitivity;
- Managing a thriving real estate agency where, among other tasks, I wrote weekly ad copy to get customers in the door; and
- Teaching junior high school English in a diverse, urban setting.

I look forward to meeting with you to discuss in greater detail your requirements and my qualifications. In the meantime, if you have any questions, please feel free to contact me at (781) 555-0112 ext. 555, or e-mail me at djones@creative.org.

Sincerely,

Doreen Jones

Enclosure: Resume

Deborah Barnes, CPRW — Nahant, Mass.

Beverly Marquez

2303 Whiteline Ave., Alexandria VA 22306, 703-555-0111

[Date, inside address, salutation]

Subject: Classified ad in March 5 Washington Post for Pharmaceutical Sales

Would a person with three years *sales* experience combined with a *degree in nursing* be of interest to you? What if that person could couple her experience with the ability to build productive business relationships and effectively interface with all levels of medical management — and was an expert at closing sales? I fear no obstacle. "Can't do" doesn't exist in my territory! If this describes the professional you want to represent your company, please give me your valued consideration.

I am interested in expanding my professional horizons by seeking new challenges within the health care industry. I have a firm understanding of the relationship between medical conditions and the various treatments prescribed for same. I believe my skills, as noted on the enclosed resume and especially when combined with my formal education as a nurse, are transferable and would facilitate my desired career redirection.

The following is a brief overview of my attributes:

- ✓ A "quick study" and a self-starter with the desire to sell surgical equipment and/or medicinals.
- ✓ An interest in medicine and a knowledge of pharmaceuticals, anatomy, biology, and symptomology. I keep abreast of medical technology and the latest treatments available.
- ✓ A demonstrated ability to negotiate transactions to successful conclusions aided by verbal and persuasive skills, sharply honed over the past few years. Currently I rank as #2 on a 10-person sales team.
- ✓ *Most importantly, through my experience, I have acquired the skills that enable me to effectively deal one on one with physicians and other members of the medical field.*
- ✓ A natural ability to rapidly gain a client's confidence.
- ✓ A stellar performance record in every major endeavor I have attempted.
- ✓ Personal values of honesty, integrity, and a powerful work ethic.

I know that resumes help you sort out the probables from the possibles. Nonetheless, I would like to meet with you and demonstrate that I have the disposition and dynamics that make for a high-impact contributor. Be assured that your investment of time will be amply repaid.

Very truly yours,

Beverly Marquez

Art Frank — Flat Rock, N.C.

GRETCHEN YOUNG, *MS*

20 S. Main Street, Columbus, New Jersey 08505 • (555) 555-0111 • gretchenyoung@email.net

[Date]

Charter University
Adjunct Search Committee
Department of Business Administration/LN0622
P.O. Box 1002
Charter, Pennsylvania 17551-0302

RE: Business Administration Adjunct Instructors

Dear Adjunct Search Committee Members:

I hope to join the Charter University faculty as a part-time, temporary Instructor. As a resident of Charter County, I am very familiar with your University and your commitment to education and community outreach. Here are highlights of my relevant qualifications and accomplishments:

Expertise / Experience I Offer

Six years of teaching experience in higher-education environments. **Focus on Corporate Communications, Marketing, and Business Writing.**

Ten years of experience in both corporate and non-profit settings; held various management positions in Marketing and Internal Communication departments.

Graduated with a Master's Degree in Marketing from the University of Kansas. Certified as a Business Communication Professional (CBP).

My passion is providing an engaging and productive learning experience to all students. My style is participatory and one that involves all students. I look forward to discussing with you how I can use my experience and knowledge to further the mission of Charter University.

Sincerely,

Gretchen Young
Enclosure

Professional instructor with academic credentials and real-world corporate experience; engage students in an active learning environment and encourage new ideas about traditional subjects.

Comments from Past Evaluations

-Professor Young takes the time to get to know her students. She wants us to succeed and it shows.

-I truly enjoyed the learning environment Ms. Young created. She doesn't stand and lecture for hours – instead she challenges us to think for ourselves and be involved.

-Professor Young cares about her students. I felt that I could always approach her with a concern. She took me seriously.

-I was nervous about taking Managerial Communications, but Professor Young made the experience enjoyable. She gave us the tools to prepare our presentations and it was a positive learning experience.

Jason Macdonald
4865 Barcelona Crescent
Toronto, ON N9G 3J1

[Date]

Mr. Julian Roberts
Pro Manufacturing
200 Morton Drive
Toronto, Canada
N9J 3W9

**RE: Industrial Electrician
Globe and Mail, [Date]**

Attention: Mr. Roberts

With over 13 years of successful electrical experience in a manufacturing environment, I would be a great fit for the position you need to fill. Spend 10 minutes interviewing me, and you'll quickly agree that I'm well qualified to do the job you want done.

In my current position with VP Plastics as a Maintenance Electrician, I am responsible for performing the maintenance and repair of machinery including electrical, mechanical, and hydraulic systems. I am also involved in implementing preventative and predictive maintenance. Additional duties include managing all power distribution in the plant and troubleshooting PLC's control systems.

I currently hold an Interprovincial Electrical License, and I have a solid understanding of electrical systems in a manufacturing environment. I am organized, work well alone or with others, and welcome the opportunity to learn new skills.

If you are interested in a self-starter and highly motivated candidate, we should speak. My resume is attached for your review and I am available for an interview at your convenience. I appreciate your time and look forward to speaking to you.

Sincerely yours,

Jason Macdonald

Elizabeth Macfarlane, CPRW — Windsor, Ontario, Canada

Joseph T. Horton

51 Silver Road
Troy, NY 12000
joseph.horton@us.army.mil

Residence: (999) 555-0111
Office: (999) 555-0112
Office Voice Mail: (212) 555-0113

[Date]

[Inside address]

RE: Red Cross Program Manager, State Emergency; Organization Job ID: 5517BR

Dear Mr. Martin:

I don't scare easily. Nor do I own a panic button. Instead, when the wheels come off, I remain alert and act calmly to deal intelligently with a crisis. My skills, experience and professional credentials make me confident that I am the ideal match for your Program Manager, State Emergency position advertised on New York's Job Bank.

I offer over 19 years of *Emergency Management*, *Security / Surveillance*, *Logistics*, and *Operations Management* experience in positions of progressive responsibility and duties. My areas of expertise include

✓ Emergency Response
✓ Disaster Planning and Response
✓ Emergency Preparedness
✓ Homeland Security
✓ Program / Project Management
✓ Team Building / Management

✓ Staff Training and Development
✓ Intelligence / Operations Analysis
✓ Information Collection / Analysis
✓ Event Planning, Interagency Coordination
✓ Sensitive Information Management

I possess an active Top Secret / SCI security clearance with a current background investigation. With strong leadership and organizational skills, I have a track record of designing and implementing emergency / disaster response programs and leading large-scale emergency / disaster response and security / surveillance operations in high-risk situations.

With strong technical / computer abilities, I am skilled at utilizing technology, databases, and computerized systems to manage emergencies and disasters. As a seasoned instructor with excellent communication skills, I am talented at training and coordinating the efforts of multiple teams of professionals. My professional credentials include a Bachelor's degree, comprehensive FEMA and security / surveillance training, Six Sigma Lean Manufacturing Certification, and IS100, IS200, ICS300, and ICS400 Certifications.

With the track record and leadership abilities that I offer, you can be assured that I will make an immediate and positive contribution to the American Red Cross. I would like to further discuss my background in a meeting with you. Thank you for your time and consideration. I look forward to your reply.

Sincerely,

Joseph T. Horton

Enc. Resume

John Femia, BS, CPRW — Altamont, N.Y.

Nicole Lawrence

123 South Street, Atlanta, Georgia 30329
(770) 555-0111
nicole_lawrence@hotmail.com

[Date]

Mr. Timothy Anderson   **RE: Retail Assistant Manager of Visual Merchandising**
Director of Marketing Management
Loach Luggage
800 Fashion Boulevard
Atlanta, Georgia 30039

Dear Mr. Anderson:

As an experienced and committed manager in the competitive world of retail, I am seeking to position myself with a successful, innovative, and best-in-class company. And that's what you are, which is why my strong background in retail management makes me a heads-on favorite for the job of Retail Assistant Manager of Visual Merchandising position with Loach Luggage.

Three years ago I was promoted to Assistant Customer Experience Manager at Alpha Inc. My responsibilities focus on creating positive customer shopping experiences, planning and implementing promotional programs, overseeing proper store operations, training and developing staff, and increasing store profitability through inventory maintenance and effective sales team coordination. During my career at Alpha Inc., sales revenue increased by 15% each year while shrink decreased by 25% each year. My store was named top retail store in the district in [date].

Continuing my education at the Art Institute of Atlanta, I am enrolled in Visual Merchandising along with Brand Strategy and Brand Marketing. I am enhancing my knowledge on consumer buying habits, creating visual displays, and learning the relationship between marketing planning and media. By expanding my understanding of the retail fashion industry, these courses are helping me to easily integrate the creative and corporate aspects of retail

Mr. Anderson, I am confident that my experience and passion will contribute to Loach Luggage's growth and profitability. I would appreciate the opportunity to discuss with you the *Retail Assistant Manager of Visual Merchandising* position and how I could fit into Loach Luggage. My resume is enclosed for your review and consideration. I will call your office on Thursday to see when we might arrange a meeting. I look forward to talking with you!

Sincerely,

Nicole Lawrence

Enclosure

Dynesha Montgomery — Atlanta, Ga.

LOUISE BERRY, LCSW, CASAC

24 Michigan Avenue, Leonia, NJ 07605
Home (201) 555-0111 • Cell (917) 555-0112 • LBerry@gmail.com

[Date]

Ms. June Schultz
Human Resources Manager
Northern Bergen Family Services Clinic
450 Main Street
Hackensack, NJ 07601

Dear Ms. Schultz:

I believe my professional skill set coupled with my clinical experience qualifies me to serve as your **Director of Programs**. In response to the job posting on your organization's website, I am enclosing my resume for your consideration. Highlights of my qualifications include:

- **Day-to-day Senior Management Experience.** More than 12 years of administrative and staff management experience at a satellite clinic providing outpatient care to more than 550 lower income patients and families.

- **Experience with Family Dynamics.** Well-versed in family interactions from two clinical perspectives — general mental health and substance abuse — and spanning a variety of cultures.

- **Strong Background — Clinically & Academically.** Provided individual, couple, and family psychotherapy, diagnosing and treating a variety of diagnoses, including depression, anxiety, and substance abuse, and in addition to having earned a Master's degree in Social Work, I am now pursuing a Master of Public Affairs degree.

I am confident that the enthusiasm and experience I can bring to your company will prove to be an asset in managing your direct service agencies.

Thank you in advance for your time and consideration. I look forward to hearing from you for a personal interview at your earliest convenience.

Sincerely,

Louise Berry

Enclosure

Laurie Berenson, CPRW — Park Ridge, N.J.

JEROME NELSON

599 Norvan Lane
Columbus, OH 98019   jnelson@yahoo.com   Cell: (305) 555−0111
                                                                          Home: (305) 555−0112

[Date, inside address, salutation]

Like many recent graduates, I am eager to begin my career in finance. Unlike others, I realize that a new bachelor's degree is not enough to qualify in today's highly competitive market. As a result, I have worked diligently to supplement my college education with hands-on experience in financial environments, equipping me with a wide range of skills as a Financial Analyst. Through my employment and educational training, I have developed the qualifications that will make me an asset to your company:

Financial Skills and Experience:

More than 2 years of experience in a corporate environment as a financial advisor along with a solid background in financial analysis, reporting, budgeting, negotiating and business/financial planning. Apply financial tools to identify, manage, and maximize investment funds.

Keen Research, Analytical and Quantitative Skills:

Adept in reviewing, analyzing and synthesizing financial data as well as viewing challenges from different perspectives to arrive at creative solutions

Computer Software Tools:

Demonstrated proficiency in learning new applications quickly, I am skilled in using Microsoft Word, Excel and Access database software. I also utilize Morningstar extensively to research data on mutual funds.

Proven Communications, Organization and Interpersonal Skills:

My collective experiences have enabled me to hone my interpersonal, written, and verbal communications skills, which include developing financial reports, interfacing with internal and external customers and delivering presentations. Cultivating and maintaining positive relationships with a wide range of personalities have resulted in a large referral network from satisfied clients. Another strength is my ability to efficiently organize and manage my day-to-day responsibilities for maximum productivity.

Based on my talents and dedicated efforts, I have been recognized for my contributions to business growth and success. If you need a highly motivated professional who grasps new concepts quickly, loves to learn and offers the personal drive, skills and confidence to succeed, I would welcome an interview and will touch base with you next week. Thank you.

Sincerely,

Jerome Nelson

Louise Garver, CPBS, JCTC, CMP, CPRW, CEIP — Broad Brook, Conn.

SIMON MASTERS

4511 Flowers Drive
Petersburg, OH 40000

330.555.0111
Email: smasters@yahoo.com

[Date, inside address, salutation]

My four favorite career words are: competitive, assertive, positive, and victorious. That's me! With the confidence that I can make a positive impact on Allies Supplies Company's bottom line, I present my resume for your advertised position of **Sales Representative**.

As you review my resume, you will discover that I am embarking on a career change. While I have enjoyed my 10$^+$ years in law enforcement and earned the respect of my peers and superiors, it is time for a change and for me to follow the advice of David Lloyd George, who said, "Don't be afraid to take a big step if one is indicated. You can't cross a chasm in two small jumps."

My ability to build effective relationships, ask the right questions to get the information I need, and manage time effectively will certainly facilitate a short learning curve as your next Sales Representative. I am self-motivated to learn about the products/services I will be selling so that I can demonstrate to potential customers how this product/service will address their needs and ease their "pain." Given my self-motivation, communication skills, loyalty, upbeat personality, character, and life experience, I am sure to soon be considered a valued addition to your sales team, as evidenced below.

> **Sales Skills Index®**— an objective analysis of an individual's understanding of the strategies required to sell successfully in any sales environment. Results for Simon Masters for **choosing either the first or second most effective strategy** in the following categories:
>
> Prospecting/Qualifying—54% ~ First Impression/Greeting—66%
> Qualifying Questions—86% ~ Demonstration—55%
> Influence—83% ~ Close—60% ~ General—69%

In anticipation that you will have questions for me, I will contact you next week to answer them and to schedule a time for a more extended conversation. Until we speak, thank you for your attention and professional consideration.

Sincerely,

Simon Masters

Enclosure: Resume

Jane Roqueplot, CPBA, CWDP, CECC — Sharon Pa.

Chapter 9

Broadcast and Prospecting Letters

. . . .

In This Chapter

▶ Feasting on a bountiful bevy of topnotch direct-mail letters

▶ Understanding techniques that make specific letters perform

▶ Questioning whether to mail, e-mail, or hand deliver

. . . .

*B*roadcast and prospecting letters are direct mail that's designed to uncover an opportunity in the hidden (unadvertised) job market; they're high-class versions of advertising flyers. When these letters are boring, trite, or mediocre and sent indiscriminately to a generic mailing list, they're treated as flyers and discarded without a thought.

On the other hand, direct mail done right can hit the jackpot, says John Lucht, career management guru and author of *Rites of Passage at $100,000 to $1 Million+* (Viceroy Press): "If you send a highly persuasive letter and resume that arrive with perfect (though accidental) timing, the decision maker *will* pay attention. Why would he or she not? On the other hand, if what you send is unpersuasive, even the neediest decision maker will pass."

Arriving online or by postal mail — or even better, hand carried by a company's employee to the company's hiring authority — these letters absolutely must catch the reader's eyes and then glue them open.

Prospecting letters and *broadcast letters* have much in common. Some argue that they're really the same genus. Maybe so. But, in my viewpoint, the difference is a matter of scale and personal connection. Here's a distinction:

✔ **Broadcast letters** are self-marketing letters sent to a large but carefully targeted roster of potential employers. You may draw your targets from commercial mailing lists.

The list is king. Even with great writing, without verifying that the list you're using is up to date and representative of the specific industry or career field you want to reach, you're sending junk mail.

✔ **Prospecting letters** are self-marketing letters sent to a much smaller and even more selective number of potential employers. They may, for example, be addressed to a potential employer you met at an event or to a member of a small professional organization whose name you obtained from the group's directory.

The 26 broadcast and prospecting letters in this chapter usually can be reshaped to use in either category — or adapted to become job reply letters (Chapter 8).

Send Postal Mail or E-Mail?

Deciding which medium is most likely to get results for your letters is a toss-up. Here are a few important considerations:

✔ E-mail is cheaper and quicker than postal mail, growing rapidly and producing similar results in many circumstances, particularly with executive recruiters and venture capital firms.

✔ Recruiters like e-mail because they can punch a button and shoot your materials to clients with ease.

✔ Conducting an e-mail campaign to employers is risky even if you can find the decision-maker's personal e-mail address. Why? Your letter and resume may disappear into the spam version of the Bermuda Triangle. Unless a company has advertised an HR (human resources) address, you have no assurance that your campaign will get to the right people.

✔ A persuasive mailing on quality paper is still the best way to forward an unsolicited letter and resume to top-level executives and other prominent decision-makers.

When you're facing an uphill search in a thin job market, a direct mail campaign comprised of broadcast and prospecting letters riding herd on your resume can produce leads you may otherwise miss. The caveat: Research the best techniques to mail your letters (whether a commercial service or a do-it-yourself effort) and follow up on leads generated by the campaign.

Techniques to Notice

Smooth moves are self-evident in a number of the letters in this grouping. But here I comment on many underlying factors and related techniques that make them winners:

✔ **Stage setters.** A social worker (Seligman) aiming for community services announces upfront what she's about and what she offers.

All fired up and ready to go, a business development executive (Adams) vividly banners her intent to take her next employer's company to the next level.

Both letters illustrate the value of using insights gained from professional branding activities (See Chapter 13) to convey a giant impression of who the candidate is and what the candidate offers.

✔ **Rookie glad-handers.** A new graduate and would-be trade support analyst (Braden) pulls out all the stops to include flattery, a reference from a mutual friend, and more honeyed words of praise, all the while framing himself within the letterhead's contact information as the best financial candidate since, well, Warren Buffet. The kitchen-sink approach is a viable option for new graduates and well illustrated in this sample letter.

✔ **Heads-up alerts.** A senior staff analyst (Deeker) trumpets her search with a headlined talent alert and chalks up a smile with her corny but creative opening sentence. Starting a reaching-out letter with the name of the prospective employer draws interest.

✔ **Global greats.** A Russian ace software engineer (Milochev) concentrates on high-demand competencies and skills, noting a Skype address that facilitates free telephone interviews. Additionally, a Skype address suggests the candidate has a contemporary outlook.

✔ **Merger strategies.** A process engineer (Moran) writes an unusual kind of prospecting letter to shore up his position in a merger of two companies. Seizing the initiative is smart in any situation where excess personnel results from a merger of two companies.

✔ **Power profiles.** A recent high school graduate and would-be customer service rep (Vincent) makes good use of an innovative profile designed to predict his behavior on the job he wants. This innovative approach addresses the ever-present question of personality fit for the job.

✔ **Foodie thoughts.** A culinary arts candidate (Cookin) offers another version of personality disclosure and background. The job seeker gambles that if she doesn't target a specific job, an employer will sort through her attractively presented qualifications and discover the perfect position for her. This presentation, the equivalent of a resume's qualifications summary, is an approach to consider when seeking virtually any good job in a specific industry or career field.

✔ **Philosophical practicalities.** A teaching professional (Woodman) expresses her loving perspective on the value of children — attention bait in the field of education. And she makes sure that the reader grasps her serious qualifications, such as certification to teach in her state's schools by stating those facts in boldface type. This format works to hook the reader with clues to one's inspirational inner person but sustains interest by trumpeting the candidate's practical qualifications.

✔ **Home helpers.** A communication by a seeker of a household management position (Adamson) differs from the typical broadcast or prospecting letter because it volunteers biographical information not found in typical job applications. This document, identified as a *personal statement,* is limited in usage to jobs such as domestics and bodyguards, where personal histories are very important. It can be used in at least two ways: e-mailed with a cover note (see Chapter 14), or left behind in hard copy at job interviews as a reminder of a candidate's personal background and qualifications.

✔ **High flyers.** An executive (Armstrong) applies for an upscale job in the consumer products industry. Grabbing the reader by the collar with a masterful accomplishment statement in boldface type at the top of the letter, he legitimizes his claims with Stand Out details and ends with an action close. (See Chapter 6.) An executive model, this letter is appropriate for alpha candidates who are itching to move on and up.

✔ **Quiet types.** A financial executive (Montgomery) writing to a recruiter immediately says he comes recommended, an opening that's likely to cause his letter to be among the first read in the crush of daily mail. He quickly sounds the alarm that his search is under the radar by marking it *confidential* in capital letters and underlined boldface type, and then placing the statement where the eye can't miss it.

In another recruiter-targeted letter, a business technology executive (Thompkins), also wants to keep his search quiet but places his underlined request for privacy at the end of the letter.

Flagging confidentiality vastly improves the chances that a job seeker's letter won't inadvertently be sent to the seeker's current boss. (Yes, that happens rarely, but it happens.)

✔ **Employer pleasers.** A candidate seeking to analyze business and technology issues (Monroe) announces upfront that he's a triple treat who can manage technology, money, and people. Such a strong combination of talents resonates with many employers, especially when the claims are backed up with numbers in a quantitative statement of accomplishments.

Another letter from an executive/administrative assistant (Dempsey) immediately states that the job seeker's objective is to make her boss's job easier. She continues to explain why her strengths and abilities are right on the pulse of the position. The tone of her letter is perfect for a position as a right-hand assistant.

Writing effective letters begins with thinking through what employers really want and writing them from the employer's viewpoint.

✔ **Repetition rewards.** A retailing executive (Lansing) chooses repetition — namely, the popular "Bottom-Line" term — and uses it three times to introduce three different accomplishments. The technique of repetitive phrasing slams home a candidate's main message.

Quick takes. A database manager (Dotreev) cuts to the chase with a brief but effective use of her career brand — efficiency while maintaining quality, aided by tenacious problem-solving skills. Short, tastefully designed letters spiced with persuasive information earn attention.

✔ **Down-times uppers.** A broadcast letter from a former entrepreneur now seeking employment (Brown) opens with a direct appeal to economically threatened small business owners. This is a difficult sale, but the seeker does a good job of explaining that he beat adversity for years while others failed as he markets his survival skills. When facing the need to stay up in down times, employers fear taking on additional labor costs. Successful job seekers focus on ways to allay those fears in their reaching-out letters.

✔ **Smart strategies.** A real estate professional (Boudreaux) capitalizes on having done such a good job that he worked himself onto the job market! He follows his clever opening with knock-out statistics before closing with a time frame to talk about making money together. A timeless tactic: Emphasizing — at first glance — impressive measurable success as an inducement to meet.

✔ **Recommendation vouchers.** A business executive (Anderson) combines an attractive design, targeted positions, and accomplishment-based text with rousing endorsements from two former employers. What's not to like about this Stand Out marketing letter?

✔ **Self-referrals.** An outdoors enthusiast and customer of a sports company (Abbott) seeks to morph from customer to employee. He writes of transferring his construction expertise to help build the company's new sports facility and then of transitioning to the position of facilities director for the completed structure. Promising to make contact at an upcoming job fair, the candidate gets a leg up on being welcomed at the company's fair booth by establishing his bona fides in advance. Psychology experts believe that we like people who are like us; identification as a customer creates instant readiness for acceptance.

✔ **Bullet pointers.** A CPA seeking employment as a controller or finance director (Kelham) makes smart use of five bulleted reasons to hire him.

In a second sample with bullet points, a supervisor (Kowal) highlights his readiness to relocate to a region of Canada that has advertised its desire to attract talented immigrants, wisely noting that his family is on board with the prospective relocation. (In a buyer's job market, employers typically resist out-of-area candidates because they don't want to pay relocation costs when local talent is available; the situation described in this letter is an exception.)

In a third sample, a sales executive (Borden) getting the word out about his availability shows how to attract attention with bullet points. In this case, the points are framed in a dotted-line rule like a theater marquee.

Modern media has conditioned readers to be receptive to bulleted lists. A variation of bulleted lists, "Five Top Tips" and "Top Ten Reasons Why" lists are especially popular.

✔ **Insider clues.** A fitness expert (Martinez) opens his prospecting letter by revealing that he's one of the fitness clan by writing, "But for those of us who are in the business . . ." By positioning himself as a fellow professional, he creates a favorable climate for following up when he's in the same city. Whether citing experience or leisure-time activities, any indication of being a good cultural fit reduces resistance to reading an unsolicited letter and considering the candidate for an interview.

✔ **Sheherazade stories.** A social worker who wants to become a pharmaceutical sales rep (Hoover) presents her qualifications in an interesting narrative that makes those qualifications come alive. She explains why her expertise as a licensed clinical social worker is a dynamite match for pharmaceutical sales, and ends with yet another compelling story. Savvy job seekers don't underestimate the power of storytelling to get their letters read, and they write as though they are speaking to one person.

On with the Letters!

The 26 letters that follow are a spectacular collection of broadcast letters (many recipients) and prospecting letters (fewer recipients). As in other chapters, the name of the professional writer of each letter appears beneath it. For more information about the writers, turn to the appendix. You'll like these gems.

Maximum message readability is the presentation criterion for each sample cover letter in this chapter. To save space in some superb but lengthier samples, I had to chop the original boilerplate text leading into the letter — most often deleting the recipient's name, title, company and address. So when you see a letter leading off with "[Date, inside address, salutation]," or some variation of that, the generic line is merely a reminder that you can't just say "Hey you, read this!" If you're not sure how to layout your cover letter, turn to Chapter 4.

Sarah M. Seligman, MSW
93 Ellington Avenue
Buffalo, New York 14111
(716) 555-0111

[Date]

[Inside address]

My Mission: Creating a World that Works for All
My Means: Community Services Administration

Dear [Name]:

One of social service's most enthusiastic and dedicated individuals is applying for a professional position with your foundation. That would be me, supported with solid experience, a new academic degree, and lots of promise.

After recently completing my MSW with a concentration in Community Services and Administration, I'm primed for a new chapter in my career where I can make a difference using business acumen and counseling skills. My resume documents chapter and verse but here are significant accomplishments and experience:

> Enhanced fundraising efforts: Identifying resources and connecting with strategic partners. Result: 160% increase in realized campaign goal.

> Direct experience: Program administration, staff and volunteer supervision, advocacy/lobbying activities, public relations, public speaking, and television appearances. Result: A thorough knowledge of programs, services, and resources in Western New York.

> Personal strengths: Professors and previous employers have commented on my "perseverance and commitment to children and families," as well as my "outstanding empowerment and advocacy capabilities."

I would very much appreciate the opportunity to meet with you to discuss my credentials and how I will benefit your foundation. I will call your administrative assistant on Tuesday morning to identify a space on your busy calendar when I can come to your office for an interview.

Sincerely,

Sarah M. Seligman, MSW
Enclosure

Freddie Cheek, MS Ed, CCM, CPRW, CARW, CWDP — Amherst, N.Y.

Henry L. Braden

Ambitious * Bright * Hard Working * Most likely to Succeed

1095 Johnson Ferry Road, Apt. 400
Atlanta, Georgia 303042
(404) 555-0111, email@email.com

[Date, inside address, salutation]

Over the past few years I have followed the masterful expansion of International Stock & Trade, as well as your leadership in electronic trading. Until recently it was through publications that I followed your company; now, Marc Kertosh, an esteemed friend whom you also know, has confirmed what I believed to be true: You genuinely champion technology innovation, customer service and employee initiative — all of which are values of utmost importance to me.

I recently graduated from the University of Georgia's Terry College of Business, Magna Cum Laude, with a degree in Finance and am also a nominee to the Beta Gamma Sigma Honor Society, the highest recognition a business student anywhere in the world can receive in a business program accredited by AACSB International. I finished my college career in less than 2.5 years while working part-time. Further, I excelled in the study of corporate finance and derivative securities courses, as you will note in my attached resume.

My initiative and drive does not end with academia. I am a licensed private pilot, conducting my training out of Peachtree-Dekalb Airport, the third-busiest commuter airport in the United States. I am well versed in situations that require attention to detail, quick interpretation and interpolation of data and multi-tasking, as such qualities are indispensable to safely transcend the rigors of Atlanta's Class B airspace.

Mr. Martin, I am very interested in pursuing a career with your company and in particular the position of Trade Support Analyst. I would greatly appreciate an opportunity to meet with you and further discuss how my qualifications dovetail with your requirements for an A-list employee. I will contact you soon to schedule an appointment, and I thank you for your time and consideration.

Sincerely,

Henry L. Braden

Enclosure: Resume

Sharon M. Bowden, CPRW, CEIP — Atlanta, Ga.

Julia Stephanie Deeker
♦ 2708 Flinstone Dr, Fort Worth, Texas 76131 ♦
♦ Home: 682-555-0111 ♦ Cell: 888-555-0112 ♦ ksdeek9987@sbcglobal.net ♦

[Date]

Mr. Garret Smith
VP Information Systems
Krispie Cream, Inc   Talent Alert:
1300 Rollins Plaza   Senior Staff Analyst
Dallas, TX 75000   On the move!

Dear Mr. Smith:

I'm betting dollars to Krispie Cream donuts (ouch!) you haven't met an IT scheduling analyst with better chops than I've acquired during my services as a senior staff analyst with specialized training in Tivoli Workload Scheduler Scheduling and Operations. Quickly, my credentials include:

- **25 years of working on various job scheduling software, solution focused, process improvement to increase proficiency work with IT applications, use groups**

- **UNIX, ESP/Encore, CA7/CA11, McAfee PGP E-Business Server, MVS/JCL for Computer Operations, MVS Operations Training, STK Tape Libraries**

- **Core strengths encompass: managing servers, systems, applications, and backups by utilizing job schedules, file transfers, disaster recovery, encryption, and media management in a secure Data Center environment**

- **Interpersonal skills for interfacing well with all levels of management**

If you currently are searching for a stand-out with my credentials, let's meet and talk about how I might contribute my technical knowledge and leadership skills to achieving your organization's strategic objectives. I can shuttle my schedule to be in your office within 48 hours of hearing from you on my cell 888-555-0112.

Sincerely,

Julia Stephanie Deeker

Enclosure

Danni M. Kimoto Barker, CPCC, CPRW — Crestview, Fla.

GREG MILOCHEV

Manezhnaya Street • Moscow, Russia 105215
+7 916 555 0111 • Skype: gregmilochev • gmilochev@email.ru

[Date, inside address, salutation]

Subject: A+ List Software Engineer ready to meet

As an internationally acclaimed and accomplished software engineering professional with an advanced degree in applied and theoretical mathematics incorporating statistical analysis, probability theory, and mathematical/computational physics, as well as many years developing and deploying popular new algorithm-based software architectures and technologies for global industry leaders, I believe my qualifications will be of great interest to you.

A more comprehensive overview of my qualifications includes publication of numerous complex technical and scientific commentaries, instruction to graduate-level students on algorithm-based software development in preparation for leading roles with major industry players, and expertise in cross-geographical team coordination to engineer effective solutions that drive company growth and technological innovation.

My current goal is to apply my highly targeted background, knowledge, and strengths to the exciting field of quantitative analysis software development within the investment banking industry. My potential contributions to your organization include:

➤ Progressive experience within global technology enterprises directing all aspects of SDLC, as well as performing R&D, market potential analysis, and coordinating with clients, staff, and third-party vendors for effective task execution.

➤ Solid history developing leading-edge tools and technologies; strong C++ programming skills as well as proficiency with all IT standards, procedures, and protocols.

➤ Demonstrated versatility to coordinate cross-platform algorithm development; equally adept in Windows and Linux OS platforms and methodologies.

➤ Team management expertise; hire, train, coordinate schedules, and monitor performance.

I would welcome the opportunity for a webcam interview to more fully discuss how my background and strengths can facilitate the achievement of your goals. I look forward to this opportunity, and I thank you for your consideration.

Sincerely,

Greg Milochev
Enclosure

Karen Bartell, CPRW — Massapequa Park, N.Y.

CHARLES W. MORAN

1450 Wingate Parkway Camberville, Georgia 31200 ✉cwm1000@hotmail.com – ☎707.555.0111

[Date, inside address, salutation]

Like you, I've been working to help resolve details of the upcoming partnership between Arista and my company, Carter Manufacturing. But after work, on the drive home, on the weekends, one measure of merit captures my attention: How soon, and how powerfully, can we use the strength of our new company to extend our ROI? How do we do that faster and more durably than our competition? I know I'd benefit from your reactions to my ideas.

Many are ready to dismiss cottonseed delinting as a potentially lucrative market segment. The market may be small, but there are opportunities that I think can **generate $12M of new revenue in the first three years alone.** In addition, demanding delinting process creates a follow on durable market for parts, supporting services, and replacement.

In addition, these factors we help beat the competition early on:

- ❏ **We have unique knowledge of processes and equipment.** I'm not just thinking about mechanical specs. Our customers know, or soon find out, delinting is as much an art as a manufacturing process. If continuing customers' dissatisfaction with our competition is a good indicator, we have mastered an art they haven't.

- ❏ **We have personal knowledge of our customers and their needs** —something of extraordinary value among customers whose cultures value personal relationships differently than we do. They've invited Joann and me to their homes to share family meals: we've been fortunate to do the same. Said another way, we "speak" their business language to mutual benefit.

Leveraging all these advantages is very doable. But, as our customers from South America and Africa have told me often, words on paper are no substitute for people speaking with people. If what you've read appeals to you, I'd like to suggest a next step. May I call in a few days to see how well my thoughts align with yours?

Sincerely,

Charles W. Moran
Process Engineer

cc: Sharon Cartwright
     Director of Human Resources

Don Orlando, MBA, CPRW, JCTC, CCM, CCMC — Montgomery, Ala.

DON VINCENT

2386 State Route 111 Parker, PA 16049 Home: 734-555-0111 dvincent@aol.com

[Date, inside address, salutation]

RE: Customer Service Representative

Please take a moment to review my resume for the position of Customer Service Representative with your organization. As a recent high school graduate, I am eager to begin my career with a reputable firm such as yours. In order to shorten the learning curve and enable you to predict my behavior on the job, I took the liberty of completing a professional behavior profile. I am prepared to offer you a copy of this profile, which further details my behavior strengths as they relate to employment. Please note the four key environmental factors listed below and the profile's description of my natural response. I am pleased to fully endorse the accuracy of the profile:

Problem Solving – Challenges

"Don will be quite cooperative by nature and attempt to avoid confrontation as he wants to be seen as a person who is easy to work with."

People – Contacts

"Don is enthusiastic about his ability to influence others. He prefers an environment in which he has the opportunity to deal with different types of individuals. Don is trusting and wants to be trusted."

Pace – Consistency

"Don is appreciative of the team concept and feels quite secure in an environment where the need to move from one activity to another quite quickly is held to a minimum."

Procedures – Constraints

"Don is independent in nature and feels comfortable in situations where the constraints are few and far between."

Thank you again for your consideration for this opportunity. I would appreciate an interview and I am available at your convenience. You may reach me any time at the following number: 734-555-0111.

Sincerely,

Don Vincent

Enclosure: Resume
View my resume online at www.resumehotlight.com/dvincent

Jane Roqueplot, CPBA, CWDP, CECC — Sharon, Pa.

123 MAIN STREET • MYTOWN, CA 09876 • (123) 555-0111
IMACOOKIN@DINEWITHME.COM • WWW.DINEWITHME.COM

IMA COOKIN

[Date]

Ms. Debra Smith
Founding Partner
Culinary Art Center
100 Boulevard West
Hometown, CA 12345

Dear Ms. Smith:

I am about passion: passion for life, food, health, community, and humanity. My passion for cooking and gardening, along with an intense desire to share my knowledge with others has led me along a path paved with extraordinary experiences and opportunities. Along the way, I have worked with exemplary artisans well known in the culinary world, affording me an unparalleled education.

I wear a coat of many colors in my current position as Public Relations and Hospitality Manager at Stovetop Culinary School, voted IACS Best Cooking School of the Year, [date]. This position is enhanced by my entrepreneurial endeavor, Dine With Me. As you look over my resume, I encourage you to also look at www.StovetopCookingSchool.com and www.DineWithMe.com.

As I continue my journey through the wonders of food and wine, I strive to enrich the lives of everyone I meet along the way, accomplishing this through collaboration with cookbook authors and publishers, cooking class curriculum coordination and instruction, and management of public and private customized events. This goal, when intertwined with my talents, experience, and personality, is a recipe for success!

I look forward to meeting with you to discuss my background and philosophy and what I can bring to your table.

Sincerely,

Ima Cookin

Linda Meehan, NRWA, PARW/CC — Sonoma, Calif.

SARAH JANE WOODMANN

1773 Circle Drive, Dallas, TX 75211
(214) 555-0111 ◆ sarahjwoodmann@aol.com

[Date, inside address]

> **I Believe**: *"The finest gift you can give anyone is encouragement.*
> *If everyone received the encouragement they need to grow,*
> *the genius in most everyone would blossom. . . "*
> *— Sidney Madwed (American poet)*

Dear [Name],

Are you currently seeking a nurturing, experienced teaching professional with proven success in encouraging students to attain not only academic goals, but also self-confidence and a positive attitude toward learning? If so, we should meet.

I believe all children are important to the future of our country — every single child. By leveraging all I have to offer — my teaching skills and training, years of experience (often with challenging special-needs students), dedication to children, caring spirit, creativity, and attitude of encouragement — I know I have made a positive impact on children in their formative years. May I do the same for your students?

* **Bachelor's Degree and Substitute Teaching Certification (Texas).**

* **Teaching and substitute teaching experience at the elementary grade level** — More than 5 years of teaching experience (teacher assistant, substitute teacher, youth and family teacher, art teacher, art director, arts counselor, and after-school program counselor) at the K-12 level.

* **Public and private educational settings** included special needs populations and inclusive-education classrooms for the Roosevelt School, Dallas Public Schools, Plano YMCA, Dallas Recreation Commission, Fort Worth Action Campers, and more.

At this point in my career I am seeking the opportunity to use my proven teaching experience and encouraging attitude to make a difference. If you are on the lookout for a teaching professional who can promote students' creativity and confidence, I'm ready, willing, and able to deliver the goods.

Thank you for your time and consideration. Please expect to hear from me next week, or, if you wish, you can e-mail me at sarahjwoodmann@aol.com.

Sincerely yours,

Sarah Jane Woodmann

Susan Guarneri, MRW, CERW, CPRW, CPBS, NCCC, DCC — Three Lakes, Wis.

ASHLEY ADAMSON

9963 Chapman Ave ▪ Tomville, AL 79432
806-555-0111 ▪ ashley_adamson@door.com

PERSONAL STATEMENT FOR HOUSEHOLD MANAGER POSITION

My career goal is to secure a position as a Household Manager; to that end, I pledge to bring my unique skills in household management and child/animal/plant caretaking, along with the highest levels of trust and respect, to my future employer.

I was born in Berlin, Germany, in October 2, 1960, and grew up in Houston, TX, following my family's relocation. I have been married to Joseph for 12 years. We have one son, Christian, who is 21 years old. My father worked for 35 years as a railroad technician and operator, and my mother was a full-time housewife and caretaker until I turned 18; she then pursued a career in clerical work. I have one older brother.

Due to my mother's physical condition, which required her to spend a great deal of time in bed while I was growing up, I found myself having to contribute to the running of the household at an early age, perhaps even more so than many other children my age. I discovered that I was a "natural" at organizing household affairs, and I enjoyed bringing my mom breakfast in bed, helping to take care of her, and ensuring that all the daily household chores were not neglected. As I developed my skills in helping to manage a household, I discovered that I could handle large-scale events, as well. When I was 16, I catered my relatives' 25th anniversary party. I planned and organized all aspects of the event, and the party was subsequently a complete success! I proved that I could not only run a household, but that I could also coordinate special events and ensure their success.

What I would like to emphasize in this statement are characteristics and strengths that contribute to my abilities as an effective Household Manager. My communication style is open and direct; I am sensitive to the needs of others, yet I am able to be firm with staff when necessary. I have experience in medical care, and I have unlimited patience in dealing with those who are affected by physical and mental limitations. I pride myself on my ability to be resourceful and "wear many hats," including household manager, caretaker, special events coordinator, staff supervisor, healthcare assistant, and construction supervisor.

My resume includes details of my work history; additionally, I have an impeccable list of references, which I will gladly provide upon request.

Ashley Adamson

Dan Dorotik, NCRW — Lubbock, Texas

TONY L. ARMSTRONG

970 Dunmore Circle
Chicago, IL 60693

Cell: 947.555.0111
tlarmstrong@aol.com

[Date, inside address, salutation]

Building high-performance, high-profit consumer products companies is my expertise. Whether challenged to launch a new venture, facilitate a complete business transformation or accelerate growth throughout markets worldwide, I have consistently delivered multi-million-dollar gains in revenues and bottom-line profits. Most notably, I:

- **Led development and launch of more than 800 new products throughout my career that have generated combined revenues in excess of $2 billion for major consumer products companies.**

My career can be briefly summarized as follows:

- In my current position as **COO/EVP** with GXT Products and Gunner Industries, orchestrated the integration of two consumer products companies into one organization and delivered 28% revenue growth and 20% margin improvement in the first year. These achievements were realized through a series of operational changes (including transition to third-party manufacturing), an aggressive new product development effort (6 new patents pending), a massive upgrade of internal IT and e-commerce capabilities (resulting in a 53.5% increase in web traffic), and unprecedented gains in productivity, efficiency, and cost elimination.

- As **Founder/President** of **Crestar Consumer Products,** built new global venture and brought to profitability in first year. Developed and patented 4 new products, negotiated strategic alliances with distributors worldwide, and penetrated new B2C and B2B markets in the US, Europe, and Asia.

- As **VP** with **Newman Consumer Products** and **Director** with **Reynolds Products,** led the sale of some of the most-recognizable consumer brands in the US. In total, facilitated development of hundreds of new products and product line extensions that generated more than $200 million in new product revenues.

These achievements are indicative of the quality and caliber of my entire professional career — identify and capture opportunities to build revenue channels, reduce costs, eliminate non-profitable products and operations, streamline core business processes, leverage technology resources, and penetrate global markets to further expand our markets, our brand recognition, and our competitive position within the industry.

Currently, I am managing a complex due-diligence process for the sale of GXT Products and, as such, am exploring new executive-level opportunities within the consumer products industry. I would welcome the opportunity to meet with you to discuss your needs for a top-level leader who can, and will, deliver positive results. I'll follow up with you next week to schedule an interview, and I appreciate both your time and consideration.

Sincerely,

Tony L. Armstrong

Enclosure

Wendy Enelow, CCM, MRW, JCTC, CPRW — Coleman Falls, Va.

MARK J. MONTGOMERY

2946 Randolph Avenue ▪ Concord, NH 03301 ▪ (603) 555-0111 ▪ markandlois@earthlink.net

[Date]

Mr. Anthony Pringle   **CONFIDENTIAL**
Elite Executive Recruiters
One North Tower, Suite 604
Boston, MA 02109

Dear Mr. Pringle:

Your firm has been recommended to me by Shad James as active in the recruitment of <u>executives with strong operational and financial backgrounds</u>.

For the past 15 years, I have held positions of <u>General Manager</u>, <u>Executive Vice President</u>, and <u>Chief Financial Officer</u> of a mid-size manufacturing firm. I have been a key player in the execution of successful turnaround situations, the development and implementation of acquisitions/divestitures, and the design of operational strategies.

- Planned and implemented the consolidation of businesses from four locations to one without the loss of any major customers.

- Introduced two new breakthrough product lines, representing $7 million in sales.

- Profitably outsourced shipping, logistics, mail, document management, and network maintenance functions previously performed internally.

- Reduced inventory costs by 25% through cycle time improvements, fewer suppliers, and JIT raw materials ordering.

At present I am conducting a confidential search, as my company has been targeted for takeover in the near future. I enjoy the challenge of creating, building, and growing an organization. Ideally, I would be interested in an executive position with a young company that has an entrepreneurial outlook and sales of less than $50 million. An opportunity to earn equity would be attractive.

I am flexible on immediate compensation if there is adequate potential for growth, but for informational purposes, my annual salary and perks total approximately $170,000. My preference for geographic location is the New England area, where most of my family resides.

Whether or not you presently have an appropriate search assignment, I would welcome a personal meeting with you or your representative for an appraisal interview. I will call you next week.

Sincerely,

Mark J. Montgomery

Enclosure: Resume

Melanie Noonan — West Paterson, N.J.

David Merrill Thompkins

19 Peter Road, North Reading, MA 01864

978-555-0111 • Cell 508-555-0111 • dmt4498@gmail.com

[Date, inside address, salutation]

I am currently exploring opportunities in Information Management/Business Strategy Development at the Director-VP-AVP levels. My expertise is within the financial service industry, a discipline in which I am very qualified; however, I would also be interested in aligning my skills with opportunities in either the insurance field or medical technology industry.

As a business technology executive, the breadth of my experience in both the business service and IT sides of the organization uniquely combines an ability to understand and significantly help optimize business—from leveraging new business opportunities and helping the sales and marketing aspects of a business to controlling costs, improving productivity, and generating greater returns. Highlights of my experience include an ability to:

- Manage relationships (customers/clients, partners, staff, managers) exceptionally well—establishing rapport and critical trust.

- Identify and surround myself with exceptionally strong people—giving direct reports the support and tools to do their jobs.

- Effectively manage system/application issues post-acquisition—designing integration strategies that reduce redundancies, streamline operations, and provide properly aggregated information.

- Expertly direct integration and systems implementation teams and processes—while being able to consistently identify and eliminate obstacles to successful project achievement.

- Understand/manage within security and privacy regulations, being ultrasensitive to confidential data and business needs.

- Ensure a bottom-line emphasis on optimizing overall operations—defining short- and long-term strategies that deliver desired results; as an innovative business strategy/technology executive, I provide the creative leadership and targeted systems design solutions that help companies stay ahead of the curve and achieve their goals.

I would value the opportunity to discuss potential opportunities with client companies you represent and to determine if my skillset is the right fit with the challenges these organizations are facing. Please consider this communication in confidence. Thank you for your consideration.

Sincerely,

David Merrill Thompkins

Jan Melnik, MRW, CCM, CPRW — Durham, Conn.

JAMES MONROE

9803 Clifton Street • Lubbock TX 79432
806-555-0111 • jamesmonroe@door.com

[Date]

**Triple Treat: Manager of
Technology, Money, and People.**

Dear Ms. Ockerman:

Analyzing business/technology issues and developing effective solutions to meet organizational needs is my expertise.

Throughout my career, I have played a key role in implementing new strategies and processes that boosted productivity, efficiency, and profitability for both my employers and their top-priority clients. Whether leading projects in oil and gas, electric, manufacturing, or network services industries, I have consistently met the challenge of solving problems through a combination of technology innovation, project leadership, and client relationship management, illustrated by the following examples from my current position:

- **99% uptime from transfer of entire IT infrastructure to Active Directory environment;**
- **80% productivity gain from build-out of Help Desk function in the Western region;**
- **65% security increase for systems and 720 users through Disaster Recovery plans;**
- **Instruction for advanced users in conducting training classes for employees.**

With a blended background that shines in management and technology, there's every chance that I can bring genuine value to your future initiatives and, at the same time, integrate smoothly within your current IT management team.

I hope you think we have lots to talk about in a meeting to discuss the benefits and strategies I can bring to your company table. I'll make it a priority to call you next week to pin down a mutually convenient time. If you need information about my experience, education, competencies, or skills before then, please do not hesitate to reach me at 806-555-0111.

Sincerely,

James Monroe

Enclosure

Dan Dorotik, NCRW — Lubbock, Texas

George Lansing

87 Landing Drive ▪ Albany, NY 54490
567.555.0111 ▪ gmonroe@cox.net

[Date, inside address, salutation]

As Director of Operations for a nationwide retail organization, I successfully innovated and introduced operational, merchandising, customer service, and employee training programs.

> **Bottom-Line: Sales climbed $25 million annually and the gross profit margin increased by 13 full points within the first year.**

As Regional Manager, I reversed a store-closing trend and turned a non-producing region into a highly profitable operation.

> **Bottom-Line: Under my management, the region achieved the highest sales volume throughout the entire company comprised of 52 regions.**

As Store Manager, I provided superior customer service increasing average sale by 50%.

> **Bottom-Line: Recognized for significantly increasing store sales, margins, and profits to record heights.**

Throughout my career, I have demonstrated my ability to identify challenges, implement effective management practices and respond to market demands. Beginning with a concept, I have created and implemented sales and marketing strategies designed to achieve bottom-line results.

Equally important has been my success in recruiting, developing, and directing teams of well-qualified management and sales personnel. By creating proactive business cultures encouraging employee participation in the decision-making process and rewarding individual contributions, I have built profitable business operations.

I am now exploring new opportunities that will allow me to continue to produce while offering new challenges. If you need a professional with my talents, I would welcome a conversation.

Very truly yours,

George Lansing

Louise Garver, CPBS, JCTC, CMP, CPRW, CEIP — Broad Brook, Conn.

DENISE DOTREEV

3 Cousins Crescent
Aurora, Ontario
L4G 9A9

Home 905-555-0111
Mobile 905-555-0112
d-dotreev@my-email.com

Targeting management roles in:
FINANCIAL ANALYSIS · DATA ANALYSIS

[Date, inside address, salutation]

The theme of my career: To locate the most efficient route possible to achieve a goal within the shortest amount of time — without sacrifice to overall quality.

Case in point: While at Top Telecommunications, I participated on a 4-person I.T. team challenge to support a weekly subscriber base of 5 million customers spanning all of the U.S. and Puerto Rico. Because of the sheer volumes of work, we uncovered new data sources as well as innovative processes and procedures that led to the drastic reduction of weekly report production times from 5 days to 1 day — a drop of 80%.

In addition, new codes were being set up in response to different cable TV packages offering a variety of network bundles. My team and I determined a way to interpret the data that improved overall staff productivity because this initiative reduced coding times and heightened accuracy levels.

Successful employees are tenacious: A resourceful problem-solver, I diligently tackle what is in front of me. I persevere until the job is done because I resolve to take on tough challenges and aspire to succeed — even in the face of challenging goals. With a solid track record behind me, I am confident that I can do the same for you.

I would be pleased to have the opportunity to set up an in-person meeting so that we may discuss your needs and how I might be able to meet them. I will follow up with you in a few days; in the meantime, you are welcome to contact me if you seek any additional information.

Thank you for your time, consideration, and attention. With a solid track record of making money and saving money behind me, I am confident that I can do the same for you.

Yours truly,

Denise Dotreev

Enclosure — Resume

Marian Bernard, CPS, CPRW, JCTC, CEIP — Aurora, Ontario, Canada

Sidney M. Brown

10 East Buffalo Grove Road ▪ Arlington Heights, Illinois 60004
sidney.m.brown@anyisp.com   Home Phone: 555-555-0111

[Date]

Mr. Elliot Winters, Chief Operating Officer
Alpha Beta Consumer Electronics
50 West Dundee Road
Wheeling, Illinois 60089

Dear Mr. Winters:

Can your company benefit from the energy of a senior manager who's a superman at dodging business bullets?

When decades got tough, this tough businessman kept turning a profit. Despite a changing neighborhood that folded many small, less well-run businesses, my independent retail appliance and furniture store (Sansone-Blackmoor, Inc. in Berwyn, Illinois) made money despite all odds. That's verifiable.

But wisdom is in knowing when it's time to transfer skills and knowledge to another venue and I'm now ready to make that career move. To help your organization grow and expand, I can bring to your table the following benefits:

→ Extensive knowledge of the major electronics and appliance brands as well as what most consumers want and expect.

→ Well-developed sales acumen; strong closing skills and talent for developing <u>and</u> retaining a productive sales team.

→ Excellent communication skills; ability to develop strong relationships with mass merchandisers, buyers, and sales representatives.

→ Skilled in establishing immediate, positive rapport with customers.

→ Awareness of how creative merchandising strategies can assure maximum inventory turns.

→ Sound bottom-line judgment.

Thank you very much for your consideration. I will contact you next week to see if we can arrange a meeting at a mutually convenient day and time, so we can further discuss your needs and how I might be able to fulfill them. Should you have any questions in the interim, feel free to get in touch with me by phone or e-mail.

Sincerely,

Sidney M. Brown

Joellyn Wittenstein Schwerdlin, CCMC JCTC, CPRW — Worchester, Mass.

JONATHAN BOUDREAUX
(949) 555-0111

234 Poinsettia St.
Corona del Mar, CA 92625
name@domain.com

[Date, inside address, salutation]

The time has come. I have finally sold myself out of a job with Happy Homebuilders!

For the past 17½ years, my real estate activities have focused on the development, leasing, management, and sale of Happy Homebuilders' commercial, industrial, and office properties, which now have all been sold. As a result, I am now looking to my colleagues to assist me in my search for an **Executive Management** position with a development / project management company where my experience and expertise will be of benefit.

During my career in the industry, I have built and led successful development, property management, and brokerage / sales organizations. I have provided the strategic, marketing, financial, and operating expertise to deliver strong earnings and sustained revenue streams and have successfully negotiated sales of retail, industrial, and office properties.

Highlights of my professional career clearly indicate my ability to identify a solid investment, pull all the players together, and deliver positive results. They include:

> ➢ Successfully negotiated leases for over one million sq. ft.
> ➢ Held management oversight for 3.5 million sq. ft.
> ➢ Completed sale transactions for over $300 million.

Is there is an opportunity with your company? I will contact you within five days to discuss ways that I might produce equally impressive results for your team. Should you have any questions before then, please feel free to call me at 949-555-0111, or e-mail me at name@domain.com.

I greatly appreciate your time and consideration.

Sincerely,

Jonathan Boudreaux

Enclosure

Gay Anne Himebaugh — Corona del Mar, Calif.

John Anderson
458 River Road ▪ Tarrytown, NY 96880 ▪ Home: 914.555.0111 ▪ Mobile: 914.555.0112 ▪ johnanderson@aol.com

"Having worked with John in a very dynamic and fast-paced environment, I was always impressed with his ability to look straight at the goal and help guide the team to the objectives. This ability was invaluable to the group when working with various organizations, people, and processes to build cohesive business and marketing plans spanning our worldwide organization."

Vice President of Marketing
Remintar Technology, Inc.

"John can be counted on to take an assignment, project, or complex problem and pull the right resources together (people and funding) to drive to success. He works to understand the customer needs, requirements, and pain points and then addresses those in creative new ways. One of the most talented individuals I have had the pleasure to work with in my 18 years."

Worldwide Vice President
of Marketing
Remintar Technology, Inc.

[Date, inside address, salutation]

As a business and marketing leader in program management and process improvements that have increased revenues and reduced costs, I offer a combination of knowledge and skill sets that will benefit your company. My expertise in leading companies through periods of growth and change has prepared me for any number of challenges that your company may be facing.

Highlights of my achievements during my rapid growth at Center Technology Inc. include:

As Marketing Manager for the global business unit:
- Led a global team of marketing and product managers to redefine the program scope, which increased storage revenue by more than $50 million incrementally in 6 months.

As Marketing Manager for the hardware program:
- Directed the reduction of over 120 marketing programs with a $13 million quarterly budget down to 8 marketing programs with an $8 million budget.
- Implemented promotions and extensive training programs to increase cross-sell of PCs and support services by over 25% and server.

As Business Planning Manager:
- Leveraged the company's global account organization and sales force to increase global accounts revenue by more than 12%.
- Improved relationships between the Americas' regional business and marketing teams through the implementation of best practices.

If you need a strategic marketing executive with strong business acumen and out-of-the-box problem-solving talent blended with extraordinary team leadership and the ability to execute tactically, then I am your candidate. I would welcome the opportunity to discuss how my vision, creativity, and skill sets could benefit your organization. May we meet?

All best,

John Anderson

Louise Garver, CPBS, JCTC, CMP, CPRW, CEIP — Broad Brook, Conn.

JONATHAN B. ABBOTT
58 Island Path
Tulosca, FL 02927
555.555.0111

[Date]

Mr. Bernard Hale
Director of Human Resources
Surf-n-Sand Sports
3837 Main Street
Tulosca, FL 02927

Dear Mr. Hale,

As a long-time outdoors enthusiast and supporter of your products, I was very excited to hear that Surf-n-Sand Sports is planning to build in my area. I would like to be considered for employment at your company in the construction phase of the new building with the goal of transitioning into Facilities Director.

In my 25 years of experience in the building industry, I have successfully managed many multi-million-dollar projects, including our local sports arena and several buildings at Tulosca Community College. My strong understanding of mechanical systems and my natural ability to lead diverse crews make me an excellent candidate for this position.

My references say I am a conscientious, proactive leader who routinely follows jobs from start to successful completion, often under deadline and under budget.

I would bring this same expertise and enthusiasm to your company. I will be attending your Job Fair next week and look forward to discussing my qualifications with you at that time.

Sincerely,

Jonathan B. Abbott

Heather Carson, GCDF, CPRW, JCTC, CWDP — Concord, N.H.

GERARD KELHAM, CPA

2265 Grove Road, Columbia, MD 21045
(443) 555-0111 ▪ gkelhamcpa@gmail.com

[Date]

*"Gerard's uncanny ability to get the
numbers right on tax accruals and deferrals
is much appreciated."*
— **Alberto Mendez, CFO, Columbus National Bank**

[Inside address, salutation]:

Are you in the market for a highly dependable, ethical **Controller** or **Finance Director** with a track record of excelling with *non-profit financial management challenges*? Someone who has guided the financial operations of an historic non-profit (labor union) through international mergers and consolidations to emerge as a resilient and profitable entity? If so, look no further. My hands-on experience managing the full array of controllership functions for the past 15 years includes proven accomplishments that attest to my enterprise-building value.

Here are five reasons to bring me on board.

1. **Cash Management:** Successfully maintained **consistent positive cash flow for 15 years** managing controllership functions for historic labor union undergoing ebb and flow of membership due to international mergers and, most recently, consolidations.

2. **Financial Leadership:** Served as senior financial advisor to Board of Directors and member of senior management team. **Doubled volume of investment assets** ($2.2 billion) during my tenure and secured 2% above-market return-on-investment (ROI).

3. **Merger Finance:** Led financial restructuring and **integration of four mergers**, including merger with an international union. Resulted in viable non-profit operations for years.

4. **Regulatory Compliance & Reporting:** Achieved **100% compliant record** with all federal and state laws and regulations, including DOL and IRS reporting. Possess in-depth knowledge of GAAP principles, as well as LM-2 reporting.

5. **Technology Integration:** Championed transition to integrated financial information systems and automated processes that **cut costs, streamlined operations, and improved member programs**, outreach, and communications.

The depth of my experience in a senior financial management role for a large union with up to 900 local affiliates and 165,000 members, combined with my up-to-date training, offers you the prospect of hiring a high-performing and trustworthy professional who can begin producing the kind of results you need — immediately.

My resume goes into the details you'll want to know. I'll contact you within the week to see if the results I offer are of interest to you. If your needs are immediate, you can reach me on my mobile phone: (443) 555-0111.

All best,

Gerard Kelham, CPA

Susan Guarneri, MRW, CERW, CPRW, CPBS, NCCC, DCC — Three Lakes, Wis.

Sergei Kowal

62 Ready Avenue South ⤙ London ON ⤙ N5T 1U8
519-555-0111 ⤙ 519-555-0112

decisive ⤙ **LEADERSHIP** ⤙ accountable

Ready to relocate

[Date]

"WorkBC" Job Fair

Re: Dream Job British Columbia

Dear Reader:

As your Web site challenges, "It's one thing to talk about jobs in theory, and quite another to get out there and find a great job." Not one to just talk, here I am. I am organized, have a positive attitude, and am willing to work hard. My resume provides solid proof of these attributes. I hope that there is a new role waiting for me in Canada's arguably most beautiful province.

Your Web site gives 10 great reasons to move to B.C., and all of them are quite compelling. Because I have school aged children, reason #4 is reason enough, but #10 — "B.C. promotes a flexible and healthy work environment" — is the best reason for wanting to work in B.C. You will read in my resume that as Supervisor, and previously as a Team Leader, I have found ways to improve staff morale and enjoyment of work life — essential for the health of the community and its businesses.

May I draw your attention to a few of my strengths?

⮑ Organization to get things done efficiently, saving time and money.

⮑ Leadership to balance business needs and employee needs; a company's sustained bottom line is interwoven with the health of its employees.

⮑ Communications to relate in earnest — and with passion and enthusiasm — to people in everyday language a company's "big picture," correlating it to the small details that will create that vision.

My family is 100% with me on this venture, and I sincerely hope that something in my resume will pique the interest of a quality B.C. employer. I will take the initiative, and will give you a call mid-week, [date]; I'm willing, ready, and able to join B.C.'s workforce.

Yours truly,

Sergei Kowal
Att: 3 pages, resume and training addendum

Stephanie Clark, BA, CRS, CIS — Kitchener, Ontario, Canada

CHARLES T. BORDEN
7733 Lionheart Lane, Alexandria, VA 22315
703-555-0111 ▪ charlestborden15@yahoo.com

[Date]

Name
Title
Organization
Street Address
City, ST Zip

I increased sales 300% for my last employer.
Can I do it again for my next employer?
The answer is a resounding yes!

Dear [Name]:

I'm looking for a new boss, but you need look no further for a **sales executive** with a track record of hitting quota challenges out of the ballpark.

Excelling with turnaround sales management challenges, I've paid my dues by orchestrating company firsts for sales performance and by lighting fires beneath mediocre territories and regions.

My resume reveals nitty-gritty details, but here's food for thought: **five fast reasons why you should consider hiring me.** These are results attained in turnaround sales management at the regional and national levels — all verifiable.

- **National Director of Sales:** Reorganized turnaround of struggling 3-year-old start-up to attain national sales quotas within 3 months for Eastern US region (PharmaSystem).

- **Regional VP:** Achieved company record for hitting regional revenue quotas in first year for long-sales-cycle, high-ticket medical equipment and devices sold to hospitals in 15-state region (MediEquipMore).

- **Regional Director of Sales:** Outperformed other regions to capture top sales ranking for capital equipment and software in four consecutive years with previously underperforming 20-state region. Won President's Club Regional Manager of the Year award (National Medical Processing & Systems Automated).

- **Regional Business Director:** Boosted historically sluggish sales record for Southern US region to near-quota (99.5%) levels within 6 months (Corp500Care).

- **Director of Marketing:** Requested by CEO to step into interim national marketing role for one year and devise winning market strategy. Achieved highest lead-generation rate in company history and top-notch sales for new product launch (Corp500Care).

Are you my next employer? Let's plan on talking soon. I'll call you next week to set up a meeting. But if you need action sooner rather than later, you can reach me on my cell phone: 703-555-0111.

Sincerely,

Charles T. Borden

Susan Guarneri, MRW, CERW, CPRW, CPBS, NCCC, DCC — Three Lakes, Wis.

ELIZABETH C. ADAMS

1141 Grand Avenue • St. Louis, Missouri 63003
314-555-0111 • eadams@email.net

[Date]

Mr. Randy Cargill, VP of Sales
Parbel Systems, Inc.
1000 Michigan Avenue
St. Louis, Missouri 63014

Psyched up to
explode sales and
gain market position

Dear Mr. Cargill:

Developing innovative strategies that blow the lid off a company's sales and advance its market position is my expertise.

My background with start-ups and small businesses has allowed me to take on and accomplish progressively responsible roles covering business development, advertising, marketing, and strategic planning. For the past six years, I have served as the Vice President of Kent Furnishing's Wholesale Division. My attached resume outlines many of my successes in this and previous roles, but I would like to call your attention to the following:

Kent Furnishing
- Tripled annual sales from $4+ million to $12 million in less than four years, which allowed the company to increase its retail locations from one to six.
- Cultivated referral base by developing newsletter and strategic e-mail campaigns.
- Increased sales and productivity while enhancing the working environment by instituting productivity assessments, employee surveys, and incentive/reward programs.

The Grayson Group
- Aggressively built business to $4.2 million in annual revenue with startup capital of less than $10K.
- Maintained profitable operations through 13 years of business; negotiated sale of business in 1999.
- Promoted highest level of customer service to gain competitive edge within a marketplace dominated by real estate investment trusts and large publicly-traded companies.

I welcome the opportunity to discuss your needs and how my capabilities can meet them. I will follow up with you next week, but please contact me at 314-555-0111 if you have any questions. I look forward to speaking with you soon.

Sincerely,

Elizabeth C. Adams
Enclosure

Michelle Penn, CPRW — Granite City, Ill.

Orlando Martinez
(714) 555-0111

7849 Greenville St., Santa Ana, CA 92705

fitnesspro888@aol.com

[Date]

Mr. John Reingold
Manager
Magnet Sports Center
7899 Qualcomm Way
San Diego, CA 92102

Dear Mr. Reingold:

Most people agree that health and fitness are becoming more important in today's world, especially because of lifestyle pressures and increased longevity. But for those of us who are in the business, fitness is not only a way of life but life-giving.

Fitness has been my passion and my career. I have thoroughly enjoyed every minute of teaching people how to understand their bodies and achieve personal fitness goals, and I am honored to have made a difference in the lives of my clients over the years.

In September, I will be relocating to San Diego and would like to continue doing what I do best — teaching people about fitness and introducing them to the wonderful mental and physical benefits it can provide. From the enclosed resume you will see that my career has been both diverse and rewarding, affording me an opportunity to reach people of all ages and levels of fitness.

I would sincerely appreciate an opportunity to meet with you and discuss how my background and experience can benefit your outstanding program. I will call your office to schedule a personal interview at your convenience.

Thank you for your time and consideration.

Sincerely,

Orlando Martinez

Enclosure

Gay Anne Himebaugh — Corona del Mar, Calif.

SUSAN J. HOOVER, LCSW
265 Charlotte Street • Hallsville, TX 75650 • (903) 555-0111
shoover@yahoo.net

[Date, inside address to hiring authority at a pharmaceutical company, salutation]

RE: Licensed Clinical Social Worker for Pharmaceutical Sales: A Great Idea!

Let me tell you a story. A patient of mine put herself in a bad situation and called me to rescue her. She had self-raised her antidepressant, and when she ran out early, her physician refused to prescribe more. The antidepressant is known for withdrawal effects. How would I advocate for my patient while communicating to a physician (whom I did not know well) that I understood her perspective?

I immediately contacted the physician, listening closely to her viewpoint, and agreeing that the patient had made a mistake (the physician's primary issue). I expressed my concern regarding withdrawal, and shut up. The doctor slowly took out her script pad and wrote what was needed. I thanked her, and asked for advice on how I could convince the client not to do this again. Not long after that the physician asked me to handle another case, which I did immediately, going above and beyond what she asked.

Can you use my communication and problem-solving skills on your pharmaceutical sales team?

As a licensed clinical social worker, I have been "selling" in the medical community for over 15 years—negotiating diplomatically with patients for changes in living and habit, as well as with medical providers for services and supplies. I work independently and believe I am valued by physicians and medical staff. The medical director of New Beginnings thought enough of my clinical skills, insight, and strong customer service orientation to (almost) convince me to stay after I was offered a job at the Healthcare Center.

I am ready for a new challenge. I enjoy exposure to the "hard science" of pharmaceutical chemistry and research, and I believe I would enjoy working with [company name].

A final story: I was the youngest student ever accepted to the Texas University Advanced Standing Graduate Program — because I had a high GPA, good GRE scores (studied madly over the summer), excellent volunteer and extracurricular experience, a good personal narrative, and top recommendations by professors. I drove down to TU on my own initiative to interview key people at the School of Social Work to see if it was what I wanted — and to stand out as one of the best, I even bought a suit.

Thank you for your interest, time, and consideration. I look forward to an interview at your convenience.

With enthusiasm to match my skills,

Susan J. Hoover, LCSW

Dayna Feist, CPRW, JCTC, CEIP — Asheville, N.C.

JACQUELINE DEMPSEY

422 Robin Hill Lane
Abbington, MA 02351

Cell Phone: 788-555-0111
E-mail: Jacqueline78@aol.com

[Date]

Ms. Carol Manning
Human Resources Manager
Barrington-Tays, Inc.
433 Old Coach Road
Dartmouth, MA 02714

*"Jacqueline was an inspiration to the staff, treating everyone
who came into this office with respect. In fact, she treated
everyone as if they were a war hero."*
— Kerry White, CEO, Caruthers Corp. (now AHK Industries)

Dear Ms. Manning:

As an experienced **Executive/Administrative Assistant**, my overall objective has always been to make my boss's job easier, and I have successfully done that. I have been supporting senior-level management for more than 14 years and have acquired the skills necessary to ensure the highest level of competence.

I enjoy my current position as a Special Event Coordinator, but this job has taken me away from the executive support positions that I have held in the past and really liked. I miss the challenges and the multi-tasked responsibilities of a fast-paced and smooth-running office. My goal is to return to an office support position, and I am looking for an opportunity as an Executive or Administrative Assistant.

As you can see from the attached resume, my previous experience in executive support and event planning has given me the overall skills, competencies, and knowledge needed to perform well in a high-level position where you are often called upon to plan meetings and events, as well as run a smooth and efficient office. My office skills are excellent, and I have outstanding time-management and organizational abilities.

As a professional dedicated to service and excellence, I am a self-starter with excellent written and verbal communication skills and work well as a team leader and team player.

I would welcome the opportunity to meet and discuss how my strengths and abilities could benefit you. I'll call you Wednesday morning to see when we can meet. Thanks so much for reading.

Best regards,

Jacqueline Dempsey

Attach.

Carol Nason, MA, CPRW — Groton, Mass.

Chapter 10

Networking Letters

- -

In This Chapter

▶ Gaining insights from a wealth of networking letters

▶ Getting to the bottom of networking moves that really work

▶ Sampling simple tips to maintain your network

- -

*O*ne of the most overused words in contemporary language is *networking.* You're urged to network your way to new friends, network your way to better business opportunities, network your way to more sales, and network your way to an attractive new job.

Networking's popularity is not undeserved: Whether pressing-the-flesh the traditional way on land — or meeting new people the newer way online (Chapters 2 and 13) — putting together a personal network is a work project highly recommended by virtually every career adviser I know. And most cite true stories to back up their convictions.

I particularly like the story of a newly unemployed technology executive who 20 years ago decided to give networking a go by writing to everyone he knew — friends, acquaintances, distant relatives, former employers, and former employees — 200 people in all.

Explaining that he'd become a freelancer, the tech exec said he was looking for work. He outlined his credentials in a letter; he did not attach a resume, presumably to avoid paralyzing readers with too much information. The newly-minted freelancer asked everyone to let him know if they had work or to introduce him to anyone they knew who might. The tech exec immediately received an offer of a temporary work project that turned into full-time employment — a networking touchdown that restarted his ultimately very successful career.

This chapter shows you what to say and how to say it when you launch a networking job project of your own.

Short Key Points about Job Networking

Entire books are written about the ins and outs of job networking. But I cut to the chase in this chapter because the focus is on communicating better to allies who can spread your word or deliver interviews. To make your networking work, review these basics:

- **The networking secret.** Successful networkers invest in people over the years. They think about personal networking as making deposits into and withdrawals from a kind of favor bank. Networking is a way of life, not a life jacket you pull out as your ship goes down.

- **The networking process.** You already may be building promising connections with people you meet in the normal course of your life. Keep a list of who they are and how to reach them. Refresh your memory with these examples of personal-network-rich activities:

  - Attending professional association and alumni meetings
  - Being helpful to your neighbors
  - Exchanging pleasantries with people like letter carriers and sales reps
  - Striking up conversations in dentists' and veterinarians' offices
  - Chatting up other parents at your child's school
  - Getting to know other volunteers on a civic project
  - Working on humane endeavors at your church

  Keep others in the picture of what you're up to; don't be the taker who calls only when he or she wants something. Use lunch hours to stay in touch. Send e-mail. Connect others. Take leadership positions in groups. Do good turns.

- **The networking benefit.** By building bridges to a group of individuals whom you are willing to help, and who are willing to help you in return, you create a safety-net infrastructure to mobilize when you're on the road again in the job world.

Networking Letters to Note

The ten sample messages in this chapter demonstrate using the ripple effect in tapping into the personal networks of others. All the samples make it easy for recipients to help the job seeker, but some have surprising twists. My comments about each call your attention to specific tactics, circumstances, and advantages:

- **Confident networkers.** No Timid Tillie, a candidate (Stitel) follows up with a telephone call on a job lead she found on an online business networking site. The candidate's letter boldly states on the upper-right screen that she's the Stand Out winner, backing up her assertion with impressive achievements.

Going for a goal with all flags flying is a modern mindset to survive turbulent times of change.

✔ **Chance encounters.** A Canadian airport executive (Callahan) turns a meeting at a pubic forum into an interview opportunity and follows up with a cover letter and resume that spell out exactly why he can be a leading candidate for an emergency services position at a larger airport.

Being prepared to write a quality cover letter and to customize a core resume are skills that capitalize on unexpected opportunities.

✔ **Postscript persuaders.** A senior chemist (Paine) opens by naming one of her former employees as her connector, which in itself suggests that she's a likeable manager, or her former subordinate wouldn't have referred her. A hard-to-miss postscript implies that she's a team player who believes in keeping managers in the loop with regular updates — an applause-line statement.

Postscripts may be the first words read on a cover letter.

✔ **Alumni endorsements.** Applying to become a business solutions consultant (Foster), a candidate connects quickly by stating that a former professor recommends the contact. Professors typically have their referral plates full with requests from current graduates. The candidate will be perceived as above average when a professor is willing to reach back five years to endorse an alumnus.

A professor's recommendation is a strong endorsement worth pursuing.

✔ **Pitching recruiters.** An aerospace executive seeking to bail out of a thinning industry pulls out all the stops (Sloan). After mentioning a mutual connection, the job seeker praises the recruiter's status. He makes a strong presentation of his crossover skills and, icing on the cake, promises to relocate if the job is good enough.

Recruiters are weary of wasting time on candidates who, at the last minute, refuse to relocate when the job requires it.

✔ **Informational interviews.** A student seeking assistance with a class project (Forbart) not only mentions the person who referred her but explains that they met through volunteer work helping animals. If the recipient is also an animal lover, the letter could stop right there and the informational interview would be granted. But the student wisely goes on to include five questions described as representative of the type she would ask in an interview, an act that reassures the reader the student is organized and respectful of the reader's time.

Consider a possible extra benefit of writing a Stand Out letter: The interviewee, impressed by the student's thoughtfulness, may choose to become an important member of the student's personal network.

✔ **Entrepreneurial networking.** An amusing subject line heralds a businessman's new venture. The entrepreneur (Galloway) cuts it short to command attention. Additional networking e-mails are likely to follow as the business becomes established and grows.

Marketing online through a network is a favorite way to bootstrap a business, especially during its start-up months. Although the business later may focus on e-mails selling products and services, career management documents are needed at launch.

✔ **Advance selling.** A financial executive (Hankerd) with exceptional government contracting expertise breaks out on his own with a networking letter after originally being filtered through a network contact.

Even when the employer doesn't read the resume in advance, the letter quality suggests that the candidate knows how to handle himself in business, confirming the mutual friend's recommendation.

✔ **Industry insiders.** A vocational rehabilitation counselor (Smith) taps a colleague, including both a capsule and a resume. Unless the friend wants the job himself, it's a good bet he'll alert her to attractive job openings. Although a job search engine can uncover the same open jobs, fellow professionals can add endorsements and inside tips.

Professional associations are fertile fields for networking letters. Nothing works better than a recommendation by a fellow professional.

✔ **Networking postcards.** A well-thought-out sample for a nonprofit executive (Gray) depicts the creative postcard model. Both sides of the postcard pull their weight. This thrifty medium stands out from other mail and allows the job seeker to spread a message widely and quickly.

Watch Out — Samples Ahead

Conventional advice suggests that in networking letters you ask for advice and help — not for a job. A direct request for employment puts people on the spot, and most of us hate to say "no" to a friend or colleague.

But results for a job seeker who *did* ask for a job — contract work to be sure, but a job nonetheless — make me question that conventional advice. The freelance technology executive I describe at the beginning of this chapter asked for work or for introductions to people who have work, and it paid off for him. My observation: As with most practices in job search, there are no absolutes. Use common sense.

Reflecting on the samples that follow puts you steps ahead of others who haven't learned to write enticing networking letters that don't sound like ransom notes.

So what can you do if your message-return rate is disappointing? Assuming you've stayed connected and you're not a fair-weather friend, rewrite your message, or engage a professional writer to do so, and try again.

JINGER STITEL

14 RIDGE MOUNTAIN DRIVE, YELLSBERGVILLE, AZ 85367
(623) 555-0111   JS81@YAHOO.COM   (602) 555-0112

[Date]

Ms. Maylene Wishburn   **Your Staffing Need: Payroll, Accounting, HR**
1 Saturn Place   **My Recommended Solution: Jinger Stitel**
Rayville, AZ 85368

Dear Ms. Wishburn:

It was energizing to speak with you Friday and be able to personally convey my
enthusiasm and excitement about the open position at Saturn! I find it amazing that
using the power of my *LinkedIn* network really led to a phone interview.

As I said, I currently work at ADP and have extensive knowledge of payroll issues.
I am seeking a new opportunity at a much smaller organization where I can be of
assistance in payroll, accounting, and human resources.

Here is how I meet/exceed your needs described in the job opening you mentioned:

♦ *Payroll, Paychex, computer, office, and accounting skills:* I process payrolls for over
  250 clients at ADP. Excellent on the computer and with spreadsheets. I have basic
  accounting knowledge, coupled with working toward B.A. in Accounting. The
  Paychex system is almost identical to ADP's.

♦ *Analysis and problem solving:* I love math! Before I was hired at ADP, I took their
  entry-level test and received a perfect score. 90% of applicants fail the test. I have
  created some innovative spreadsheets and letters that have been implemented
  throughout the office.

♦ *Familiarity with HR:* I have assisted with HR duties, including new and terminated
  workers and processing paperwork. Working for ADP and Douglas Rentals required
  knowledge of and compliance with many different legal, tax and governmental
  policies and procedures. I am used to navigating a myriad of important
  requirements.

I will contact you next week to see if I can help make your Saturn dealership run more
smoothly.

It was my pleasure. A hearty thank you for your time.

Jinger Stitel

Enclosure

Gail Frank, NCRW, CPRW, JCTC, CEIP — Tampa Fla.

WARREN CALLAHAN

2270 Valleyview Road, Grande Prairie, AB T3E 2P7   wcallahan@shaw.com   (403) 555-0111

[Date, inside address, salutation]

Following our intriguing conversation at the Airport Authority Open Forum on April 19, I have attached a copy of my resume for your review, in anticipation of a need for Emergency Services Operations leadership within the Grande Prairie Airport Authority.

The Grande Prairie Airport expansion project presents significant and exciting growth opportunities for the entire northern region of Alberta. I heartily agree with you: The importance of substantial emergency preparedness and response infrastructure to support transportation, warehousing, tenant, and public safety and security requirements cannot be overstated.

As a potential member of your team, I offer the following expertise and experience to improve the effectiveness of safety and security operations with the GPAA:

> ➢ Over 30 years of career experience in emergency operations here in Grande Prairie, with 5 years of experience in a senior management role.

> ➢ Proactive change leadership in technological and operational improvements.

> ➢ Established reputation and positive working relationships with local and regional emergency service partners.

> ➢ Visionary innovation with a verifiable record of accomplishments increasing cost savings and decreasing administrative burdens.

I feel strongly that I could make a significant contribution to the future success of the Grande Prairie Airport Authority. I would be happy to make myself available to discuss your vision for Emergency Services Operations within your organization in greater detail. Let's talk!

Sincerely,

Warren Callahan

Enclosure: Resume

Susan Easton, CRS, BFA — Prince George, British Columbia, Canada

MARIA L. PAINE, PH.D.
19 Dorothy Place, Syracuse, New York 13572
H (315) 555-0111   C (315) 555-0112   MLPaine@adelphia.net

[Date, inside address, salutation]

Re: Senior Chemist and QC/QA

A former direct report, Sam Quintesse, and I reconnected at a recent alumni event. Sam suggested that I might be ideal for your quality team and, after hearing about the tremendous work you're heading up, I think he's onto something.

My background includes 10 years' experience contributing to the success of quality operations in support of research and manufacturing at the department, plant, corporate, and global level. Performance appraisals have noted my commitment to controlling costs and ensuring on-time product release. My strengths in relationship building have enabled me to train, mentor, and motivate a highly accomplished team of chemists.

My standout qualifications include:

- Utilizing a variety of troubleshooting and problem-solving methods, including root cause analysis, Pareto charts, CAPA, brainstorming, and collaboration to achieve cost savings and improve productivity.
- Auditing raw material and product release testing, bio/batch manufacturing, methods validation, and regulatory compliance for international distribution.
- Coordinating chemistry lab investigations to maintain facility compliance with cGMP, FDA, ICH, 5S, and ISO regulations and guidelines.

My attached resume offers additional details. I'd be happy to tell you even more about what I can do for your high-rated company in an onsite meeting. I'll give you a call on Tuesday to inquire about your availability. Thanks very much for taking the time to meet me by letter.

Sincerely,

Maria L. Paine, Ph.D.

P.S. I'm faithful in keeping management painlessly in the loop by providing updates of progress through regular readable reports and quality control presentations.

Freddie Cheek, MS Ed, CCM, CPRW, CARW, CWDP — Amherst, N.Y.

KEVIN S. FOSTER

44-64 70ᵗʰ Road ▪ Forest Hills, NY 11375 ▪ 718-555-0111 ▪ kevinfoster@gmail.com

[Date]

Mr. Leonard Clemmons, CEO
Infosource Inc.
34 West 47ᵗʰ Street
New York, NY 10036

Dear Mr.Clemmons:

My former professor, John Severnis, recommends that I contact you regarding your current opportunities for **Business Solutions Consultants**. With **over five years of experience in IT business solutions roles**, I strongly believe that my background meshes well with the needs of your organization.

In my current role at Compusource Limited, I conduct extensive IT audits and needs assessments to optimize the operations infrastructure and improve customer servicing.

    ✓ In just one year I created a ticket tracking system to minimize problem-resolution time, built operational scripts and flowcharts to streamline product delivery, and wrote inaugural company policies and procedures.

Prior to my position at Compusource, I was a technology consultant for IBM, where I project managed an Exchange migration program for 25,000 users.

    ✓ At IBM I rolled out a 7,000-seat NT/Exchange and Outlook initiative, authored a "how to" repository for users, and significantly trimmed server down time and crashes by auditing server logs.

Excited by your opportunity and impressed by your company's services, I would welcome the chance to meet with you in person. My resume is attached for your review. Thank you.

Sincerely,

Kevin S. Foster

Attachment

Barbara Safani, MA, CERW, NCRW, CPRW, CCM — New York, N.Y.

Thomas R. Sloan
700 West Paces Ferry Drive
Jacksonville, Florida 32211
(904) 555-0111
email@email.com

[Date]

Mr. Arnold Williams, Recruiter
Global Executive Search
253 Arlington Expressway, Suite 300
Orlando, Florida 32216

Dear Mr. Williams:

Gerry Maronni says you're the go-to recruiter for aerospace aces ready to fly in new directions. Reflecting on my highly successful professional experience within the aerospace industry, I've decided it's time to pursue new challenges.

My primary interest is in working as chief executive for a large corporation, possibly in a division-level capacity, or for a small company that's poised for growth. Yes, I pledge to relocate for the right job.

Why can I transition easily to another industry? My ability to quickly identify *areas of concern, evaluate potential solutions,* and, most importantly, *make the changes necessary to turnaround situations* are my greatest strengths.

I'm savvy in the business world: My aerospace industry experience has tuned me into the relationship between sales, government regulations, and overall production and productivity. These areas are evidenced in my resume but here is a sampling of my notable accomplishments:

- ☑ Reorganized/restructured departments, processes, and operations resulting in annual sales growth from $5 million in [date] to $200 million today

- ☑ Maximized knowledge of and experience with government regulations resulting in the procurement of funds for training and tax exemption for capital expenses totaling almost $200,000

- ☑ Developed and implemented daily performance reporting techniques that led to a 25% increase in production

Thank you for your consideration of my resume, and I look forward to talking soon. I'll follow up within 10 days.

Sincerely,

Thomas R. Sloan
Enclosure

Sharon M. Bowden, CPRW, CEIP — Atlanta, Ga.

[Date]

Ms. Carol Miasma, Vice President
Executively Trainers, Inc.
2567 Ridgedale Drive, Suite 351
Cambridge, MA 02138

Dear Ms. Miasma:

Bertha Scherberg, who does contracting work for you, has spoken very highly of your knowledge during our volunteer work at the Cambridge Humane Society. Bertha thought you would be perfect to make suggestions for my *class project* on corporate leadership training services. Could I schedule a 30-minute interview with you to get answers to some of my questions about your field?

I am a full-time student at Boston University in the Masters Adult Education program and in the process of making a career switch from Marketing to Corporate Training and Consulting.

I chose my project topic because after graduation next year I am interested in working for a corporate training firm or similar type of job in the business sector.

The project is designed to help understand the role of Human Resource Development in an organization. The kinds of questions I have are:

- What kinds of background do most people in the field have?
- What are the most important skills needed?
- What kinds of training and counseling are offered to clients?
- How is a corporate training firm structured?
- Is there data to support the success of corporate leadership training services?

Any handouts, perspective, and tips you might have will be greatly appreciated. I will call you in the next few days to see if I can schedule a short time with you and experience your workplace firsthand.

Thanks in advance!

Giles Forbart
2345 Charles Place, #411
Cambridge, MA 02138
Cell: 617-555-0111
gforbart@yahoo.com

Gail Frank, NCRW, CPRW, JCTC, CEIP — Tampa, Fla.

Subject: Ted's excellent new venture

Dear Howard,

I am happy to share some exciting news. After 17 years in the high tech arena, I am launching Jupiter Tech Appliance. This new company provides a platform for information sharing and partnership development. Because I respect your opinion and value our relationship, I'd like you to check out my new website, www.JupiterTechAppliance.com. Let me know what you think and please share this Web address with your associates.

If you run across any potential clients or partners, I'd love to hear about it. Look out for my new blog, articles, and speaking engagements.

Thanks for your encouragement as I delve into this new phase of my career!

Yours truly,

Ted

Ted Galloway
Chief Business Development Officer
Jupiter Tech Appliance
www.JupiterTechAppliance.com
(714) 555-0111

Tamara Dowling, CPRW — Valencia, Calif.

GRIFFIN M. HANKERD

1732 Resort Rd. gmhankerd1@aol.com Home: 313-555-0111
Utica, MI 48233 Cell: 787-555-0112

[Date]

Mr. Jim Edwards
Chief Executive Officer
US Connect, Inc.
8750 W. Pleasant Ave.
Jackson, MI 49272

Dear Jim:

Since we've been unable to connect personally and have been speaking through Tony Mancini for the past week or so, I wanted to get my resume to you before our July 7 meeting for your review.

With over 25 years of success in linking finance to business operations, the value I bring to US Connect extends far beyond that of a typical **Chief Financial Officer**. Not only am I effective in developing strategic plans, budgets, and forecasts, I know what it takes for operations, marketing sales to successfully execute them to deliver strong and sustainable revenue, profit, and performance results.

My career has included CFO roles in $140 million base operations, with over 2,000 personnel. I provide a unique combination of tools and direction to continuously navigate financial, market, and operational success as measured by:

- **Best Practices Implementation** to boost the value of employee productivity and process improvements.

- **Payroll and Travel Expense Management** for US Army personnel and Joint Task Force in Baghdad, Iraq.

- **Project Management** for Air Force Defense Team. As project manager, completed 135 sites on time and $750,000 under budget.

I have built financial teams from the ground up, implementing financial systems and facilitating merger integration and change management initiatives that have directly impacted the top and bottom-line.

Aware of the caliber and reputation US Connect holds in the marketplace, I look forward to our continued discussion next week as the first of many positive communications.

Sincerely,

Griffin M. Hankerd

Enclosure

Erin Kennedy, CPRW — Lapeer, Mich.

SALLY SMITH

123 ABCD Circle • Anywhere, SC 29666
(864) 555-0111 • name@ bellsouth.net

[Date, inside address, salutation]

It was good to see you at the last conference. Since then, I've learned that change is in the air in my agency and I've decided to research my options sooner rather than later. Can you help me by letting me know of any attractive job openings you hear about that you think I'm qualified to fill? Here's a capsule of my background:

As a quality-driven, visionary team member with more than 9 years of experience providing rehabilitation services and managing caseloads in multiple locations in the southern part of Alabama, I feel confident in my abilities to generate winning results. I have 9 years of combined experience in providing career counseling and job placement assistance to persons in career transition: displaced from disasters, high school students, college students, retirees, persons who were being laid off/downsized or losing jobs that were being off-shored.

My past roles ranged from Senior Vocational Rehabilitation Counselor, District Supervisor, and Disaster Relief Counselor. A sample of my accomplishments:

* **Honored with the Employee of Year** distinction by the Department of Rehabilitation.
* **Wrote successful grant proposal** that received funding to implement a technology showcase for persons with mild to severe hearing impairments to be able to test products to ascertain the effectiveness for their personal needs.
* **Co-authored legislation** with Senator Doe for Senate Joint Resolution No. 123 that acknowledges American Sign Language as a true language to be recognized by the state of Anywhere, public schools, colleges, and universities.
* **Quantifiable successes in job placements** by placing over 40 clients in competitive employment each fiscal year.

Charlie, my resume is attached. I'd like to stay in the South. Please give me a call if you hear about something, and I'll get right back to your lead's hiring authority. You know I appreciate your efforts. Thanks so very much.

All best,

Sally Smith

Kristen Jacoway, CRC, CPRW, CCC, CPBS — Seneca, S.C.

Width = 5 ½″

Dr. David B. Gray
123 4th Street
Dover Neck, NH 12345

Dear Mr. August:

Do you know organizations in the music and arts field that may be looking for someone to help support the mission and goals of that group?

I was referred to you by Carson Hex, who spoke highly of you as someone knowledgeable in the local arts field.

I am in the early stages of seeking to put my years of experience in nonprofits to work for an arts organization. A brief summary of my background is on the reverse side. Perhaps we can meet over coffee. I will call you next week to see what date and time might work for you. Thanks in advance. ~*David*

Height = 4 ¼″

Okay, you can't buy even a postcard stamp this cheap, but you get the idea.

Julius August, President
Islington Street Arts Association
987 Islington Street
Portsmouth, NH 98765

Width = 5 ½″

Dr. David B. Gray

Cell: 360-860-3343
dbgray@yahoot.com

Objective: To provide executive leadership to non-profit organization supporting the arts in the Seacoast area.

With over 25 years leadership experience in the non-profit arena, am able to provide organizational development, strategic planning, membership, marketing, and financial development guidance and leadership. Am entrepreneurial, having co-founded with my wife, Leslie Wellworth, Gentle Healing Wellness Center in Portsmouth. Have counseling training and wrote my doctorate on pastoral counseling. Currently working as a an educator, am versed in the arts of mentoring and coaching.

A member of Continuing Education in Fund Raising (CONFR). Proficient in Office, also Filemaker Pro database software. A good storyteller and a good listener. Can write and edit newsletters and case statements.

I'm available to start full-time with two weeks notice.

Height = 4 ¼″

Dr. David G. Pheaner, CWDP — Greenland, N.H.

Chapter 11

Resume Letters

. . . .

In This Chapter

▶ Introducing the resume letter, a heckuva hybrid

▶ Fixing on the finer points of a resume letter

▶ Eyeing an exhibit of Stand Out samples

. . . .

A *resume letter* is a self-marketing document that combines a cover letter and a resume. (The resume is *not* separate.) Also called a *value proposition letter*, a *job letter*, and a *res-u-letter*, a resume letter typically is two pages but sometimes only one page — or one page with a twist, which you see in a couple of the following samples.

Often overlooked and vastly underused, a resume letter works particularly well when a resume is riddled with hard-to-explain gaps and other problems.

Typically used in a targeted mailing campaign, a resume letter attracts notice because it reads more like a story than a document. Occasionally, a resume letter spills over into other document categories, such as job reply letters, when a formal resume doesn't present the candidate in the best light.

Don't Let Your Great Design Be Ambushed

You can send your resume letters by back-to-the-future postal mail or by e-mail, but if your letter contains graphic design elements as do two in this chapter (Tremaine and Brohman), as well as samples in other chapters, postal mail is the safer choice. Here's why:

The resume letter that turned a casino man back into a chemist

The best resume-letter story I've ever heard is the happy ending to an extremely difficult challenge: finding a management job for a middle-aged chemist who had nearly gambled away his career. The big win was pulled off by Paul A. Hawkinson, the legendary former publisher and editor of *The Fordyce Letter,* a gold-bar publication in the recruiting industry.

Hawkinson, himself a top recruiter before journalism struck, made an annual fact-checking pilgrimage back to the trenches where he served as an unpaid agent for a test-case job seeker who was wrestling with a really hard problem.

One of those years, a decade ago, Hawkinson took on the cause of a chemist who at age 50 left his profession to take a fling dealing cards at a local casino. Five years later, at age 55, the chemist suffered career-changer's remorse and desperately wanted to return as an executive to the chemistry workplace. But that workplace had changed during the five years the chemist was away. Having missed half a decade's technical advances, the chemist's chances were slim to none.

Yet Hawkinson managed to pull victory out of nearly certain defeat. How did he do it? He chose the resume letter route. After sending a well-written resume letter by postal mail to a custom list of owners of small chemical companies, Hawkinson was following up on the phone when he discovered a caretaker CEO job the chemist could fill while the owner took an extended two-year trip out of the country. Interviewed and hired, the chemist was back in the game.

And it all started with a resume letter.

Sending design-dependent letters online may create "very ugly cover letters," Jim Lemke explains. Lemke, the technical reviewer for this book, reports that while most applicant tracking systems retain the native format (MS Word, for example) for both resumes and cover letters, others do not.

"Cover-letter formatting gets messed up in some systems because the system keeps only the resume in native format and converts cover letters to text," Lemke says.

You can, of course, call the HR office at a target company where you plan to send a graphically-enriched cover letter and just ask: "Does your applicant tracking system retain cover letters in native format or convert them to text?" And to double check, ask the same question about resumes.

Keep an Eye Peeled for Good Writing

Among six resume letter samples in this chapter, you find a range of formality and presentations:

✔ **Top qualities.** A savvy lawyer (McKinney) seeking to relocate to a senior-level legal counsel position in a multinational corporation writes an elegant letter detailing his value proposition. The candidate uses no gimmicks, just hard-core competence to sell himself.

A market-tested financial executive (Miller), aims high with a superbly constructed letter written in industry terms that confirm he is who he says he is.

Busy executives can more easily read letters than study resumes. For that reason, supporters of resume letters believe that they are less likely than a cover-letter-and-resume package to be bucked down to the human resource department never to be seen again.

✔ **Returning moms.** By contrast to the formal and traditional letters, a mom (Baker) wants to re-enter the auto industry job market after a two-year absence because of illness and a wish to consider other career fields. She begins with an informal "hook" approach that disarms the reader. Adding to that overlay of charm, the job seeker adds a summary of impressive experience, capping her letter with three powerful testimonials.

Job market reentry issues are good reasons to let the resume letter carry the message.

✔ **1-2 twists.** A blue-collar candidate (Tremaine) relocating to Toronto sends a one-page resume letter that politely asks if he may send his resume (to communicate the matched-pair concept, I also show you the resume in this chapter). But he initially sends only the Stand Out resume letter itself. This graphically-enhanced letter is a fusion of essential skill facts with testimonials and branding statements, a mixture that breathes life into a job application.

A job reply letter for a facilities director (Brohman) illustrates a different kind of a 1-2 twist. Starting with a persuasive first page, the candidate attaches an equally riveting accomplishment sheet. The beauty of an accomplishment sheet is that not only can it work as a second page of a resume letter, but it can also be used in additional ways; if the resume letter is sent online or incorporated in a Web portfolio, the categories on the accomplishment sheet can be hyperlinked for more information. Additionally, the accomplishment sheet in hard copy can be left behind at job interviews.

The creativity displayed in the 1-2 twists of resume letters snares attention.

✔ **Short sweets.** A marketing director (Moran) uses a one-page job reply letter, a variation of the resume letter. He begins with a way-of-the-world statement that works because he prefaces it with "As you know." Otherwise such statements risk being perceived as overbearing. The rationale given for changing jobs — working closer to his home — seems reasonable in a time of record-high transportation costs.

Responding to a job ad with a one-page resume letter is an option to mute age issues before an interview

Unveiling the Resume Letter Samples

Resume letters are designed for targeted mail campaigns, postal or online. Should you use a resume letter to reply to an advertised job opening when the ad requests a resume? Probably not. But if your flawed resume is likely to kill your chances, you have little to lose by trying the resume letter in its place. Take pains to make it informative and persuasive.

As you read through the six resume letters in this chapter, notice how well each addresses the classic concerns of a harried employer:

✔ I don't know who you are.

✔ I don't know your work and your reputation.

✔ I don't know what you have that I want.

✔ I don't know why I should read about you, wasting time I don't have.

✔ I don't know why I shouldn't trash your letter right now.

Maximum message readability is the presentation criterion for each sample cover letter in this chapter. To save space in some superb but lengthier samples, I had to chop the original boilerplate text leading into the letter — most often deleting the recipient's name, title, company and address. So when you see a letter leading off with "[Date, inside address, salutation]," or some variation of that, the generic line is merely a reminder that you can't just say "Hey you, read this!" If you're not sure how to layout your cover letter, turn to Chapter 4.

Thomas Rory Moran III

173 Golden Hills Avenue
Canton, ID 00000

trmoran333@earthlink.com

Home: 333-555-0111
Cell: 333-555-0112

[Date, Inside address of ABC Foods, Inc.]

Posted Position: Marketing Director

Dear [Name]:

As you know, achieving sales and marketing success in today's competitive marketplace requires a creative and strategic thinker who has the ability to establish profitable and lasting relationships, increase revenue growth, and maintain value-added service. My accomplishments in sales and marketing mirror these achievements and are measured by solid results. With over 20 years of consistent success in marketing, sales, and management, I have delivered on all bottom-line sales projections through precise strategic planning and comprehensive marketing services. I would greatly value the opportunity to sit down with you to detail and document these results.

Therefore, it is with pleasure and genuine enthusiasm that I offer my services for your posted position of Marketing Director with ABC Foods, Inc. Please note that my versatility includes excellent business-to-business marketing skills in addition to proven leadership in management and top-notch product presentation and communications skills. Currently employed as Business Development Manager with one of the country's largest sales and marketing firms in the grocery industry, I now seek a position within a company that is closer to my home and where I can continue to provide optimal performance in sales growth and market share.

Allow me to briefly call your attention to some of my accomplishments and qualifications:

o Hold financial supervision of $5.8M in combined annual accrual
o Personally assimilated three new lines that substantially grew business volume
o Generating 9%+ sales volume, year-to-date, over last year's results
o Managed three major grocery lines with combined sales volume of $68M
o Highly respected leader and seasoned manager with an MBA degree in Business Management
o Analytical, organized, and able to conceptualize to meet changing dynamics of the food industry

With the focus of seeking a position with long-term growth and advancement, I would welcome the opportunity to discuss with you how I could make similar valuable contributions to the success of ABC Foods and to further demonstrate my ability to deliver effective solutions. I will call next week about a good time to meet with you. Thank you for considering my application.

Sincerely,

Thomas Rory Moran III

Enclosure

Edward Turilli, BS, MA, CPRW — North Kingstown, R.I.

SUSAN L. BAKER

123 Hollywood Dr. ♦ Oceanside, CA 92057
Cell: 760-555-0112 ♦ Home: 760-555-0111 ♦ Email: susan500baker@yahoo.com

Mr. Antonio K. Garcia, Director of Service   [Date]
BMW Dealers, Escondido
123 Auto Park Way
Escondido, CA 12345

Dear Mr. Garcia:

Any claim that the grass is greener outside the auto-industry-fence is a myth! At least it is for me.

After 20 years of rock-solid experience in our industry, a series of outside opportunities briefly tempted me to cast eyes elsewhere. But not for long.

My inner voice keeps shouting loud and clear that the auto side is where I belong, and that's why I'm selectively contacting you. Hopefully, you will see how adding me to your quality operation will be a big win for BMW Dealers.

My progressively responsible experience includes **service management, service consulting,** and **service writing.** *Initiative, drive,* and *positive attitude* teamed with *customer satisfaction* and *product know-how* have contributed to my documented success:

★ Service Manager, Star Mercedes Benz, Carlsbad, CA: Managed all customer service operations. Hired, trained, and supervised a culturally-diverse workforce of 15. Additionally, as a member of a leadership management quartette, co-managed a separate department of 33 full-time workers. I drove a customer satisfaction winning score in the 90s, up from a failing score in the 70s, when I took responsibility. [dates]

★ Service Manager, Star Honda, Carlsbad, CA: Managed all customer service operations, as well as oversight of equipment purchasing and building maintenance. Hired, trained, and supervised a staff of 44 employees. Initiated cross-skills training, attained State of California "Green Shop" certification. [dates]

★ Service Manager/Service Advisor, Planet Acura, Porsche, & Audi, Carlsbad, CA: Maintained customer satisfaction score of 90% or higher for 10 years with increasing responsibilities, including managing all used-car reconditioning. Promoted to service manager position where I maintained customer service transactions for all three car lines. Utilized manufacturer marketing tools to create customer-satisfaction-measurement mailings, and management of "units in operation" reports. [dates]

SUSAN L. BAKER Page 2

What about dealership operation skills? I am up to speed and ready to roll in software skills, including Word, Excel, Outlook, and PowerPoint; as well as Visio, Publisher, and Project.

What about interpersonal skills? How many references shall I provide? I think you'll find that my brand in our industry is this: Susan is a thoroughly competent professional who understands that integrity and fair-dealing are essential to remaining viable in business for the long run. She's liked by bosses, coworkers and direct reports for her ability to deal genuinely and without arrogance, or when things don't go her way, without bias or pettiness.

I will contact you on Tuesday afternoon to see when we should meet, and to answer any questions you may have concerning my commitment to again water greener grass on a team providing great customer service and boosting profits.

Sincerely yours,

Susan L. Baker

Good words for Susan:

"Although I thought I should have been saving money on a lower priced car, I kept returning to the Porsche dealer because I was treated with such respect by Susan Baker. She really understands how to keep customers happy with their service. She once sent a car at four in the morning to pick me up when, rushing to the airport, I had an accident rolling across roadside brush and wound up with flat tires and tumbleweed and little purple flowers growing out of the grill. She's an American treasure."
— Norma Luna, Porsche owner and customer

"When Susan was the handling the customer service ops at Honda, she hired me, a woman, giving me a chance to show I could do the work right along with the guys. I'll never forget her fairness in opening an opportunity for me. I'm still here. Thanks, Susan."
— Leslie Lubinski, service writer

"Susan Baker is so good that if after 30 days on the job, anyone who hires her isn't satisfied with her work, I'll pay that salary out of my own pocket."
— Cory Miller, former Mercedes dealership owner.

Tom Tremaine

8 Snowdrop Avenue ▸ Toronto ON M5T 3N2 ▸ 416-555-0111   50 Dundalk Road ▸ Milton ON N5T 6H8 ▸ 905-555-0112!

▸ **Local Route Service Driver "careful, dependable, professional"**

"Tom goes out of his way to help others, whether a customer or fellow colleague...trustworthy, dependable individual who strives to improve the quality of the work atmosphere...first to greet me every morning and always carries forth a positive attitude."

- Vince Kaine, colleague!

"Tom has a positive attitude...very strong work ethic...super dependable and is a great part of our team."

- Josie Ross, colleague

"I truly enjoy providing outstanding service; gratitude for a job well done motivates me; smiles of thanks motivate me; a hand-shake and 'thanks again, Tom' motivate me."

- Tom Tremaine

[Date, inside address of Security Shredding Inc.]

▸Re: Local Route Service Driver

Dear [Name]:

I find that Security Shredding's goals and mine — providing exemplary client experience — are very much aligned. Please note that although I presently reside in Milton, I am relocating to the Toronto address above shortly and am available immediately.

I pride myself on a job well done, on going the extra mile to deliver outstanding customer service, and on motivating or contributing to my team. Success is seldom, if ever, achieved on one's own.

In response to the qualifications needed of a local route service driver's position, you will find me:

▹ Very energetic. I consider a 70 km cycle a perfect day, and thoroughly enjoy working physically and working outdoors.

▹ Sales and customer service oriented. I find those two go hand in hand. The best way to secure future sales is through referral. The best way to gather referrals is through exemplary service.

▹ Experienced in driving large vehicles, with a valid BMZ license in good standing.

I would enjoy the chance to present my abilities, energies, and personality in person. I will call within the next five days to see if I may send you my resume. If you prefer to skip to the next level and schedule an interview at your convenience, please call me at 905-555-0112. Should I not be available, please leave a message, and I will return your call within 24 hours.

Yours truly,

Tom Tremaine

Tom Tremaine

8 Snowdrop Avenue ▹ Toronto ON M5T 3N2 ▹ 416-555-0111   50 Dundalk Road ▹ Milton ON N5T 6H8 ▹ 905-555-0112I

▶ **Local Route Service Driver "careful, dependable, professional"**

▶ **What you can expect:**

Energy, motivation, personality. Hardworking and enthusiastic individual, with winning customer service skills, and the ability to motivate and instruct staff. Positive thinker who models leadership behaviours. A true team player, contributing his best, and ensuring his team's best performance. Addresses your bottom line. Known for going above and beyond.

▶ **Employment History:**

Outdoor Activity Facility, Milton ON   [dates]
Supervisor, Rental & Tech Shop
Supervise sales & technician staff; oversee equipment maintenance; facilitate Low Ropes & Vertical Challenge course delivery to corporate customers & camps.
▹ Hire, train, supervise staff varying from 6 f/t summer to 12 p/t winter staff.
▹ Schedule staff in 2 areas, for adequate coverage of 14-hour days during ski season.
▹ Train staff in ski sharpening, base tuning to service 200 pairs/week, bringing in revenue of over $7500/week; increased upsell by 30% by offering varying packages addressing different needs.
▹ Maintain fleet of 600 pairs of skis and boots, 210 snowboards and boots; 100% safety met and maintained; ensure proper equipment testing is performed 2x per season.
▹ Service up to 600 skiers per day; trained staff for efficient, safe service delivery.
▹ Deal with customer concerns promptly;
   · issues never escalate to higher management; offer 100% customer service satisfaction.
   · instituted customer service initiative offering beverage vouchers in times of service delays.
▹ Facilitate High Ropes course with 100% safety to up to 60 children/day & for corporate team-building.

Waste Management, Brampton ON   [dates]
Driver
▹ Provided dependable recycling service to residential neighbourhoods.
▹ Proven ability to operate a variety of trucks provided employer with scheduling flexibility.

Personal Sabbatical   [dates]
Set and achieved personal athletic goals to develop stamina, resilience, and perseverance.
▹ Contestant in cycling races; 24 Hours of Summer Solstice, Ontario Cup Series, etc.

Sport Store, Oakville ON   [dates]
Assistant Manager
▹ Hired, trained & scheduled part time staff; delivered new product training several times per year.
▹ Addressed store security and decreased related losses.

Major Sport Store, Mississauga ON   [dates]
Department Manager / Bicycles and Exercise Equipment
Managed 10 staff; responsible for sales, equipment assembly and customer service.
▹ Enhanced work efficiencies to increase repair volume without additional staff.
▹ Cross-trained staff for improved customer service and to address staff scheduling issues.
▹ Reduced returns by trouble shooting complaints and providing in-home service calls.
▹ Regularly exceeded daily quotas; instrumental in store attaining sales of up to $50,000/day.

Sidebar

▶ **AWARDS**

▹ Customer Service Awards
▹ Community Service Award, Metropolitan Police Services Board, Toronto

▶ **CERTIFICATIONS**

▹ BMZ license in good standing
▹ St. John Ambulance, CPR & First Aid
▹ MSDS, WHMIS & Fire & Safety
▹ Vertical Challenge Course, Level 1

▶ **EDUCATION**

▹ Ontario College of Art, Graphic Design/Illustration Diploma
▹ Sheridan College, Art Fundamentals Certificate

...careful...

...dependable...

...professional...

Stephanie Clark, BA, CRS, CIS — Kitchener, Ontario, Canada

Walter Brohman

521 Bishop Street ❖ Cleveland, Ohio 44114 ❖ (440) 555-0111 ❖ wbrohman@gmail.com

Facilities Management | Property Management | Project Management | Operations Management

[Date]

Ms. Martha Erickson
Vice President of Operations
Excelsior Builders, Inc.
100 Jackson Circle
Cleveland, Ohio 44114

Re: Facilities Director position posted on Craig's List

Dear Ms. Erickson:

Track, measure, and monitor everything. That's my motto. How else could I effectively manage a 400-acre commercial property?

For the past 8 years, my employer has benefited from my drive towards efficiency in operations, equipment maintenance, inventory control, and staff management. Our facility's productivity has increased 35% during my tenure, as has the commitment and loyalty of our employees who stay at their posts for at least 2-3 years from date of hire.

I can do the same for your organization.

Whether you're seeking departmental restructurings, inventory liquidation, materials usage analysis, internal training programs, or regulatory compliance initiatives, I will find ways to increase margins and impact Excelsior's bottom line. My expertise extends into technical project management as well, having coordinated the implementation of an Access database to house financial data across 7 departments. Following this implementation, I took it upon myself to train our leadership team on building and generating customized reports and e-mail templates to better serve our clientele.

The cherry on the sundae? My background is in construction. As a carpenter, painter, plaster worker, and concrete worker, I've done the jobs of the people I'll be managing at Excelsior, which means I can earn immediate respect from your vendors, contractors, and in-house staff—respect that will most certainly yield consistent and exponential productivity.

Thank you for taking the time to consider my candidacy for this exciting opportunity that's come about in your Facilities division. How soon can we talk? I'll call you before Friday.

Sincerely,

Walter Brohman
<Enclosure>

Walter Brohman

521 Bishop Street ❖ Cleveland, Ohio 44114 ❖ (440) 555-0111 ❖ wbrohman@gmail.com

Facilities Management | Property Management | Project Management | Operations Management

Management professional with 8 years of supervisory experience spanning the following areas:

- Reorganizations
- Labor Reallocation
- Logistics Planning
- Health & Safety
- Systems Development
- Records & Inventory
- Client Relations
- Staff Retention

PROFESSIONAL EXPERIENCE

MEYERS RESEARCH, INC., Cleveland, Ohio   *[dates]*
Global research and education non-profit situated on 400-acre campus, with annual facilities budget of $1.2M.

Senior Facilities Manager ([dates])   *Department Manager ([dates])*
Asst. Department Manager ([dates])   *Construction Manager ([dates])*

STRATEGIC PLANNING & OPERATIONAL INITIATIVES

- *Increased labor efficiency 35%* across landscaping, installations, chemical applications, equipment maintenance, and inventory while reducing manpower 25% and budget 50%. Set company record of manicuring entire 400-acre property in a single week.
- *Reduced direct labor costs 25%* (cutting headcount by 8) via outsourcing of non-essential services.
- *Restructured 3-unit facilities department* into 2 units, establishing an entirely separate division to house 216 pieces of equipment.
- *Spearheaded implementation of Access database* to replace spreadsheets from 7 departments.

MATERIALS & EQUIPMENT COST MANAGEMENT

- *Saved over $160,000 per year in equipment costs* and materials costs by implementing expense-tracking system and formal budgeting parameters.
- *Realized $60,000 gain through liquidation* of obsolete computer components and equipment all of which were identified via newly implemented warehouse inventory tracking system.
- *Minimized overall materials usage* and corresponding floor staff by as much as 65%.

WORKFORCE DEVELOPMENT & SUPERVISION

- *Boosted staff retention rate* by designing research classes for 350 staff running on a 6 month rotating schedule. (75% of attendees reported feeling more committed to their jobs afterwards.)
- *Oversaw delivery of 15-20 facility-wide trainings* on OSHA standards, software technologies (e.g. Visual Basic, Microsoft Office), and vehicle and equipment usage. Ensured pesticide operators and service personnel obtain 3-5 trainings per year for state-mandated certification.
- *Managed 25 employees with 7 direct reports* across 2 departments including warehouse.

BACKGROUND & EDUCATION

Prior to transitioning into management role, worked in construction industry as a foreman, carpenter, painter, plaster worker, HVAC assistant, and concrete worker for bicoastal commercial and residential properties.

Associate of Arts in Liberal Studies, Remington Community College, Toledo, Ohio

Cliff Flamer, MS, NCC, NCRW, CPRW — San Francisco Bay Area, Calif.

JERRY L. MILLER
215 West 69th Street • New York, NY 10023 • H: 212-555-0111 • C: 917-555-0112
jerrylmiller@msn.com

_____

[Date]

Mr. Harry Deiner, Managing Director
The Mellon Group
101 Park Avenue
New York, NY 10174

Dear Mr. Deiner:

A survey by *Global Investors* of 200 plan sponsors identified the top factors for choosing a transition manager. Trading capacity and the manager's ability to find liquidity from diverse sources was number one, followed by cost containment; stellar project management skills; a keen ability to identify and deter portfolio, operational, and business risk; analysis and reporting capabilities; and unwavering integrity.

With four years' experience providing market structure expertise in institutional sales environments including Gemini Partners and Lisker Limited, and a 12-year track record of building and leading sales trading desks for such reputable firms as Bank of New York, Lehman Brothers, The Beck Fund, and Wachovia Securities, I have built a knowledge base that supports the key competencies of a successful transition manager and makes me a valuable asset to a firm seeking someone to fill this critical role.

Throughout my career, the companies I have been affiliated with experienced unprecedented change. Whether the change was precipitated by an inaugural desk, a new account, an expanding operation, or an organization in need of turnaround solutions, I was always able to embrace the change and deliver superior results in very short time frames. During my tenure at Gemini Partners, I identified the need for and orchestrated a comprehensive audit of the firm's trade systems, resulting in a 450% reduction in monthly transaction fees and close to a 25 basis point increase in fund performance. At Lisker, I streamlined a new system integration and eliminated project spillovers by leading prospective client consultations to qualify organizational risk management needs, articulate solution alternatives, and structure financial risk monitoring practices. Through the development of a proprietary ranking system at The Beck Fund, I changed the way order execution efficiency was measured to successfully mitigate risk and reduce costs.

Each trading desk that I led experienced exponential growth. With that growth came enormous change and stress. Year after year I leveraged the positive aspects of change to mentor and motivate teams that contributed record-breaking earnings for the firms they supported. At Bank of New York, I expanded the customer base by 750% in 14 months and was credited with being the catalyst that led the nation's largest biotechnology hedge fund, with $650M under management, to change their prime broker to Bank of New York.

Lehman Brothers presented a different type of challenge that included a culture change and a shift to profitability which was evidenced by an 85% jump in non-syndicated sales trading credits over a one-year period. Wachovia Securities afforded me the opportunity to become the company's first head trader, and I successfully led the firm through the acquisition of over $8B in new business.

In addition, I have held executive sales positions and marketed electronic trading, risk analysis and reconciliation software, and institutional market research services for Bener Technologies Inc., ERP Brokerage Systems, and Research Focus Ltd. My extensive knowledge of the tools available on the market to manage trades and risk would afford the firm that employs me a competitive advantage when choosing future trade management systems.

Confident that my skill set can be of significant value to your organization, I would like to have the opportunity to speak with you in person regarding my credentials and I will follow up with you next week to discuss the opportunity for a face-to-face meeting.

Sincerely,

Jerry L. Miller

Barbara Safani, MA, CERW, NCRW, CPRW, CCM — New York, N.Y.

William P. McKinney
4920 Magnolia Cove Drive
Houston, TX 77100
wpm@gmail.com ▪ Mobile 555-555-0111

John E. Jones, Jr., Esq.
General Electric
Senior Vice President, Legal Affairs
1 Van Antwerp Road
Niskayuna, New York 12309

Dear Mr. Jones:

Realizing you have the full view of GE's legal landscape, I wanted to contact you directly (I have issued my resume and profile with human resources through your corporate website), and perhaps open a dialogue regarding the potential of my joining your company in a senior-level legal counsel role. My resume reflects my background and successes, and the following are highlights of what I believe represent my unique value to your team:

- Ten years of experience as a corporate officer and senior-level executive contributing to high-level strategic and tactical business and legal matters for a US Fortune 500 enterprise with worldwide brand recognition.
- Seventeen-year legal career with specialization in corporate law, international business law, intellectual property rights/protection, licensing, patent enforcement, market access, export control, and other matters pertinent to a large, diverse business.
- Acuity to trade shifts and barriers — regulatory, licensing, competitive, geopolitical — business issues, legal matters, policies, ethics, and corporate responsibilities of conducting business internationally.
- Vast experience in corporate development, transactional, and commercial matters — financings, mergers, acquisitions, joint ventures, co-licensing agreements, domestic/international business startups, service/product rollouts, commercial negotiations, capital purchases, service purchase agreements, and leases.
- Superior business acumen, crisis management expertise, high-caliber cross-functional management qualifications, and proven leadership talents.

William P. McKinney Page 2

With experience and an acute and continuing interest in the consumer electronics sector, I maintain a broad knowledge of the industry's relevant and contemporary international business activities, commercial trends, regulatory matters, and legal affairs. I am confident that my skills and abilities will transfer immediate value to you in the following capacities:

- Weighing in on business strategies and legal initiatives that will steer the evolution of global positioning.
- Facilitating avoidance, relief, and remedy against intellectual property infringement, licensing validity/compliance, countervailing, importation safeguards (global-country- or region-specific), market disruption, or other unfair trade threats or injuries.
- Advancing GE's influence and protecting its interests by applying and/or developing in-depth knowledge of industry standards currently impacting the global marketplace.
- Navigating — with financial sensibility — legacy IPR matters, conceiving and executing offensive strategies, and creating and implementing preemptive actions and policies.
- Avoiding/mitigating risks and costs associated with corporate initiatives and international transactions.
- Contributing my strong network of global, political, and corporate contacts to execute winning lobbying strategies.
- Furthering GE's goals of continued growth through strong, and sustainable legal affairs governance.

Though secure in my current position, I am confidentially conducting a search for a new professional challenge within another global enterprise with considerable international business activities. The precise area of law I am involved with is not my primary concern
    I am very well qualified for senior-level corporate counsel roles in a variety of capacities; what is crucial to me in joining another organization is that I serve in a position in which I can contribute to a team-based endeavor and make a positive impact on the larger organization.

If you can free up a bit of time in the next two weeks, I welcome the opportunity to meet with you in person. In the meantime, thank you for your time and consideration; I look forward to speaking with you.

Sincerely,

Bill McKinney

Chapter 12

Thank-You and Follow-Up Letters

· ·

In This Chapter

▶ Learning from a game-changing collection of post-interview letters

▶ Perceiving the true purpose of follow-up messages

▶ Taking advantage of your last chance to win the job

· ·

The biggest self-defeating mistake that too many people make when writing thank-you letters is merely being polite. Politeness is a good thing, but good manners aren't nearly enough to dramatically raise the odds of your getting the job you want in a competitive marketplace.

You need to write *job clincher letters*, as pro writer Don Orlando terms them Follow-up messages really are sales letters!

In your resume and during your interview, you sold yourself on being a great fit for the job — superb qualifications, competencies, skills, experience, and interest — all punctuated with true and lively tales of accomplishments. Don't stop the winning streak that got you this far. Instead, use what happened during the interview to build on it!

The Mechanics of Sales Power

One typical way to begin a follow-up letter is by expressing appreciation for the interviewer's time and for giving you a fresh-from-the-front-lines update on the position. Other ideas:

✔ Think outside of yourself: Remind the interviewer of what you specifically can do for a company, not what a company can do for you. Draw verbal links between a company's immediate needs and your qualifications — You want A, I offer A; you want B, I offer B.

✔ Elaborate on your experience in handling concerns that were discussed during the interview. Write brief paragraphs about how you solved problems of interest to the company.

✔ After researching an issue that the company is wrestling with, include a brief but pertinent statement of your findings, perhaps even enclosing a relevant news clip about the matter.

✔ Add information to a question you didn't fully answer during the interview.

✔ Overcome objections the interviewer expressed about offering you the job.

✔ Reaffirm your interest in the position and respect for the company. You need not dish enthusiasm with a shovel, but adding a couple of statements about your zest for the company and for the position are basic requirements.

In this digital age, most people send e-mail thank-you letters. Doing so is usually fine for garden-variety jobs, especially when the hiring decision is going to be made within a few days or so. But for an important job, a typed dead-tree-industry letter is more impressive and memorable; send it by postal mail, or if time is short, via an overnight delivery service. The letter can run two, even three pages, if it is flush with white space and easy to read.

Some people swear by handwritten notes, but even when the penmanship is good, a note doesn't readily lend itself to a sales tool when you're going for the win. Even when you're addressing it to your old college roommate.

Letters to Remember You By

Although most jobs are won or lost during the interview, sometimes the finalists are so approximately equal in qualifications that the best-remembered candidate wins the position. Letters can revive memories.

Pay attention to the finer points in the following samples from professional writers credited at the bottom of each letter:

✔ **Serious summaries.** In an understated but highly effective online letter to a nonprofit organization's selection committee, a candidate (Motneau) summarizes the three main concerns of the committee, both numbering and underscoring them.

Another summary sample, this one from a contender for an emergency control management position (Scott), uses a version of the two-column "you want — I offer" formula. "Your Needs" and "My Qualifications" head up the matching language.

An alternate version of the matching formula appears in the two-page sample for a hopeful (Cary) who seeks an unspecified human resource position. The candidate headlines key concerns by repeating the phrase "I have met the challenges of . . ."

Yet another candidate competes for a position as a senior budget analyst (Woods) by listing six key competencies in bullet-bold statements.

A letter that gets straight to the point by summarizing core job requirements represents an aspirant (Daniels) who seeks to become a national accounts manager in an industry in which he lacks experience.

Thank-you letters are a contender's last easy chance to cement a "best of the bunch" image. They are especially valuable to stimulate favorable memories when a candidate interviewed early in the selection process is followed by equally strong competitors.

✔ **Human glimpses.** A candidate for a teaching assistant position (Byers) at a school for the hearing-impaired refers to her nurturing personality — "Feeling empathy and relating well to others are in my DNA."

Another candidate (Phillips) shows her human dimension to nab a competitive slot in a physician assistant degree program. How? She describes her project to surgically assist two poor children from Bolivia.

Revealing admirable human characteristics and sharing an unusual story are other Stand Out techniques that make a candidate unforgettable.

✔ **Combination competencies.** A bidder (Scardino) for an industrial video maker's production job doesn't have the exact experience desired (but it would be a mistake to baldly state that fact). Instead, the candidate gamely asserts that a combination of facets in his background qualify him for the position.

Zeroing in on the most important job requirements — those that specifically fit the candidate's qualifications — makes a persuasive case for winning the offer.

✔ **Postscript deal-sealers.** A legal administrative assistant (Morris) reminds the interviewer of her mastery of the position's required skills and comes across as a pleasant person to work with. Her P.S. assures the reader that she's a quick and enthusiastic learner.

A candidate seeking an IT solutions analyst position (Patel) uses a postscript to call attention to one more impressive reason to hire him.

A postscript is eye candy. Shrewd writers don't waste this valuable space on "oops-I forgot" statements, but instead use it to impel the reader's interest. (See Chapter 6.)

✔ **Thoughtful enclosures.** A new graduate (Anthony) reminds the interviewer that he has a leg up on a human resources position because of his education and internship experiences. As a topper, he encloses a relevant article about a topic discussed during the interview.

Including a tidbit of information helpful to the employer — a print news clipping, a link to an online news clipping, an obscure but vital industry report, follow-up information on a topic discussed during the interview, useful Web site addresses — reinforces a candidate's positive image.

✓ **International flavors.** A candidate (Danzig) wishing to become the director of an international programs center at a United Arab Emirates university expresses her interest with an online letter following a video-conference meeting. Correspondence with potential employers out of country is more traditional and formal.

Globalization, new technology, and shifting job markets mean that candidates with a modern mindset go to the front of the line.

✓ **Hard-selling pitches.** A commercial real estate sales manager (Anderson) writes a strong and convincing letter explaining why he can deliver deals even in a city where he doesn't know the real estate turf.

Reinforcing an ability to bridge a divide — using rationales of crossover skills (see Chapter 7) and networking skills (see Chapter 10) — a motivated job seeker can wind up on the right side of a hiring decision.

✓ **Resurrection letters.** After two weeks of deafening silence, a competitor (Chapman) for an employee relations coordinator reconnects with humor and subtlety.

Any approach other than a whiney or accusative "Why haven't you had the courtesy to get back to me?" is a good move when silence sucks up the oxygen in a job search. Humor is a winner.

Set Your Eyes on Stand Out Samples!

In the samples to come, you find Stand Out ways to market yourself with a thank-you or follow-up letter. As in other chapters, the name of the professional writer of each letter appears beneath it. For more information about the writers, turn to the appendix.

Maximum message readability is the presentation criterion for each sample cover letter in this chapter. To save space in some superb but lengthier samples, I had to chop the original boilerplate text leading into the letter — most often deleting the recipient's name, title, company and address. So when you see a letter leading off with "[Date, inside address, salutation]," or some variation of that, the generic line is merely a reminder that you can't just say "Hey you, read this!" If you're not sure how to layout your cover letter, turn to Chapter 4.

Subject: VP, Marketing position; Selection Task Force

Dear [Name of Task Force Chair]:

Thank you and each of your task force members for taking the time to meet with me this week to discuss the position of *Vice President, Marketing*. I enjoyed our discussion about your organization, its philosophy, and its goals and objectives for the years ahead.

I highlight again some of the key initiatives I would explore as vice president. The goals I would strive to meet are threefold: (1) strategic growth and development; (2) brand consistency and growth; and (3) appropriate uses of Internet technology.

With respect to <u>strategy</u>, I will create a roadmap for the organization's growth which will include benchmarks for assessing goals. As you may recall, I created strategic plans of this nature in connection with my earlier leadership role for Fire Solutions America, which included creation of a blueprint document that I subsequently used in consulting activities with other companies.

With respect to <u>brand consistency</u>, I will review all uses of the brand in print and online media to ensure that it is being accurately represented. In addition, I will conduct an internal audit of the brand among members and volunteers to get their perceptions of the brand. This audit, together with an understanding of what competing organizations are doing, will assist in developing a platform to determine how far to grow, expand, and stretch the brand.

Finally, each of the above goals involves the use of <u>Internet technology</u>, particularly an assessment of the social media landscape. To meet the goal of effectively using Internet technology, I will conduct research to determine where members go for information on business issues, including their favorite blogs and online publications. Information of this nature will help identify destination sites for the syndication of content to position the organization as a thought leader.

As you can see, I welcome the opportunity to discuss my qualifications further or answer any questions you may have. I hope "It's a go!"

Sincerely,

Kevin Motneau
E-mail: k_motneau@gmail.com
Phone: (928) 555-0111
Cell: (928) 555 - 0112

Linda Tancs — Hillsborough, N.J.

MARY SCOTT

142 Centre Blvd • Dale, TX 78616 • (512) 555-0111 • mary.scott@email.com

[Date, inside address, salutation]

Thank you for your time and courtesy during our meeting on Wednesday. I was pleased to learn more about your organization's history and current requirements. The more I learned, the more enthusiastic and eager I became to take on this exciting new position, as I feel totally confident that your needs and my qualifications go together like salt and pepper.

Your Needs	My Qualifications
A proactive individual with both Facilities and Event Management expertise.	✓ Solid history delivering facilities and event coordination and management across diverse industries and sectors.
Emergency Control Management to ensure campus safety and security including evacuation planning, building security, and access control.	✓ Administration of company Emergency Response Program, along with oversight of 70-member Emergency Control Force Team to plan and conduct a full range of safety and emergency evacuations and procedures.
Individual to provide leadership in short- and long-range space planning and renovation management.	✓ Solid, award-winning experience in long-range building and space planning to promote development, reorganization, and renovation of company facilities.

I appreciate your consideration and am excited by the prospect of leveraging my award-winning skill in Facilities and Event Management to facilitate your organization's immediate and long-term success. An additional copy of my resume is enclosed for your convenience. I look forward to speaking with you again soon.

Sincerely,

Mary Scott

Enclosure

Karen Bartell, CPRW — Massapequa Park, N.Y.

KIMBERLY ANN BYERS

1773 Circle Drive, Dallas, TX 75211
(214) 555-0111 ◆ email@email.com

[Date]

Dr. Catherine McKennick, Director
Ms. Janet Carlys, Co-Principal
Pine Grove Speech School
1225 Middletown Avenue
Dallas, TX 75211

Dear Dr. McKennick and Ms. Carlys:

Thank you for taking time from your busy schedules to meet with me yesterday regarding the position of **Teaching Assistant**. Your passion for what is best for your students was evident, as was your genuine warmth and contagious enthusiasm.

I am confident that I can meet your performance expectations as a member of the Pine Grove Speech School team. The desired attributes you mentioned most often in our meeting follow, along with my matching qualifications and teaching philosophy.

Team player — Just as I took the initiative to refill your water cooler without being asked, I will pitch in to help in any way needed. My maturity and proven teaching ability will be an immediate asset in this position. In addition, I will gladly contribute to cultural and artistic enrichment functions through my own activities and the guest artists I can secure.

Nurturing personality — Feeling empathy and relating well to others are in my DNA. My belief that every child should have a fair shake is a strong draw for me in fulfilling this developmentally critical role for your students.

Focus on mainstreaming — Your goal of educational mainstreaming indicates the high value you place on having your pre-scholars master independence. My career and life values resonate with this philosophy of encouraging and supporting independence and learning as tools for attaining happy and well-developed lives.

I enjoyed our meeting and believe that personality-wise I can be a good fit on your team. As an experienced teacher, substitute teacher (Texas certification), and arts and recreation program facilitator, I have successfully dealt with difficult and emergency situations. You can count on me!

My references will enthusiastically confirm that I am a dependable and flexible team player with a gift for nurturing and teaching children. Will you give me the opportunity to prove that I can deliver the exceptional results that your pre-schoolers deserve? I'm counting on you!

Sincerely,

Kimberly Ann Byers

Susan Guarneri, MRW, CERW, CPRW, CPBS, NCCC, DCC — Three Lakes, Wis.

GERALD S. SCARDINO
3344 Cliff Ave • Darwin, FL 79432
806-555-0111 • gsscardino@door.com

[Date]

Mr. Ted Shackshaw, Production Manager
ABC Health Services School
5401 34th Street
Lubbock, TX 79423

Dear Mr. Shackshaw:

What a pleasure it was to speak with you earlier this week regarding your current opening. I appreciate the time and information you shared about your department's current needs and goals.

After reviewing our conversation, it is evident that a key aspect of this position is the ability to work with others and help medical professionals develop curriculum that improves the quality of video production. As we discussed in our interview, I have worked successfully with many diverse groups, including staff and administration. **My strong background both in education and video production has allowed me to develop the skills necessary for helping others plan and implement an improved video lesson.**

I look forward to hearing from you again so that we may continue our discussions regarding your organization's needs and the benefits I could contribute towards meeting them.

Again, thank you for your interest, Mr. Shackshaw.

Sincerely,

Gerald S. Scardino

Dan Dorotik, NCRW — Lubbock, Texas

MICHAEL D. WOODS

8857 Sherman Ave > Brandywine, MD 20613 > ☎ 301-555-0111 (H) > 301-555-0112 (M)
woodsmd@aol.com

[Date]

Sampson Accounting Solutions, Inc.
Attn: Stephen Stone, Chief, Financial Management Division
1234 Rush Mount Blvd.
Falls Church, VA 22665

SUBJ: Senior Budget Analyst Interview

Dear Mr. Stone:

Thank you so much for taking the time to interview me on [date] for the Senior Budget Analyst position. I consider it a privilege to have been considered among those best qualified. To wit:

- **Subject matter expert in budget procedures, reports, and related requirements to compile, organize, and submit budget requests**

- **Familiarity with Treasury Department appropriation accounts, elements of resource, and subsidiary accounts utilized in order to review budget estimates, adjust and reconcile accounts, and research/extract/compile data for reports**

- **Capacity to fully grasp accounting/budgetary terminology, codes, and procedures to ensure that obligations and expenditures are properly recorded**

- **Ability to apply the principles and practices of budget formulation to review, edit, and consolidate budget estimates, and to adjust data on related forms and schedules**

- **Insight to apply administrative budget regulations and procedures associated with the preparation and maintenance of Internal Operating Budgets**

- **Comprehensive knowledge of all phases of the planning, programming, budgeting, and execution system (PPBS) as it is implemented and executed**

I hope that once the matrix is done for all the applicants I will be among those recommended for selection. I look forward to hearing from you in regard to your decision.

All best,

Michael D. Woods

Phyllis Houston, PARW-CC, NRWA — Upper Marlboro, Md.

Patricia Morris

327 South Street ~ Burlington City, NJ 08016
456-555-0111
Pmorris2@verizon.net

[Date]

Ms. Marie Carr, Esquire
Applied Legal Services
222 Hwy. 70, Suite 24
Medford, NJ 08055

Dear Ms. Carr:

It was a pleasure meeting with you last Friday. Thank you for providing me with the opportunity to interview for the *Legal Administrative Assistant* position now available with your firm. After learning more details about your job requirements and objectives I can assure you that my contribution can be an excellent answer to your current challenges and needs.

As discussed, I have advanced experience in Microsoft Office and specialized skills in the area of legal terminology and court documents. This combined expertise will facilitate a quick learning curve regarding your organizational preferences and allow me to become an immediate asset.

Should you have any additional questions, please feel free to contact me. Again, thank you for the enlightening interview and your time, and allow me to confirm my interest in the position. Learning more about your organization has only made me eager to become a dedicated member of your staff, and I am looking forward to hearing from you.

Sincerely,

Patricia Morris

P.S. I believe I omitted reference during our interview to the advanced courses I have taken in legal terminology over the last few months. I plan to continue my education with evening courses in the fall.

Kathleen Marshall, NRWA — Medford, N.J.

DEV PATEL

123 Lake Drive ◆ Arlington, MA 01933
Telephone/Fax: 617.555.0111 ◆ Mobile: 617.555.0112
E-mail: email@email.com

[Date, inside address]

Attn: Don Smith, Principal Engineer

Dear Don:

I enjoyed meeting you and the team on June 13th and 21st and want to reiterate my strong interest in the <u>Solutions Analyst</u> position. I understand that you are looking at additional candidates, and I'd like to take this opportunity to review what I can bring to this role for the ISMIBC Corporation.

My experience has been a combination of pre- and post-sales, always centered on the business aspects of IT. My roles have involved exchanging knowledge between Sales/Marketing and Engineering/Services departments, with a strong customer focus.

I enjoy change and look forward to a role that constantly challenges me with something new. I have successfully worked independently and in groups. More specifically, I've gathered requirements from various experts and stakeholders, analyzed and synthesized the information and written functional, product, and technical specifications, in addition to being the primary responder to RFIs and RFPs.

While not an engineer from the information storage and management industry, I believe my years of varied experience in pre- and post-sales, customer focus, and people skills will bring the fresh perspective ISMIBC Corporation is seeking.

I look forward to hearing back from you.

Regards and best wishes,

Dev Patel

P.S. Did I mention that last week I received my certification in IT architecture / project management?

Judith L. Gillespie, CPCC, CPRW, CEIP — W. Melbourne, Fla.

Peter Anthony

12 Park Street, Tampa, FL 12345
(941) 555-0111, panthony@email.com

[Date]

Mrs. Lori Gumbo
Human Resources Manager
Any Corporation
123 Career Way
Tampa, FL 12345

Dear Mrs. Gumbo:

It was a pleasure to speak with you earlier today. I hope that you are even half as excited about my application materials and skills as I am about the opportunities for business graduates within your organization.

As I detailed in our discussion, I graduated with honors and excelled in the business department through the creation of clubs and participation in internship experiences. My career portfolio showcases my accomplishments. Although we did not have time to look through the portfolio today, just give me the word to set up a mutually convenient time to do so.

To reiterate some of the things we spoke of, I would be able to immediately help the organization with the creation of a human resources/new employee manual because of my previous internship experience. I was encouraged because you mentioned this as an immediate need. Because of my skills and the rapport I developed with the staff during my group interview, I have reason to believe that I would be an excellent addition to your team.

After leaving your office, I was fortunate enough to find the enclosed article in the local newspaper regarding the company turnover issue we discussed. I hope you find it of interest.

Sincerely,

Peter Anthony

Haley Richardson, CPRW, JCTC — Riverview, Fla.

QUICKY ANDERSON

◆ 946 Cedar Lane Nashua, New Hampshire 14532 ◆ (619) 555-0111 ◆ qanderson@gmail.com ◆

[Date]

Mr. Steven Wexler, President
Princeton Equity Services
190 Wabash Avenue, Suite 120
Chicago, IL 60661

Dear Steve:

Since leaving our meeting on Thursday, I have thought at great length about our discussion, the tremendous opportunity that appears to be present in the Chicago market, and the value I bring to your organization.

First and foremost, I am a dealmaker and marketer, able to identify and capture opportunities that have driven strong revenue and asset performance. I tackle each new project with a two-pronged focus: (1) negotiate the best possible transaction that, as trite as it may sound, truly is a "win-win" deal for all partners; and (2) create strategic and tactical marketing programs that consistently create value, dominance, and earnings.

My efforts can easily be measured by gains in the value of real estate holdings and improved project cash flows. Full financial documentation can be disclosed (without conceding the confidentiality of Maxxen Properties). I have maximized the value of each asset under management and transitioned "average" properties into "top" performers.

You're right. I have never worked in the Chicago market. However, I have demonstrated my ability to build presence within other new markets nationwide (e.g., Atlanta, Southern California). Further, I have an extensive network of contacts across the country, many of whom are well connected in Chicago and will be of significant value in facilitating the start of my own regional network.

I have always been fortunate in that networking is a natural process for me. I am able to quickly ascertain who it is that I must establish a relationship with, identify the appropriate channels to do so, and quickly begin the process. In turn, despite often unfamiliar territories and personalities, I have quickly established myself in key markets nationwide. I am not daunted by challenge, but rather motivated to succeed and beat the odds.

I hope that you and I have the opportunity to continue our discussions and certainly appreciate the amount of time you spent with me last week. I guarantee that I can not only meet your expectations, but exceed them.

Sincerely,

Quincy Anderson

Enclosure

Wendy Enelow, CCM, MRW, JCTC, CPRW — Coleman Falls, Va.

Jana B. Phillips
404 Shipwatch Lane
Alpharetta, GA 30005
(770) 555-0111
email@email.com

[Date]

Mr. Mark Matthews, PA-C
Director of Admissions
Emory University Physician Assistant Program
1400 Clifton Road, Suite 500
Atlanta, GA 30322

Dear Mr. Matthews:

Thank you and the Emory Admissions Committee for providing me the opportunity to interview for the Emory Physician Assistant Program. Emory's PA Program remains my first choice. My reason for writing to you is threefold: to emphasize my continued interest in your program, provide you with an updated resume, and to advise you of a recent opportunity that has arisen providing me with "real-world" experience helping the medically underserved.

During a recent trip to Bolivia, a patient called our attention to two very poor young children who needed surgery. The patient asked Dr. Robert Mitchell, the orthopedic surgeon whom I support, if he could help. After reviewing the X-rays, Dr. Mitchell agreed that yes, indeed, the two kids are in dire need of surgery but said it would have to be done in the United States. That's where I entered the scene: Dr. Mitchell asked me to serve as the primary fundraiser and liaison for this humanitarian project.

Over the next few weeks, I will reach out to such facilities as the Ronald McDonald House to house the children and their families while they are receiving treatment. (I've been a fund raiser for Ronald McDonald for several years while I was at Georgia Tech.) Additionally, Dr. Mitchell and I will be working to recruit surgeons and find a facility to take on these cases. It's a great feeling to know that we can make a significant impact on the lives of these two little children.

The broad scope of the Emory PA Program provides me with all of the essential elements I seek in order to become a well-balanced Physician Assistant, and I want the opportunity to be a part of that community. Thank you for your time and consideration and I look forward to hearing from you soon.

Sincerely,

Jana. B. Phillips

Attachment

Sharon M. Bowden, CPRW, CEIP — Atlanta, Ga.

MACKENZIE CHAPMAN
2073 Pyramid Way ~ Cottonwood Heights, Utah 84121

(801) 555-0111 **mchapman@comcast.net**

Mr. Alexander Cole
Human Resources Manager
Titleman Associates
1430 Collard Way
Salt Lake City, UT 84108

Did the dog eat my resume?
Never mind — here's another!

Dear Mr. Cole:

Two weeks ago I provided my resume for consideration for the position of *Employee Relations Coordinator*. I am sure you received quite a response and have needed to devote time to reviewing the qualifications of each candidate. If I missed your call, I wish to reiterate my interest in the position and assure you that *my qualifications not only meet but exceed your hiring requirements.*

In brief, my qualifications include:

- Extensive experience in training curriculum development and presentation
- Strong customer service and team-building skills in a retail environment
- Customer focused, driven, and dedicated to the pursuit of excellence

I can easily meet at your convenience. I am confident that I will convince you that I have the skills you need as well as the enthusiasm, energy, and dedication that characterizes your best employees.

Enclosed is another copy of my resume for your convenience in reviewing the benefits I bring.

Best regards,

Mackenzie Chapman

Enclosure: resume

David J. Jensen, CPRW, CEIP — Salt Lake City, Utah

ELAINE DANZIG

400 Johnson Road • Endicott, NY 13760 • 518-555-0111 (H) • 518-555-0112 (C)
edanzig@email.com • skype: elainedanzig

[Date]

Mr. James Peters
Dean, College of Business Sciences
Shaj University
P.O. Box 4444
Abu Zaby, United Arab Emirates

Dear Dean Peters:

Thank you for your time and courtesy during our videoconference meeting on Thursday. I was pleased to learn more about your University and its requirements, and appreciated the impressive and informative Forbes Magazine article on Shaj University. Shaj University is appealing to me on many levels, e.g., as a modern university, as one committed to the education and advancement of women, and as an institution dedicated to the progress of the United Arab Emirates and its people.

After discussing the Directorship position at length, I am convinced that your requirements and my qualifications are a close match. With my expertise in *budgetary planning and expense management, domestic and international programs development, strategic business alliance formation, staff and operations administration, and strategic planning and marketing,* my ability to direct the Center's current and future operations is well-developed.

I appreciate your consideration and am excited by the prospect of leveraging my award-winning skill in international programs expansion and mission and vision attainment to help drive your university's immediate and long-term success. Enclosed is an additional copy of my resume for your convenience. I look forward to speaking with you again soon.

Sincerely,

Elaine Danzig
Enclosure

Karen Bartell, CPRW — Massapequa Park, N.Y.

BOYD CARY

10293 Cedar Street
New Orleans, LA 78874

(661) 555-0111
bcary@aol.com

[Date]

Charles Taylor, President
PYD Technologies
120 Robert Trent Avenue
Columbia, SC 27104

Dear Charles:

First of all, thank you. I really enjoyed our conversation the other day and am completely enamored with the tremendous success you have bought to PYD. There are but a handful of companies that have experienced such aggressive growth and can predict strong and sustained profitability over the years to come.

I would like to be a part of the PYD team — in whatever capacity you feel most appropriate and of most value. I realize, of course, that you already have an HR Director who has successfully managed the function throughout the course of the company's development. It is not my intention to compete with Leslie Smith, but rather to complement her efforts and bring new HR leadership to the organization.

Let me highlight what I consider to be my most valuable assets:

I have met the challenges of accelerated recruitment:

* In [date], I launched a recruitment initiative to replace 50% of the total workforce in a 900-person organization. This was accomplished within just six months and was the key driver in that organization's successful repositioning.

* In [date], when hired as the first-ever HR executive for a growth organization, I created the entire recruitment, selection, and placement function. Over the next two years, I hired more than 50 employees to staff all core operating departments.

* Between [date] and [date], I spearheaded the recruitment and selection of technical, professional, and management personnel. This was a massive effort during which time I interviewed over 300 prospective candidates throughout the U.S. and Europe.

I have met the challenges of employee retention:

* During my employment with Helms Financial, we were staffing at an unprecedented rate. The faster an organization grows, the more critical the focus must become. Costs associated with recruitment can be significant and must be controlled. Following implementation of a market-based research study, I was able to reduce Helm's turnover 35%, saving over $350,000 in annual costs.

PYD Technologies, Boyd Cary
[Date]
Page Two

<u>I have met the challenges of international human resource leadership:</u>

- Throughout my tenure with Laxton Data, I led the organization's International Employment & Employee Relations function. This was a tremendous experience during which time I developed strong qualifications in both domestic and expatriate recruitment, compensation, benefits administration, and relocation. Further, I demonstrated my proficiency in cross-cultural communications and business management. I traveled extensively and am comfortable in diverse situations.

<u>I have met the challenges of organizational change through development and acquisition:</u>

- Each of the organizations in which I have been employed has faced unique operating and leadership challenges. These situations have been diverse and included high-growth, turnaround, and internal reorganization. Each has focused on improved performance and accelerated market/profit growth through development of its human resources and management competencies. To meet these challenges, I have created innovative, market-driven organizational structures integrating pioneering strategies in competency-based recruitment and performance.

- Most recently, I orchestrated the workforce integration of two acquisitions into core business operations. This required a comprehensive analysis of staffing requirements, evaluation of the skills and competencies of the acquired employees, and accurate placement throughout the organization. The integration was successful, and all personnel are now fully acclimated and at peak performance.

I hope that the above information demonstrates the value I bring to PYD — today and in the future. You will also find that my abilities to lead and motivate are strong and have always been the foundation for my personal success.

I look forward to speaking with you and would welcome the opportunity to meet Mr. Williams. Again, thank you for your time and your interest. I wish you continued success in your efforts.

Sincerely,

Boyd Cary

Wendy Enelow, CCM, MRW, JCTC, CPRW — Coleman Falls, Va.

1220 East Algonquin Rd, #14A   **STEVEN M. DANIELS**   Home: 555.555.0111
Schaumburg, Illinois 60173   steven.daniels@anyisp.net   Mobile: 444.555.0112

[Date]

Mr. James Moore, Vice President
Worldwide Waterfalls
3170 S. River Road, Suite 4B
Des Plaines, IL 60018

Dear Mr. Moore:

Thank you for taking the time to meet with me yesterday. I really enjoyed visiting with you and
appreciated learning more about the **National Accounts Manager** position within Worldwide
Waterfalls. This sounds like an exciting opportunity and one I would enjoy.

Drawing on my diverse *sales background* along with expertise in *prospecting, cold calling,* and
proposal preparation across multiple industries, I know I can learn the waterfall business
quickly and be up to speed in a relatively short timeframe. If offered this position, I will accept it
without hesitation! Pardon the pun, but you sold me!

I look forward to hearing from you about the next step in the interview process. If you have any
other questions, please feel free to contact me at your earliest convenience.

Standing by,

Steven M. Daniels

Joellyn Wittenstein Schwerdlin, CCMC, JCTC, CPRW — Worcester, Mass.

Part IV

Online Messages: Sample the Best

The 5th Wave   By Rich Tennant

Dear Ms. Hoppner,
I look forward to my interview for the position of Conservation Coordinator. I think my position on recycling stands on it's own merit.

In this part . . .

The way you call employers' attention to your qualifications online comes with a few different opportunities than the traditional cover letter. This part contains 34 more outstanding samples that show you how to impress with branding statements, online profiles, and online cover notes.

Chapter 13

Branding Statements and Online Profiles

*I*n an ancient legend that shows up in various cultures, blind men who had never seen an elephant decide that each would examine one small part by touch and, based on their own individual experience, figure out what an elephant looks like. Unsurprisingly, they each came up with a different perception. The man who feels the elephant's leg, for example, says an elephant is like a pillar, but the man who touches the elephant's tail says an elephant is like a rope.

The take-away: Different people can have distinctly different perceptions of the same thing.

That thought perfectly describes what I found when I went looking for examples of professional branding statements and online profiles. Opinions vary among experts about everything from the length of the documents to whether they should be written in the first or third person. That's why this chapter presents an assortment of sample styles on both branding statements and online profiles.

Styling Your Professional Brand

Branding is a marketing concept and tool. It is a way to stand out from the teeming masses of competition for the best jobs. Without getting too philosophical about *professional branding statements* — also called *personal branding statements* and *branding briefs* — here's how I see a professional branding statement's contribution to your job search.

Your professional brand is the essence of who you are in the workplace. Your brand reflects your professional reputation — what you're known for (or would like to be known for). When your reputation is a good one, it includes marketable distinctions like positive characteristics and achievements.

Breaking the concept into manageable pieces, professional branding statements explain

- Your specialty — who you are
- Your service — what you do
- Your audience — who you do it for
- Your best characteristic — what you're known for

Put all the pieces together, and you end up with something a little like this:

> *I'm a Computer Technology Manager and Biomedical Engineer keeping the machines running smoothly from desktop to the treatment room. Not for my health, for yours. — Chris Welch*

As Alison Doyle, the Job Search guide for About.com, explains, "There may not be much difference between personal and professional branding, but from my perspective, your professional brand is what matters to a potential employer, networking contact, or anyone who can help you find a job or grow your career."

You can use professional branding statements in many ways, including the following:

- Incorporated into cover letters, online profiles, and other job search messages
- Printed on the back of business cards
- Incorporated in elevator speeches (really quick pitches)
- Spoken in job interviews ("Tell me about yourself")
- Used in networking connections

An extra benefit of writing a professional branding statement is that doing so wonderfully concentrates your mind in answering the questions, "Who am I and why am I in this workplace?"

Professional branding for the little guy

We easily get that Tiger Woods' brand is golf excellence and Angelina Jolie's brand is movie stardom. But what about mere mortals who can't make such distinctive claims?

Joe Turner and Sue Swenson have suggestions. Authors of *Paycheck 911: Don't Panic . . . Power Your Job Search!* (Swenson Turner Publications, 2008), they recommend that you begin to think about your professional brand by first deciding how you are accountable to the bottom line. Does your job make or save money for an employer? You may directly make money for the company through production or sales. Or, realizing that time is money, you may be an administrative assistant who routinely spares a boss untold mundane minutia each day, saving the company time and money it can invest to make more money elsewhere.

Capitalizing on your status as a maker or saver of money, move on to flesh out a professional branding statement that recognizes the skills and benefits you bring to a lucky new employer. Among many examples of professional branding statements given by Turner and Swenson in their book are these two:

> *I am a seasoned administrative assistant whose specialty is client-phone relationship building, creating a solid bond with our clients that strengthens the sales link with my company.*

> *I am a safety coordinator with a strength in training and program implementation that helped reduce workers' compensation claims by 37 percent over a four-year period for my current employer.*

Take thoughtful moments to craft your professional branding statement and be inspired by how others did it.

Bringing on the branding samples

The dozen professional branding statements that follow were created by free-agent writers whose names appear beneath their work.

A Whiz of a Sales Executive

I was born knowing about selling the sizzle, not the steak. An executive risk taker, I drive business to the next level. Application of enthusiastic confidence generates new customers and competitively positions products. I consistently overcome obstacles and generate product loyalty while increasing company's profits and global market recognition.

Kathleen Marshall, NRWA — Medford, N.J.

A Teacher Who Uses Appealing Learning Technique

As a dedicated educator, I stimulate curiosity and make learning approachable and rewarding for all students. I implement a unique teaching technique that successfully addresses individualized learning variables by incorporating sight, written, and hearing applications in all material presentations. I get good outcomes: Improved test results by 50% and decreased student drop-out rates by 25%.

Kathleen Marshall, NRWA — Medford, N.J.

A Turnaround Ace

I rescue troubled companies. I have a documented track record of business development, operational planning, and leadership.

My ability to find solutions that lead to success, foster team cohesion, pursue excellence, and work with a high degree of integrity has become my brand. In one case, I led a company through unparalleled growth and success, increasing revenue from $30 million to $60 million. In another, guided a company through a downturn, shifting from a privately owned company to a public company. In still another, managed significant software changeover/upgrade for more accurate and timely processing of accounting functions, inventory reports, and financial statements.

Sheri K. Czar, CPRW — Lake Oswego, Ore.

A Helpful Career Coach

I leverage my avid love of learning and mastery of online technology to facilitate career management for trend-setting professionals who strive to be dynamic and high achieving in their business.

Kristen A. Jacoway, CRC, CPRW, CCC, CPBS — Seneca, S.C.

A Career Management Natural

Before I moved into the trenches of actually experiencing the workplace or studying its dynamics, I successfully — but informally — advised legions of friends on their career choices.

Now, after gaining HR generalist employment in the allied health field and completing the HR certificate program at the University of Lowell, I realize that the ability to guide individuals in career management issues comes naturally to me.

Gail Frank, NCRW, CPRW, JCTC, CEIP — Tampa, Fla.

A Change Agent in Human Affairs

As a catalyst for positive change, I have a history of engaging board and staff members to generate new ideas and increase overall performance. I am adept at establishing policies, procedures, and technologies to enhance efficiency, financial health, and service to organize constituents. I enjoy building and strengthening strategic alliances. My passion is to guide nonprofits, specifically those focused on youth empowerment, to achieve new heights.

Tamara Dowling, CPRW, MCRS — Valencia, Calif.

A Lawyer You Bring to Win

Results-focused trial attorney with a 90% case success rate and repu-tation as a crack investigator who brings over 10 years of litigation expertise to any legal endeavor. Tenacious in pursing firm's goals and maintaining its tradition for excellence, I apply strong communication and interpersonal skills to achieve consistently successful mediation.

Kathleen Marshall, NRWA — Medford, N.J.

A Super Science Marketing Specialist

Recognized for 20+ years of success in linking science-based achieve-ments with decisive market leadership to build high-performance organi-zations with significant financial rewards. Led strategic and operational breakthroughs in proactive health informatics and communications tech-nologies, evidence-based prevention and care management products, and cost-effective healthcare delivery systems. Pioneer in wellness and pre-vention programs, disease management and population health.

Wendy Enelow, CCM, MRW, JCTC, CPRW — Coleman Falls, Va.

IT is me, Tracy Hammond.

With more than 10 years of interesting experience in Information Technology, it's been my work and my pleasure to contribute to major initiatives that increased revenue, brought repeat business, and fueled company growth. I feel good every time I deliver challenging projects on time and under budget. Some little girls play with dolls; I played with computers. I grew up to become an accomplished Senior Consultant in my career field.

Michelle Penn, CPRW — Granite City, Ill.

A Woman Who Speaks "Solutions"

One of the costliest and most painful points in any project is when fail-ures in communication regarding scope and requirements cause delays, functional gaps, and scope creep.

Analysis is primarily about communication: asking the right questions, listening to the answers. It's about documenting and communicating capabilities, expectations, and outcomes. It's about speaking everyone's language.

I have contributed to the success of a variety of projects in analysis and IT roles for over eight years. I'm all about timely execution, clean and clear communication, and consistent leadership.

I speak business. I speak technology. I speak solutions. My fluency will save you time, frustration, and money.

I'm listening.

Kate Herrick — Bellevue, Wash.

Meet The Big Three Guy: Software, Projects, Solutions

Stan Wilson   Software Engineer

→111 Greenland Crescent → Toronto ON → M3H 3P3 →
→H. (555) 555-0111 → C. (555) 555-0112 → softwareguy@hotmail.com →

Software Development   **Project Management**   **Client Solutions**

Highly motivated software developer with strong programming skills and a talent for identifying and implementing innovative technology solutions that align with client objectives and corporate goals. Outstanding leadership, problem-solving, and analytical skills using cutting-edge development tools and industry knowledge. Diligent project execution with precision and patience.

Tanya Taylor, CHRP, MCR — Toronto, Ontario, Canada

An Entrepreneurial Technologist Who Gets Results

I possess keen instincts and intelligence, am results driven, and have an aptitude for solving business technology problems. Years in the trenches have fine tuned my background as a trainer, leader, and supervisor. Weighing the combination of these factors, I am certain I can be an impact contributor at the outset.

The following contrasts a "before and after" picture depicting how my background enabled a profit center to grow…and what I can do for you as well:

Before	*After*
2 Video Systems and no integrated AV program or systems, with staff of one (me)	20 Video Systems and 4 integrated AV seminar rooms across 8 buildings within 2 years and a doubling of connectivity inside of one year. Support team of 4.
Minimal training and support	Established a full training and support program designed from scratch including all user guides and training materials.
A lack of awareness among executives of the technology's usefulness in terms of marketing product	Enlightened executive staff to the point where we now support 200 videoconferences per month and a daily logjam of back-to-back VC meetings every day.
Video success approximating 40%	A consistent 96% resulting in quicker or more imminent market entry per product culminating in millions of dollars of added revenues.

Art Frank — Flat Rock N.C.

The B words: Boasting versus branding

To claim that you are the best swimmer in the world is bragging. But to back such a claim by winning eight gold medals while setting seven world records as did Michael Phelps in the Beijing Olympic Games is — drum roll — branding.

Bragging is boasting, often in an obvious or arrogant manner to make oneself seem more important. Branding, on the other hand, is based on more than empty rhetoric any copywriter can dream up. Believable branding must stand up to inspection in the glare of bright light: Do you walk the walk when you talk the talk?

Creating Your Online Profile

Online profiles are creatures of many hues. They range from (short) keyword-driven text messages, to (long) documents with Hollywood production values and reams of descriptive writing. Here's the short and long of crafting an online profile.

Short stories

The *online executive bio* — also called *online executive summary* and *online executive brief* — is used to advance employment or business objectives. The profiles are searchable: Employers can search for the profiles they want, such as financial manager, pipefitter, and so on. Nourished by keywords, a short profile — about 200 words or fewer — is found on social networking sites and job boards. The short profile includes a link to a full resume (or more — see the "Long stories" section that follows) but omits a photo. When an online executive bio captures interest, the recruiter clicks through to a candidate's resume.

What can you do when you're filing a resume in a large bureaucratic system and fear it won't be seen by the right decision-maker? Federal job expert Kathryn Troutman encourages her clients to e-mail a short executive bio as an introduction letter to an agency hiring manager, and to confirm by postscript that a full resume is available in the official federal system.

Long stories

The *online profile* originally developed as an instrument of social engagement on such social networking sites as MySpace and Facebook. The early expressions of online identity mentioned or linked to many personal factors — pictures, gender, home town, occupation, alma mater, and taste in music and romantic relationships. Socially focused pages have evolved into social marketing presentations for commerce and careers.

In contrast to online executive bios, online profiles are multi-link creations that appear on Internet networking sites like LinkedIn and Visual CV.

Long online profiles present some combination of features from a wide range of digitally-based options:

- Professional branding statements
- Qualifications summaries
- Accomplishment sheets
- Blogs
- RSS (Real Simple Syndication) feeds
- Reports and press releases
- Publications, books, newsletters
- Videos, videoclips, audio bites
- Recommendations, testimonials
- Association memberships, affinity groups
- Honors
- Interests, hobbies
- Connections to other people
- Photos
- Resumes available in three variations — PDF, MS Word, and text

Elaborate online profiles with flashy graphics and serial links (like a nest of boxes, each of which fits into the next larger box) are updated and slicker versions of earlier Web portfolios. The high end of the long online profiles are usually professionally produced for high-achieving professionals who are always open to employment offers they can't refuse and for entrepreneurs who use the profiles as an advertising medium to attract business.

For more information about online profiles, check out Chapters 2 and 16.

Never in history has so much information been available about so many people. And the information is for all eyes on publically accessible Web pages. Hundreds of millions of people worldwide have expressed their likes and dislikes — and sometimes their innermost feelings. Corporations use profile information to specifically market products to you. Identity thieves use profile information to rob you. Think before posting.

Online profiles are yet another facet of the expanding body of job search message tools and are represented by the following eight samples that follow.

Tenured Educator specializing in Special Education, Reading Recovery and Community Outreach

BA - Elementary Education, MA – Administration of Special Education. A dedicated and caring educator with advanced degree and 12 years of classroom experience. Committed to helping all children become successful learners. Recognized for consistently creating and maintaining classroom atmospheres that are stimulating, encouraging, safe, and adaptive to the varied needs of students. Exceptional interpersonal skills; able to establish and maintain cooperative, professional relationships with students, parents, colleagues, administrators, and community. Rewarded for the ability to incorporate hands–on materials, Provide individualized instruction, cooperative learning techniques, and technology. School Board member and administrator. Areas of specialty: state and federal law and regulations, individual education plans, problems of low- and high- disability students, mainstreaming, special education curricula, staff management, parent education, communications and community relations, budgeting, professional standards and ethics, Head Start, Title 1, ESS, grant writing. Mentor, tri-athlete, licensed private pilot.

Resume and complete reference information are available

Contact: janedoe@gmail.com

Debbie Ellis — Houston, Texas

Financial Management Analyst / Budget Analyst / Resource Manager

5+ Years, Bank of America Corporation
5+ Years, Financial Management Services
BS, Financial Services

Areas of Expertise:

- Consolidated operating budget management
- Performance and accountability reports
- Improve internal controls
- Research and analyze budget shortfalls
- Budget forecasting
- Activity-based costing
- Resource management
- Planning and defining objectives
- Monitoring and analyzing trends
- Spreadsheet and report designs
- Narrative writing, briefings and presentations
- Efficiency processes
- Problem-solving, solutions and recommendations for managers
- Customer Service, research and follow-up

Kathryn Troutman — Baltimore, Md.

LEGAL SECRETARY / PARALEGAL – 5 years of experience

- AS, Paralegal Studies – Sullivan College, Lexington, KY
- Highly proficient in word processing, data entry, and Dictaphone transcription using Microsoft application software; noticed for maintaining consistently superior levels of accuracy
- Organized, efficient, and thorough; maintains flexibility in changing work assignments
- Perform well under stress, taking pressure off superiors and peers
- Proficient in the planning and execution of multi-faceted projects in time-critical environments
- Dependable and successful problem resolution and time-management solutions
- Outstanding record of performance, reliability, confidentiality and ethical business standards
- Computer skills include Microsoft Word 97, 2003, 2007 Windows XP, Word Perfect; familiarity with Excel, PowerPoint, and Access. Typing rate 90 WPM
- Complete resume and superior references available

Criminal / Civil Law, Powers of Attorney, Complaints, Domestic Relations, Divorce, Exhibits / Witness Lists, Affidavits, Adoption, QDRO, Subpoenas. Probate, Personal Injury, Motions, Wills, Client Interviewing, Orders,   Estates, Real Estate, Research, Worker's Compensation, Mortgages / Deeds, Title Search.

Contact: sallysmith@yahoo.com; Louisville, KY - 555-555-0111

Debbie Ellis — Houston, Texas

Scientist / General Engineer / Mechanical Engineer / Project Manager / Program Manager / Naval Architect – BIOTECHNOLOGY

17 yrs in Navy R&D on naval, aerospace and sensor platforms
7 yrs in private sector R&D on Biosensor platforms
Master's in Mechanical Engineering, University of California Los Angeles, 1995
Master's in Engineering Management (EMGT), George Washington University, 1991
Bachelor's in mechanical Engineering, 1985, Virginia Tech, Blacksburg, 1985
NAVSEA Certified Submarine Hydrodynamics Trials Director, 1991
Granted Confidential and Top Secret Clearances

Expertise:
- Biosensor R&D
- Sensor networks and sensor concepts
- Hydrodynamics
- DOD and US Federal Government Contractor
- Small Business Innovative Research (SBIR)
- Program Manager, Program Developer
- Project Manager, R&D, Testing, Evaluation, Intellectual Property Licensing
- Concept demonstration team lead for engineers, researchers
- Innovative Methods Designer

Kathryn Troutman — Baltimore, Md.

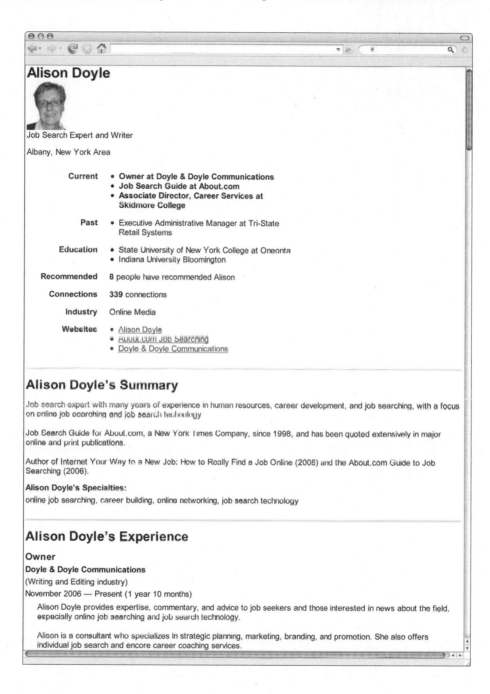

Alison Doyle

Job Search Expert and Writer

Albany, New York Area

Current	• **Owner at Doyle & Doyle Communications** • **Job Search Guide at About.com** • **Associate Director, Career Services at Skidmore College**
Past	• Executive Administrative Manager at Tri-State Retail Systems
Education	• State University of New York College at Oneonta • Indiana University Bloomington
Recommended	8 people have recommended Alison
Connections	**339** connections
Industry	Online Media
Websites	• Alison Doyle • About.com Job Searching • Doyle & Doyle Communications

Alison Doyle's Summary

Job search expert with many years of experience in human resources, career development, and job searching, with a focus on online job searching and job search technology

Job Search Guide for About.com, a New York Times Company, since 1998, and has been quoted extensively in major online and print publications.

Author of Internet Your Way to a New Job: How to Really Find a Job Online (2008) and the About.com Guide to Job Searching (2006).

Alison Doyle's Specialties:

online job searching, career building, online networking, job search technology

Alison Doyle's Experience

Owner

Doyle & Doyle Communications

(Writing and Editing industry)

November 2006 — Present (1 year 10 months)

Alison Doyle provides expertise, commentary, and advice to job seekers and those interested in news about the field, especially online job searching and job search technology.

Alison is a consultant who specializes in strategic planning, marketing, branding, and promotion. She also offers individual job search and encore career coaching services.

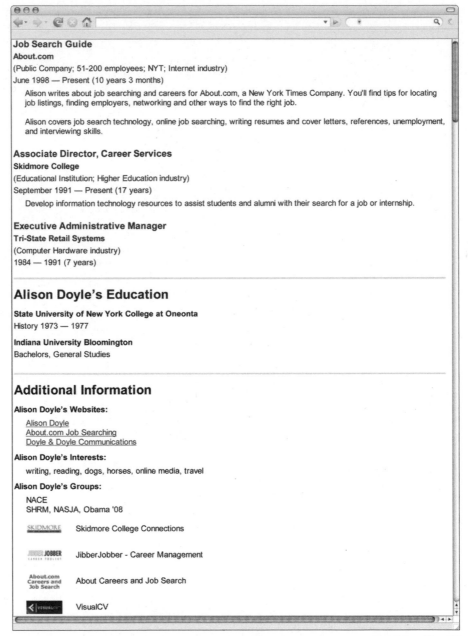

Job Search Guide

About.com

(Public Company; 51-200 employees; NYT; Internet industry)

June 1998 — Present (10 years 3 months)

Alison writes about job searching and careers for About.com, a New York Times Company. You'll find tips for locating job listings, finding employers, networking and other ways to find the right job.

Alison covers job search technology, online job searching, writing resumes and cover letters, references, unemployment, and interviewing skills.

Associate Director, Career Services

Skidmore College

(Educational Institution; Higher Education industry)

September 1991 — Present (17 years)

Develop information technology resources to assist students and alumni with their search for a job or internship.

Executive Administrative Manager

Tri-State Retail Systems

(Computer Hardware industry)

1984 — 1991 (7 years)

Alison Doyle's Education

State University of New York College at Oneonta

History 1973 — 1977

Indiana University Bloomington

Bachelors, General Studies

Additional Information

Alison Doyle's Websites:

Alison Doyle
About.com Job Searching
Doyle & Doyle Communications

Alison Doyle's Interests:

writing, reading, dogs, horses, online media, travel

Alison Doyle's Groups:

NACE
SHRM, NASJA, Obama '08

SKIDMORE — Skidmore College Connections

JOBBER — JibberJobber - Career Management

About.com Careers and Job Search — About Careers and Job Search

VISUALCV — VisualCV

Alison Doyle — Albany, N.Y.

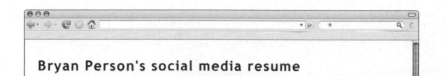

Bryan Person's social media resume

Evangelizing the tools, best practices, and conversations of social media.

Overview

I am a passionate social media evangelist who thrives on teaching business professionals and organizations how to use the tools of the online social Web, including blogs, podcasts, RSS readers, wikis, presence applications, and social networks.

How do I do that?

Blogging:
I have been writing about about social media since April 2006. BryanPerson.com is a mix of practical advice for using social media, commentary on the goings-on in other PR and marketing blogs and podcasts, and reflections from in-person networking events/conferences that I attend and organize.

Community organizing:
A big part of the power of social media happens when online conversations turn into face-to-face meetings. To that end, I organize monthly Social Media Breakfasts for Boston's online PR, marketing, and entrepreneurial community.

Podcasting:
New Comm Road made its debut in May 2006 and has evolved into a highly-respected PR and social media podcast. The show's trademark segment is the "New Comm Road Map," where I provide listeners with step-by-step advice for using a new online tool or implementing a social media program.

Click below to stream a recent episode about how to use Google Reader.

Focusing on the connected professional:
In my role as an interactive content producer for Monster, I regularly write about the ways that workers can use the tools of new media to build their personal brand and raise their professional profile.

****

Comment on this social media resume.

Contact information

E-mail:
bperson AT gmail DOT com

Phone:
+1 (781) 413-5846

Skype: Bryper
Yahoo Messenger:
bperson745
AIM: NewCommRoad

Social media links

My work history:
* LinkedIn profile

My current projects:
* BryanPerson.com
* Social Media Breakfast

Podcasts I edit:
* IDRA Classnotes
* The We Show

My best work:
* Purpose-built del.icio.us portfolio page

Events I've organized:
* CaseCamp Second Life
* PodCamp Boston

What I'm reading:
* Google Reader shared items
* del.icio.us shared items

Presence:
* Twitter posts

Social networks:
* Flickr photos
* Facebook profile

With inspiration from Christopher S. Penn's Social Media Resume.

Brian Person — Austin, Texas

Where to post profiles

The problem with writing about technology is that something changes immediately after publication. But here's a short list of Web sites where you can familiarize yourself with a wide variety of online profiles and to consider when posting your own profile.

- ✔ LinkedIn — www.linkedin.com
- ✔ Facebook — www.facebook.com
- ✔ ZoomInfo — www.zoominfo.com
- ✔ Spoke — www.spoke.com
- ✔ VisualCV — www.visualcv.com
- ✔ MySpace — www.myspace.com
- ✔ College Grad — www.college grade.com
- ✔ Ziggs — www.ziggs.com
- ✔ Jobfox — www.jobfox.com
- ✔ XING — www.xing.com
- ✔ Hoovers Connect — www.hoovers connect.com
- ✔ ExecuNet — www.execunet.com

Presenting the profile samples

Chapter 14

E-Mail Cover Notes

*W*hen you're rushed for time and need to move fast to get your resume out and about quickly, consider using an e-mail cover note to introduce it.

E-mail cover notes — kid siblings to cover letters — have grown in use by orders of magnitude in just the past decade. By comparison to cover letters, the cover note kids are very short — usually one to three brief paragraphs. You typically send an e-mail cover note in text, not as an attachment. Your resume may follow in text or be attached in an MS Word or PDF document.

When you need to do a more persuasive job of self-marketing than a few brief paragraphs allow, follow a cover note with a cover letter and a resume attached in a single Word or PDF doc, or in separate docs. When you do send two attachments, one for your cover letter and the second for your resume, add a message like this:

> *Two documents are attached — my cover letter and my resume. Please review. Thank you.*

This request, although terse, may put pressure on recruiters to open and look at the e-mail's attachments.

Here are a few tips for writing your cover notes:

✔ The subject line of your e-mail sparks a reading of your cover note, which sparks a reading of your resume. Power each one with a sales message that causes the reviewer to keep on scrolling.

- Use names of mutual friends or other connections, list matching qualifications to job requirements, and try for fresh, eye-catching phrasing, unless you're applying for seriously serious work like buttoned-down banking or brain surgeon jobs.

- Practice writing the long story short until you get the hang of it. Send your finished work to yourself and read it over the next day to judge whether it's still as brilliant as it was the day you wrote it.

Cover Notes Offer Spanking Smart Start

The 18 cover notes that begin on the next page are examples of the kind of message you can send online to introduce your digital resume. Generally, cover notes are more informal than cover letters. The names of their writers are printed beneath each sample; a directory of all writers appears in this book's appendix. I comment on each cover note:

- **Nurse Uses Top 10 Lure.** Employers are impressed with candidates who are in the top 10 percent of their class. Even in a talent-short category, such as RNs with a bachelor's degree, the candidate, leaving little to chance, mentions other positive points as well.

- **Assistant Headlines Industry Experience.** A candidate for a job on the plant floor adds references from previous employers to establish his ability to do the job that he wants.

- **Executive Features Big Name Background.** Employers may use "Fortune 100" and the names of premier brands as keywords. *Keywords* are search terms that recruiters search for to choose the most qualified candidates.

- **Paralegal Scores in Talent-Short Specialty.** A paralegal uses the subject to banner herself as careful, specialized in trademarks, and professionally trained.

- **Multilingual Consultant Fits International Desk.** The candidate makes clear that he can work in the global marketplace and speaks several languages.

- **Designer Stands Out with Skills, Education.** Using bullet points to flag qualifications, a candidate spreads out a cover note to take advantage of white space and openness for easy reading.

- **Events Director Shines with Achievements.** Quantitative achievements (measuring with numbers) are effectively used in this cover note.

✔ **HR Manager Stresses Experience, Excellence.** In a field where managers often are conservative, a candidate plays it safe with a traditional approach. Experience and reliability ("rock-solid") are positive attributes.

✔ **Young Banker Asks for Short Phone Interview.** A candidate who posted his resume on a specific Web site was advised that a given employer had reviewed it. Immediately the candidate followed up expressing interest in continued exchanges.

✔ **Professional Confirms Group Insider Status.** "Ask the man who owns one" was a classic slogan for an automobile line suggesting that customers are the ultimate authority on the value of a product. Echoing that theme, a candidate applies for a job at a social networking service she regularly uses.

✔ **Adjuster Concisely States Expertise.** A thoroughly seasoned claims adjuster responds to a posting on a company's Web site in a straightforward manner. Creativity may not be appreciated so much in insurance payment processing occupations.

✔ **Retail Manager Covers Key Points.** A manager who has been around long enough to know all the verses in the retail repertoire bags attention with an offer to make money for a new employer, cites frequent promotion to back up his claims, and interjects a smile at the end.

✔ **Unusual Networking to Social Agency.** The candidate uses editorial rather than advertising content to spot an individual who can influence her future and makes a bold move to meet her potential benefactor. This sample can also be considered a networking cover note. By any classification, the uncommon strategy paid off in real life with a new job.

✔ **Networker Follows Up Job Lead.** The seeker of an office manager position puts the mutual contact in the subject where it can't be missed.

✔ **Law Graduate Offers to Travel to Interview.** The new graduate not only mentions his contact in the subject but also compliments the employer and offers to travel back home to interview on the Fall break.

✔ **From Friend to Friend: Help!** This cover note is a classic way to tap into a personal network to line up a referral.

✔ **Transitioning Marine Sells His Skills.** A military service member, who may be on board ship or overseas, suggests immediate contact by telephone or online as a means of encouraging the employer not to hire anyone before interviewing him.

✔ **Hot Shot Learns from Mistakes.** No shrinking violet, the assertive sales manager also shows humility and willingness to learn new things.

**Nurse Uses
Top 10 Lure**

Subject: Top 10% of Class Nurse Candidate

Dear Ms. Johnson:

Having recently graduated from The Ohio State University, my enthusiasm and desire to assist others is deep and authentic. I graduated in the top 10% of my class and received numerous awards of achievement for my volunteer work in the community and a local hospital.

Please consider the following resume for the Pediatric Unit Registered Nurse position I found posted on your website on June 12. I hope you will be as happy about my credentials as I am about the prospect of working in such a renowned facility.

Standing by,

Kathy Lloyd
(123) 555-0111

Haley Richardson, CPRW, JCTC — Riverview, Fla.

**Assistant Headlines
Industry Experience**

Subject: Experienced Joe Smith for Manufacturing Assistant position

Dear Mr. Paul:

With more than five years of experience in our industry, I submit with great interest my resume for consideration as a Manufacturing Assistant with TRU Manufacturing. While browsing job postings on HiringBoard.com, I was delighted to see an opportunity that so closely pairs with my qualifications.

In addition to my résumé you will find letters of recommendation from past employers who will testify to my quality of work managing staff and production lines.

I look forward to an interview. I will contact you early next week to ensure you've personally received my application materials, to answer any questions you may have, and to schedule a meeting.

Sincerely,

Joe Smith
(123) 555-0111

Haley Richardson, CPRW, JCTC — Riverview, Fla.

Subject: Marketing Director with Fortune 100 Experience

Dear Ms. McGill:

For more than 12 years, I have helped premiere brands, such as Brown Software and Ace Enterprises, achieve revenue gains of up to 18%. Bridging numerous parties to drive multi-million-dollar projects to on-time, on-budget delivery is what I do best.

My expertise in direct marketing, strategic communications, and online advertising has enabled me to lead a wide range of initiatives in a highly-competitive market. This along with my creative development expertise makes me an ideal match for your Marketing Director position.

I have dedicated my career to creating synergy amongst diverse partners and would love to do the same for Worldwide Data. My resume is attached. I will be calling you the week of July 4th to schedule a time for us to explore what I have to offer. Thank you for your consideration.
Sincerely,

Jon Banner
(703) 555-0111
JonBanner@email.com

Tamara Dowling, CPRW — Valencia, Calif.

Subject: Law Firm; Meticulous Trademark Paralegal

Dear Mr. Bates:

I am pleased to submit my resume and various writing samples in the event that an opportunity should arise in your trademark department.

In addition to my paralegal certification from a leading university, you will note that I have significant experience in the preparation of licensing agreements and in trademark management. Given my extensive experience in maintaining international portfolios, researching infringements and maintaining logo enforcement programs, I can undertake significant responsibility early on without the need for costly training.

I will call periodically to determine the firm's hiring needs. Should you wish any additional information on my background in the interim, please do not hesitate to call me at 999-555-0111.

Thank you for your consideration.

Sincerely, Jane Williams

Linda Tancs — Hillsborough, N.J.

Multilingual Consultant
Fits International Desk

Subject: Part-Time Opportunity-International Career & Transition Consultant

Dear Ms. Saxenos,

I recently became the member of XYZ Association and noted in its newsletter your posting for a part-time opportunity-international career & transition consultant. **I am the perfect fit for this!**

1. MBA (Human Resources), a Certified Career Professional, have 10+ years of experience working with people, in USA as well as in INDIA.
2. Fluent in English, Hindi, and can understand/speak Punjabi very easily.
3. Working part-time in my private practice and am looking for challenging subcontracting opportunities.
4. Good networking abilities, resourcefulness, and excellent communication/ interpersonal skills.

I am confident in my ability to make an immediate contribution to ABC Partners. I would welcome an opportunity to talk to you to discuss my qualifications and candidacy in further detail. After you read my resume, I look forward to hearing from you. Thank you.

Sincerely,

Dhruv Patel
774-555-0111
Skype: dpatel

Divya Gupta, MBA, ACCC, CPRW — Naperville, Ill.

Transitioning Marine
Sells His Skills

Subject: Delivery facility operations; supervising skills; Navy trained

After reading your online job posting for an EXPRESS DELIVERY FACILITY OPERATIONS COORDINATOR, my qualifications would like to introduce themselves to your requirements. I will leave the U.S. Marine Corps in two months after a ten-year assignment [identify persuasive civilian matching points — such as overseeing high-volume unloading operations and redistributing urgent materials]. These duties demanded team leadership skills, strong communications ability and careful time management. My resume is just a quick click away.

I will relocate to Louisville in June. I'd appreciate a telephone or online interview before then if you'd like to have a sharper picture of how I could meet the needs of your firm. Please reach me at (826) 555-0111.

Joyce Lain Kennedy — Carlsbad, Calif.

Hot Shot Learns from Mistakes

Subject: Confident, achieving sales manager; ethical; proven results

As a sales manager, I've beat my numbers 99.9 percent of the time. What about that last tenth of a percent? I tried, failed, learned something, and never missed again. For me, it's time to move up. My resume suggests what I can do for you.

I would like to discuss with you why this position has my name on it, and I'll call you at the beginning of next week to see what your schedule allows. Or if you need to reach me sooner, my number is (691) 555-0111.

Joyce Lain Kennedy — Carlsbad, Calif.

Events Director Shines with Achievements

Subject: Record breaking Special Events Director saw your ad

Dear Name:

Fortune was smiling on us when I read your advertisement for a Special Events Director — I've acquired exactly the experience you ask for. With success in implementing strategies that improved event-related objectives, I am certain that I can achieve this level of performance as a member of your management team. Representative achievements include:

* 150% profit improvement and a 3,450+ increase in attendance for a key Colorado Springs Event

* 75% productivity increases for 2 consecutive years through a complete revamp of a Special Events/Promotions division

* 34 new accounts captured through a stronger marketing message and the consolidation of multiple marketing materials

My résumé is attached for your consideration. Let's talk!

Sincerely,

Joe Clooney
(481) 555-0111
j_clooney@mail.com

Dan Dorotik, NCRW — Lubbock, Texas

**Designer Stands Out
with Skills, Education**

Subject: Very Talented Graduate for **Instructional Designer**

Dear Mr. Kyzer:

Noting your posting on Monster for an Instructional Designer, I have a solid background in the areas of:

* Needs Analysis
* Instructional Design that focuses on systematic continuous improvement
* Facilitation of web-based training programs
* One-on-one training and coaching
* Content Development
* Customer Service
* Sales

I will complete a master's program in Instructional Design at the University of Massachusetts in May, focusing on Adult Learning Theory, Content Development, and Organizational Development.

I believe that the position you have advertised is an excellent fit with my qualifications.

I'll call you next week after you've had time to check out my resume.

Sincerely,

Shelby Barnum
MyEmail@Usa.Net
Phone: 555-555-0111

Sharla McAuliffe, CPRW — Burlington, Mass.

**Professional Confirms
Group Insider Status**

Subject: Responding to You: Successful PR & Advertising Pro

Dear [Name]:

A headline of "Pop Songstress Athena Quits Singing Career" would, of course, draw my attention. But no more than your posting for a public relations and advertising professional for my favorite social networking site, NetSocialTime.com! My undergraduate degree is in communications. As you will see on my resume, I currently work as a consultant for a major brand consultancy, a position that affords me the opportunity to hone the considerable writing skills that are key to this position. Please do not hesitate to contact me for any additional information. As an avid user of your social networking services, I especially look forward to hearing from you.

Teresa St. Vincent Pauday
TSVP1@marquee.info
123-555-0111

Linda Tenes — Hillsborough, N.J.

**From Friend to
Friend: Help!**

Subject: Will you do your pal Steve a favor?

Hey Bob!

I was checking out some job openings online and noticed there is a position listed for a sales rep at EFG Corporation. Didn't you mention that company is one of your vendors? From the description given in the posting, I'm sure I have the necessary qualifications they are looking for. I would greatly appreciate any help you can give me in making a connection with the person who is doing the hiring.

I'm attaching a copy of my resume with the hope that you will forward it to your contact at EFG. I'm assuming you have a good relationship with him. Be sure to tell him you've known me for 12 years and can vouch for my character, so that he would be more likely to pass my resume along to the hiring manager.

I'll call you in a few days to see how things are going.

Thanks a lot!

Steve

Melanie Noonan — West Paterson, N.J.

Unusual Networking to Social Agency

Subject: Experienced Leader of Challenged Youth

Hello Ms. Fischl:

Your recent wedding announcement in the New York Times caught my eye. After reading about your senior management role with The Next Generation Foundation, I was curious to learn more. A perusal of the Foundation's website yielded your e-mail address so I decided to write and introduce myself. I too work in the field of not-for-profit management and have great references.

At this time, I am selectively searching for my next career challenge. I am particularly fond of organizations that focus on building leadership qualities in physically challenged young people. From my included résumé, you will see strong evidence of my involvement with educationally related organizations.

After reading the news column, I understand this note may reach your inbox while you are honeymooning in Hawaii. Hawaii has got to be one of the most fantastic vacation spots on earth! If you decide to return, I would very much enjoy meeting with you.

Sincerely, Anne Mitchell
annemitchell@mail.com
(401) 555-0111

MJ Feld, MS, CPRW — Huntington, N.Y.

Young Banker Asks for Short Phone Interview

Subject: Thanks for reviewing my credentials on JumboTalent.com

Dear Ms. Smith:

Thank you for reviewing my credentials on [a targeted resume distribution Web site]. After discovering that you had done so, I visited your company's Web site. Wow! I am very impressed with the client companies you serve and the variety of positions which are available.

As my résumé indicates, I have 3+ years of progressive experience within a prominent retail banking organization in the Boston, Massachusetts, area. Among my strongest skill sets are client relationship management and branch operations oversight. Due to organizational changes within my company, I am seeking outside opportunities in retail banking where I can take my career to the next level.

I will call you next week to see if we can arrange a short phone conversation to further discuss my background in relation to your client assignments in the Greater Boston area.

I look forward to connecting next week.

Sincerely,

Robert Erickson
R_erickson@anyisp.com
555-555-0111

Joellyn Wittenstein Schwerdlin, CCMC, JCTC, CPRW — Worcester, Mass.

**Adjuster Concisely
States Expertise**

Subject: Top Performing Claims Adjuster

Ms. Rogers,

I offer 23 years of progressively responsible experience with demonstrated ability, distinctive qualifications, and stellar performance related to conducting complete liability, coverage, and bodily injury investigations. My professional profile documents the ability to determine validity of claims, verify coverage, establish value of losses, and negotiate settlements within limits of authority.

My resume for the Field Claims Adjuster position listed on your company website is attached. I look forward to hearing from you or your designated representative regarding what I should expect next regarding the interviewing process. Thank you in advance for both your time and consideration.

Respectfully Yours, Maxwell Jones
M_jones@mail.com
(528) 555- 0111

Phyllis Houston, PARW-CC, NRWA — Upper Marlboro, Md.

**Retail Manager
Covers Key Points**

Subject: Store Manager Racks Up Profits For You?

Hello Ms. Harrison:

As an experienced store manager, I have a big-numbers track record in operations management, merchandising, and customer service. I would like to parlay my expertise into assisting your company in exceeding its revenue goals at the Huntington location.

My leadership skills are best demonstrated by my frequent promotions. As the attached resume indicates, I also have significant experience in sales analysis and expense control. And finally, I'm a hard worker. Anyone who's been in retail for more than 30 minutes has got to be!

The opportunity to interview would be most welcome. I'll check back with you very soon. I hope we can profitably connect.

All the best, Mary Jane Farrell
mjfarrell@mail.com
(204) 555-0111

M.I Feld, MS, CPRW — Huntington, N.Y.

Networker Follows Up Job Lead

Subject: Office Manager: Paul Gold refers Betty Larson

Dear Ms. Carlson:

Your colleague Paul Gold, whom I met at a recent networking event, informed me of the opening within your organization for a competent Office Manager. He spoke briefly about the qualifications and requirements but couldn't provide a lot of detail. He asked that I contact you for more information.

I am attaching my resume to this e-mail in an effort to see if we have a match concerning the requirements of the position and my qualifications. Please contact me if you have questions and to schedule a time to talk in person.

As you probably know, Paul Gold thinks your organization is special and that you are a wonder. I'm fired up about exploring this opportunity with you.

All best,
Betty Larson
B_larson@yahoo.com
(123) 555-0111

Haley Richardson, CPRW, JCTC — Riverview, Fla.

Law Graduate Offers to Travel to Interview

Subject: John Timmons Referral to You

John Timmons gave me your name and volunteered to get in touch with you about my credentials. As a soon-to-be graduate (with honors) of The University of Iowa Law School and an undergraduate degree in International Business/Finance and Spanish, I am eager to begin a professional career in contract law in the Houston market. John was adamant that your firm "is the best there is" and that I need to visit with you. My professional resume and accompanying cover letter are attached for your perusal.

I'll be on fall break the week of October 12th and would be happy to travel back to Texas to meet with you should your schedule permit. Thank you for your time and I so look forward to your reply.

Best regards,

Richard (Trey) Alvarez III
r_alvarez@mail.com
(731) 555-0111

Billie R. Sucher, MS, CTMS, CTSB, JCTC, CCM — Urbandale, Iowa

HR Manager Stresses Experience, Excellence

Subject: HR manager, experienced, rock-solid

When your organization seeks a dynamic, results-proven Human Resources professional with strong communication and leadership skills, then I believe we were made for each other!

I encourage you to review my resume, which supports my desire and ability to exceed your expectations and goals by utilizing my talents as an accomplished HR Manager to support your exceptional work.

Highlights of my background include:

- Progressive leader with over five years' experience as a Human Resources Manager.

- Hands-on expertise in all functional areas of strategic human resources management working in both unionized and non-unionized environments.

- Strong educational background that includes a Master of Human Resources Management.

For more detailed information or to schedule an interview, please call (555) 555.0111 or send a message to tnt_hr@hotmail.com.

Many Thanks,

Latoya Johnson, CHRP, MHMR

Tanya Taylor, CHRP, MCRS — Toronto, Ontario, Canada

Part V
The Part of Tens

In this part . . .

Dig into short chapters rife with quick bits about job letters. In them, I offer guidance on avoiding unnecessary mistakes and ways to best represent who you are when you're writing online profiles. Cozying up to the chapters in this part is a directory of the professional writers whose work appears in this book.

Chapter 15

Ten Urban Legends to Toss

In This Chapter
▶ Myths that undermine your chances to book interviews
▶ Mistakes and misconceptions that keep you unemployed

Cover letters live in the misty atmosphere of urban legends. Many people think they're an optional exercise in the job-finding game, evaluating cover letters as baggage that no one pays attention to. (Chapter 1 discusses that point in detail.)

People for whom cover letters are off the radar may cut corners in a variety of ways. For instance, they use canned pitches or address their correspondence to a title rather than to a human. Or they softly mumble hopes that employers will find it in their hearts to call them for interviews.

They accept on face value cover-letter urban legends, such as the ones that follow. But, after reading this book, you know better, right?

It's Okay to Send Your Resume without a Cover Letter

False! That is, unless you like sending your resume into other people's dumpsters. Make sure that a results-oriented cover letter is a sidekick to your resume.

When your letter — or other job-finding document — opens up with a compelling first paragraph (see Chapter 6), readers ask "What happens next?" or say "Tell me more." Sales points confirming your benefits for a specific employer follow, concluding with your promise to follow up. Your cover letter stamps a personality on your resume — a personality that the reader may find tough to reject out of hand.

Your Cover Letter Summarizes Your Resume

False! A summary of your resume and your resume with a summary seem a little repetitive, don't you agree? Use a cover letter to add a warm handshake to your resume and to concentrate on why the employer should be interested in you and why time interviewing you would be well invested.

Your cover letter puts your resume in context, drawing attention to your benefits and presenting non-resume material that can make the difference between you and your closest competitor when the interviewing decision is made.

A Cover Letter Merely Transmits Your Resume

False! Your cover letter is much more than a routing slip for your resume. Your letter is also ultimately a silent force, enticing the reader to scour your resume. A number of employers believe cover letters are more important than resumes when choosing candidates to interview. If your cover letter doesn't flesh out the person presented in your resume, you may never get to meet its reader.

You Can Routinely Use a Generic Greeting — "Dear Employer"

False! Put yourself on the other side of the desk. Imagine that your job is to screen applicants, and that every letter you read begins with "Dear Sir" or "Dear Gentlepeople" or "Dear Job Application Screener" or, worse, "To Whom It May Concern." In effect, you're saying "Dear Nobody." How would you feel if you were that nobody? Aim for respect, respect, and respect.

Research your target organization (see Chapter 4) until you have the name and gender of the person who will make the hiring decision (usually the line manager) or the interviewing decision (usually a company in-house screener or outside third-party screener). Double-check for correct spelling and proper titles. (See Chapter 4 for more information about the anatomy of a cover letter.)

Admittedly, despite your best efforts, sometimes you simply cannot uncover the name of the decision-maker or the screener reading your letter. When you can't uncover the correct name and must rely on a generic greeting, the salutations "Dear Employer" or "Dear Hiring Authority" are as good as any.

What can you do to properly address blind online job postings when you have no clue to the employer's identity? Usually very little, but if the address of a Web site is in the posting (other than that of a job board), take a flyer and visit Allwhois (www.allwhois.com) to uncover the name of the Web site's owner and contact information. Allwhois automatically locates the appropriate "whois" database server for a particular domain name, queries that database for information about the domain name, and returns all available data.

Keep Your Cover Letter Really, Really Short

False! The length of your cover letter depends not upon absolute rules of measurement, but upon the amount of content you must convey to show why you should be interviewed.

After advising flexibility over page count, here are my personal preferences: When the letter escorts a resume, I suggest limiting the letter to one page; when the letter substitutes for a resume (see Chapter 11), two pages is an appropriate length — unless you're that rare master of long-copy advertising pitches, in which case you can go on as long as the reader doesn't sink into slumber.

Devote one paragraph to each salient point. The short-paragraph technique maintains your letter's richness even when skimmed in the blink of an eye. Make your Stand Out cover letter just long enough to accommodate all your main-selling-point benefits and to motivate the reader to review your resume and meet with you.

A Handwritten Cover Letter Is Best — It's Personal

False! Although the vast majority of cover letters and resumes are transmitted over the Internet today, a small number still travel by paper.

For those job letters on paper, handwriting is certainly personal, but the downside is two-fold:

> ✔ Employers may assume you're in a time warp and costume yourself in cobwebs if you don't use a computer's word processor.
>
> ✔ They may be unable to read your penmanship.

If an employer wants a sample of your handwriting for analysis, the employer will request one. Your only handwriting in a cover letter should be your signature at the end, written in black or blue ink.

If You Can't Find a Job, the Letter Is at Fault

False! Your marketing materials, such as a cover letter or resume, can become an easy focus for your anxieties about a job search. Many of the moving parts of the employment process are frustratingly placed beyond your control — voicemail keeps you from reaching a preferred employer, job openings for your target seem to go underground, and interviews fail to spark job offers.

By contrast, the preparation of a cover letter and resume is entirely under your control. When things go wrong, blaming the marketing materials is convenient but justified only when you aren't being given interviews.

Job seekers often think that if only they can whip their marketing materials into perfect shape, the other parts of the search will turn out favorably. Not really. The truth is, all parts of your search must be up and running.

The Letter Is Your Chance to Discuss Your Personal Life and Feelings

False! Your resume talks about you; your cover letter talks about your intended employer — and how your employer can benefit from the splendid assets you offer.

Rambling on about personal feelings, situations, and long-term ambitions in an employment letter is a monument to self-interest, but worse — it's boring. An exception can be made when you're seeking to relocate (provided you offer to pay for the relocation). Many employers appreciate the desire to be near family as a reason to relocate. No need to go into your uncle's stint in the nursing home; having family in the area is enough.

Include Salary History and Expectations in Your Cover Letter

False! Save the salary discussion for the interview. You can be eliminated at this stage if your salary history is considered too high, too low, or too static. My advice is not to get into it in advance because it's not in your best interests to do so.

If a job posting requests such information, write that your salary is negotiable. When the employer's application software won't accept the word *negotiable*, use a wide pay range for the job that you research on www.salary.com, www.payscale.com, or www.indeed.com. Add that you'll be happy to discuss the issue during an interview.

Yes, you will be excluded from consideration by employers who are ticked off that you didn't follow their directions to reveal your pay history, expectations, or both in advance. Unless you're desperate, it's a chance worth taking.

After You Send a Letter, the Ball Is in the Employer's Court

False! No matter how terrific you are, unless they need you right this very second, most employers have no time for hunting you down. If you don't get an automated acknowledgment that your letter and resume arrived, call or e-mail to confirm receipt.

But when you do receive confirmation, you don't show genius by calling and asking, "Did you get my resume?"

Another situation: Suppose you have faithfully followed up with phone calls as promised, but the clock is ticking and nothing is happening. One tactic is nudging the employer with e-mail. Here's a sample campaign:

1. **Send the following message:**

   I hope you've had a chance to review my resume (sent 9/3/XX), which shows my experience and education in convention management. I'll be glad to fill in any blanks — what else would you like to know?

2. **If radio silence is your answer, try again.**

Since my last note, I've uncovered two recent articles about your organization that make me even more certain that my communications skills and bilingual competencies would be valuable in your operations department. If you haven't seen the articles (identify by name), I'll be happy to pass them along if that would be useful. Would you like to receive them?

3. **Ugh. Still no answer. Keep trying.**

   Since we haven't been able to make contact, I'll check back with you next week — unless another time would be better. What do you think?

Most people would rather take a punch in the gut than undertake an apparently unrequited job chase; they challenge whether e-mail campaigns work. Sometimes yes; sometimes no.

Even when a serial e-mail follow-up does work, success may not arrive overnight. A newly graduated MBA used e-mail to find employment as a product manager for a Web site. He got to know the brass at the site by doing what he termed "the e-mail slow dance" for nine months before the offer came. Even then, the MBA, who describes e-mail as "less threatening than a phone call," had to call and tell the hiring manager that it was time to step up and make an offer.

How many times should you keep banging your head on a wall of silence? Until you get an e-mail or phone conversation going, or until the employer threatens to call security.

Tony Beshara of Dallas, Texas, is a high performer who runs one of America's ultra successful job placement firms. As I mention in my book *Resumes For Dummies,* 5th Edition, I asked Beshara how many times he follows up on an employer before calling it quits.

His succinct answer: "I move on after about 15 calls spread out over two months."

Chapter 16

Ten Tips for Top-Rated Online Profiles

Online networking for a job search, which I describe in Chapter 2, has opened the floodgates for professional online profiles — the kind you place on such networking sites as LinkedIn or Facebook.

Think of a professional online profile as a kind of digital billboard used for passive networking that never sleeps. You put yourself out there, hoping employers will find you and like you for their jobs. When your profile looks like a match for a job they want to fill, you hope they'll invite you to join them for a face-to-face interview — an interview that can lead to big things in your future.

You want an edge over countless competitors who are taking the leap to posting their profiles online. Here are ten ways to gain a competitive edge. I compiled these tips with the invaluable and expert help of Debbie Ellis, an award-winning Master Resume Writer (MRW) and Certified Professional Resume Writer (CPRW). Houston-based Ellis is president of the Phoenix Career Group (www.phoenixcareergroup.com), a consortium of top professional job document writers and coaches.

Do Establish Your Expertise

Pay homage to your online profile as you would to the information in your resume. Focus the content on your professional expertise, benefits, and accomplishments.

Be sure to include your current and past employment, education, and industry.

Skip personal information, such as date of birth, height and weight, and marital status unless you're in show business or are looking for a job outside the United States where American anti-discrimination laws don't apply.

Scatter relevant keywords throughout your profile because that's how search engines go about chasing people to interview. Find the hot keywords by reading job ads and job descriptions that interest you.

Check out for free the thousands of keywords on Kathryn Troutman's Keyword Tree, located at `www.resume-place.com/nspstree`. The feature includes keywords for technical, administrative, management, and analytical occupations for entry-, mid-, and senior-level jobs.

What about adding a photo of yourself? There are two schools of thought on this issue: (1) Some advisers say a photo's a must to attract attention. (2) Others, particularly those with wide experience in hiring issues, oppose the inclusion of a profile photo partly because employers fear exposure to failure-to-hire lawsuits based on such things as race, age, and gender. What's more, a potential employer may decide you remind her of a much unloved relative and you're toasted to a crisp. (The same pros and cons apply to linking your video resume to your profile.)

Add links on your profile to other sites that show your work portfolio.

You know this, but I'll say it anyway: Double-check for typos and grammatical flubs.

Do Captivate Your Audience

Start out with a bang by creating an opening summary that sells hard. Remember that online profiles are digital billboards that readers whiz by if a message doesn't grab attention, much as motorists zoom by flabby highway billboards. Size up what's important to employers in your sights by studying job ads, and then write a list of your matching experience, competencies, skills, and education; load them into your summary.

Do Write Outside the Box

Start reading online profiles and you'll marvel at how many "results-driven, people-oriented, problem-solvers" there are out there skating across the Web wonderland. Good clichés, but clichés they are. As an aspiring Stand Out writer, you'll work hard to paint fresh word pictures that help readers understand your specialness.

Use specifics. Be authentic (the opposite of phony). And within the bounds of business communication, write like you talk.

Do Rightsize, Not Supersize

Set your sights on making your profile neither too long nor too short.

There's no rule about exact profile length. The litmus test is: *Does including this information enhance my perceived qualifications for the type of job I seek? Will it help me land an interview? Have I omitted information critical to landing an interview?* Make every word sell you.

One tip to save space and construct a concise communication is to eliminate mentions of *I* and minimize the use of articles. For example, this:

> *I developed a solar-energy lighting fixture that increased the company's profits by 11%.*

. . . Is better like this:

> *Developed solar-energy lighting fixture that increased profits by 11%.*

Chapter 5 gives you the details about choosing the right words for selling your qualifications.

Do Write Robust Headlines

Another secret to successful profile writing is the power headline! Move to the other side of the desk for a moment and put on your recruiting hat: Suppose you're staring at a pool of 300 profiles that match your keyword search; which ones do you read all the way though? It's the headline that pulls you into the profile.

As an example, pretend you're one of the recruiters at Netshare.com, a subscription service for professionals and executives seeking six-figure jobs. They initially see only the first six lines but can click to read an entire profile if its headline pulls them in. Which kind of headline would excite your interest to read further?

> ***Senior Sales & Marketing Executive***
>
> ***Experienced Executive helping accelerate technology to market***

Thought so.

Don't Oversell Your Versatility

In an effort to appeal to the largest number of potential employers, some people make the mistake of cobbling together their qualifications and come off looking like jacks of all trades (but masters of none). Employers usually look for specialists, not generalists. (An exception is the mini-business where the workforce must wear more than one hat.)

If you cannot resist broadening your professional niche, at least stick to occupations in the same job family (see www.onetcodeconnector.org), the same career field (such as accounting, urban planning, or insurance underwriting), or the same industry (such as aerospace or retailing).

Even when an employer is interested in you as a candidate, unnecessary occupational spread can dim your appeal. Suppose your profile says that you're an award-winning Web designer and also notes that you're available for employment as a restaurant room manager in the evening. The employer may think technology design and foodie gigs are odd-couple talents and prefer that you spend your evenings thinking great design thoughts. An inappropriate fact on a canned profile can cause second thoughts about your value.

Most effective: Be very specific about who you are professionally and what you offer and don't keep adding bells and whistles to show that you can be everything to everyone.

Don't Overdo Overused Self-Praise

Hold back on empty adjectives like *superior, exclusive, outstanding,* and so forth when you describe your skills or qualities. Without backing up your claims, no one believes them anyway. Factually explain how you made or saved money for the company. How you delivered on a goal. How you received top marks for performance.

You're more likely to be believed when you include comments on your work from others, such as coworkers, bosses, and customers. (Read about reference commentaries in Chapter 3).

Don't Regurgitate Your Resume

Your resume is a core part of your online profile but remember that, as the infomercials say, wait — there's more. Flesh out your profile with data that will help you be chosen for an interview. A cultural fit with the employer is a key factor; add such information as your participation in amateur sports (competitiveness), five favorite books (thinking quality); and civic service organizations (community-orientation), for instance.

Politics? No, unless you're applying to a political party. Religious affiliation? No, unless you're applying to a church or ministry.

You won't always have the option of giving the reader a glimpse of you as a person as well as a professional. When a site's requirements limit you to two or three paragraphs, make them keyword-rich and stick to function and industry, as illustrated in the following profile written by professional cover letter writer Debbie Ellis.

> **Senior-level IT executive (CTO, VP/IT)   Fortune 1000**
>
> Consummate management professional, passionate leader, and high-performance individual. 20+ years' experience in executive-level IT management roles. Expert in partnering IT with enterprise strategies, initiatives, and multi-site, cross-functional operations. Technically proficient in contemporary / emerging technologies, project management approaches, best practices, benchmarks. Successful in meeting time, budget, and quality goals. Qualifications: IT Strategy; Systems & Network Architecture; Large-Scale Implementations & Conversions; IT Optimization; Project Planning, Budgeting, Scheduling & Lifecycle Management; Project & Application Portfolio Management; Internet & Web; Help Desk & Technical Support; Vendor Contracts; Technical Training & Skills / Career Development; IT Team Leadership; Department / Operations; P&L; Due Diligence; Post-M&A Integration / Transition; Change Management; Budget & Resource; Risk Management; Internal & External Customer Service.
>
> Complete resume and contact information online, www.johnjones-resume.com.

Don't Be a Victim to Perilous Posting

Don't post anything you don't want an employer to see. Instead, control your "label" for those times that hiring managers go shopping. Treat a Facebook or LinkedIn page with the care you give a resume. Use privacy settings thoughtfully and make sure that pubic messages or images you post don't cheapen your professional image.

Try not to post anything an identity thief can use to steal from you. Treat all personal identity information like a classified document. Do not put your home address, social security number, driver's or professional license numbers, or family information in your profile. Restrict contact information to your phone number and e-mail, and, if you have one, a box address at a post office or package mailing store.

A Web of opportunity is also a Web of risks. Take good care of yourself as you network even after you have a job.

Don't Play Hide and Seek

In choosing where to park your profile, be visible and be selective. Start with one or two sites, adding others only when you see a clear and present payback for the considerable time you spend actively networking.

Quality and quantity are the big questions when you're picking sites. Who's using the site? How many are using the site? A network is most useful when it's gained a critical mass of people who can do you some good. LinkedIn, for example, has more than 23 million users, including executives from all the Fortune 500 companies. Facebook has more than 80 million active users globally. But LinkedIn has a professional and business focus, while Facebook has a much larger social component.

As you explore your options among online sites that post profiles — such as ZoomInfo, a business directory; Spoke, a business directory and social network; and Jigsaw, a business directory and social network — be wary about biting off more than you can manage.

Internet job search expert and publisher Peter Weddle (www.weddles.com) sums up my thoughts about time management and expectations for online networking:

> *As helpful as online networking can be, it is a supplement to, not a replacement, for traditional networking. Despite what technophiles and Internet enthusiasts will tell you, landing a dream job still requires human interaction. That interaction can begin on the Web and even be enriched there, but it cannot occur exclusively online for one simple reason: Real people, not virtual ones, fill jobs.*

Appendix

Directory of Job Letter Writers

* * *

*T*he professional letter writers whose work appears in Chapter 3 and Parts III and IV are experts at creating the quality of self-marketing job search documents you need to stand out from your competition.

The writer's name appears at the bottom of each sample. This appendix presents each writer's contact information, a glossary of professional certifications, and a directory of five professional writing and career-development organizations to which many of the sample writers proudly belong.

The following directory lists each sample writer's name, certification designations, firm name, location, telephone, and e-mail address. Web site, blog, and fax and toll-free phone numbers are included when available.

Susan Barens, CPRW, IJCTC
CAREER DYNAMICS
Olmsted Falls, Ohio
Phone: (440) 610-4361
Fax: (440) 427-8835
E-mail: careerdynamics1@aol.com
www.yourbestmarketingtool.com

Danni M. Kimoto Barker, CPCC, CPRW
Barker & Associates, LLC
Crestview, Fla.
Phone: (850) 543-2060
E-mail: barker.danni@gmail.com
www.barkersolutionsllc.com

Deborah Barnes, CPRW
Nahant, Mass.
Phone: (781) 598-1127
E-mail: debnahant@comcast.net

Karen Bartell, CPRW
Best-in-Class Resumes
Massapequa Park, N.Y.
Phone: (800) 234-3569
Fax: (516) 799-6300
E-mail: kbartell@bestclassresumes.com
www.bestclassresumes.com

Laurie Berenson, CPRW
Sterling Career Concepts, LLC
Park Ridge, N.J.
Phone: (201) 573-8282
Fax: (201) 255-0137
E-mail: laurie@sterlingcareer
    concepts.com
www.sterlingcareerconcepts.com
Blog: blog.sterlingcareerconcepts.com

Marian Bernard, CPRW, JCTC, CEIP
The Regency Group
Aurora, Ontario, Canada
Phone: (905) 841-7120
Fax: (905) 841-1391
E-mail: marian@neptune.on.ca
www.resumeexpert.ca

Sharon M. Bowden, CPRW, CEIP
SMB Solutions
Atlanta, Ga.
Phone: (404) 264-1855
Fax: (404) 264-0592
Email: Sharon@startsavvy.com
www.startsavvy.com

Vicki Brett-Gach, CPRW
BEST RESUME, LLC
Ann Arbor, Mich.
Phone: (734) 327-0400
Fax: (734) 913-0633
E-mail: bestresume12345@aol.com
www.BestResume12345.com

Heather Carson, GCDF, CPRW, JCTC, CWDP
Second Start
Concord, N.H.
Phone: (603) 228-1341
Toll-free: (866) 313-7837
Fax: (603) 228-3852
E-mail: hcarson@second-start.org
www.second-start.org

Freddie Cheek, CCM, CPRW, CARW, CWDP
Cheek & Associates
Amherst, N.Y.
Phone: (716) 835-6945
Fax: (928) 832-6945
E-mail: fscheek@cheekand
   associates.com
www.CheekandAssociates.com

Stephanie Clark, CRS, CIS
New Leaf Resumes
Kitchener, Ontario, Canada
Phone: (519) 505-JOBS (5627)
E-mail: stephaniec@newleafresumes.ca
www.newleafresumes.ca

Joyce Cutler, CPRW
Avail Resumes
Colts Neck, N.J.
Phone: (732) 616-4082
E-mail: AvailResumes@verizon.net
www.availresumes.vpweb.com

Sheri K. Czar, CPRW
First Impression Career Services
Lake Oswego, Ore.
Phone: (503) 636-4558
Fax: (503) 636-0688
E-mail: shericzar@comcast.net
www.firstimpressioncareerservices.org

Dan Dorotik, NCRW
100PercentResumes.com
Lubbock, Texas
Phone: (806) 783-9900
Fax: (806) 993-3757
Email: dan@100percentresumes.com
www.100percentresumes.com

Tamara Dowling, CPRW
www.SeekingSuccess.com
Valencia, Calif.
E-mail: td@SeekingSuccess.com
www.SeekingSuccess.com
Blog: www.SeekingSuccess.com/Blog

Susan Easton, CRS, CEIC
Competitive Edge Career Services
Prince George, British Columbia, Canada
Phone: (250) 964-1138
Toll Free: (888) 964-1138
E-mail: NewCareer@cecs.ca
www.cecs.ca

Wendy S. Enelow, CCM, MRW, JCTC, CPRW
Enelow Enterprises, Inc. ~ Executive
Gateway to $100,000 to $1+ Million Jobs
Coleman Falls, Va.
Phone: (434) 299-5600
E-mail: wendy@wendyenelow.com
www.wendyenelow.com

Dayna Feist, CPRW, JCTC, CEIP
Gatehouse Business Services
Asheville, N.C.
Phone: (828) 254-7893
Fax: (828) 254-7893
E-mail: Gatehous@aol.com
www.BestJobEver.com

MJ Feld, CPRW
CAREERS by CHOICE, Inc.
Huntington, N.Y.
Phone: (631) 673-5432
Fax: (631) 673-5824
E-mail: mj@careersbychoice.com
www.careersbychoice.com

John Femia, CPRW
Custom Resume & Writing Service
Altamont, N.Y.
Phone: (518) 872-1305
E-mail: customresume1@aol.com
www.custormresumewriting.com

Cliff Flamer, NCC, NCRW, CPRW
BrightSide Résumés
San Francisco Bay Area, Calif.
Toll Free: (877) 668-9767
Phone. (510) 444-1724
E-mail. writers@brightside
    resumes.com
www.brightsideresumes.com

Arthur I. Frank
Resumes "R" Us
Flat Rock, N.C.
Phone: (828) 696-2975
Toll Free: (866) 600-4300
Fax: (828) 696-2974
E-mail: af@afresumes.com
www.afresumes.com

Gail Frank, NCRW, CPRW, JCTC, CEIP
Employment University
Tampa, Fla.
Phone: (813) 506-8442
E-mail: gailfrank@post.harvard.edu
www.EmploymentU.com

Louise Garver, CPBS, JCTC, CMP, CPRW, CEIP
Career Directions LLC
Broad Brook, Conn.
Phone: (860) 623-9476
Fax: (860) 623-9473
Email: LouiseGarver@cox.net
www.CareerDirectionsLLC.com

Judith L. Gillespie, CPCC, CPRW, CEIP
Career Avenues by Judy
W. Melbourne, Fla.
Phone: (850) 524-2917
Fax: (321) 953-8361
E-mail: judy@careeravenuesbyjudy.com
www.careeravenuesbyjudy.com

Susan Guarneri, MRW, CERW, CPRW, CPBS, NCCC, DCC
Guarneri Associates
Three Lakes, Wis.
Toll-free: (866) 881-4055
Skype: susan.guarneri
Email: Susan@Resume-Magic.com
www.Resume-Magic.com
Blog: blog.careergoddess.com

Divya Gupta, ACCC, CPRW
ConfidentCareer.com
Naperville, Ill.
Phone: (630) 364-1848
E-Mail: divya@confidentcareer.com
www.confidentcareer.com

Kate Herrick
Bellevue, Wash.
E-mail: kate@kateherrick.com
www.kateherrick.com

Gay Anne Himebaugh
Seaview Secretarial Solutions
Corona del Mar, Calif.
Phone: (949) 673-2400
Fax: (949) 673-2428
E-mail: resumes@seaviewsecretarial.com

Phyllis G. Houston, PARW/CC, NRWA
The Résumé Expert, Mobile Resume Service
Upper Marlboro, Md.
Phone: (301) 574-3956
Fax: (301) 574-1191
E-mail: phyllis_houston@msn.com

Kristen A. Jacoway, CRC, CPRW, CCC, CPBS
Career Design Coaching
Seneca, S.C.
Phone: (334) 332-7990
Fax: (800) 725-8019
E-mail: kristen@careerdesign
coach.com
www.careerdesigncoach.com

David J. Jensen, CPRW, CEIP
Ascension Writing Services
Salt Lake City, Utah
Phone: (801) 755-4364
E-mail: djensen962@msn.com

Erin Kennedy, CPRW
Professional Résumé Services
Lapeer, Mich.
Toll-free: (866) 793-9224
E-mail: ekennedy@prores
writers.com
www.proreswriters.com

Elizabeth Macfarlane, CPRW
Maximum Career Solutions
Windsor, Ontario, Canada
Phone: (519) 966-2819
Fax: (519) 974-3504
E-mail: inquiries@maximum
careersolutions.com
www.maximumcareer
solutions.com

Kathleen Marshall, NRWA
Gatewayresumes.com
Medford, NJ
Phone: (609) 367-5361
E-mail:kmarshall@gateway
resumes.com
www.gatewayresumes.com

Sharla McAuliffe, CPRW
Burlington, Mass.
E-mail: sharla@usa.net
www.linkedin.com/in/sharla

Linda L. Meehan, NRWA, PARW/CC
WebWords Resumes
Sonoma, Calif.
E-mail: Linda@WebWordsResumes.com
www.WebwordsResumes.com

Jan Melnik, MRW, CCM, CPRW
Absolute Advantage
Durham, Conn.
Phone: (860) 349-0256
Fax: (860) 349-1343
E-mail: CompSPJan@aol.com
www.janmelnik.com

Karen Mitchell
Limelight Career Consulting
Lititz, Pa.
Phone: (717) 468-9601
Fax: (717) 626-3443
E-mail: karen@limelightcareers.com
www.limelightcareers.com

Dynesha Montgomery
Atlanta, Ga.
Phone: (251) 423-2561
E-mail: dynesha_montgomery@yahoo.com

Carol Nason, CPRW
Career Advantage
Groton, Mass.
E-mail: nason1046@aol.com
www.acareeradvantageresume.com

Melanie Noonan
Peripheral Pro, LLC
West Paterson, N.J.
Phone: (973) 785-3011
Fax: (973) 256-6285
E-Mail: peripro1@aol.com

Don Orlando, CPRW, JCTC, CCM, CCMC
The McLean Group
Montgomery, Ala.
Phone: (334) 264-2020
Fax: (334) 264-9227
E-mail: yourcareercoach@charterinternet.com

Michelle Penn, CPRW
Granite City, Ill.
Phone: (618) 877-1538
Fax: (618) 877-1688
E-mail: MPenn@
ResumeResultsOnline.com
www.ResumeResultsOnline.com

Phoenix Career Group Inc.
Debbie Ellis, President
Houston, Texas
Phone: (800) 876-5506
International: (281) 361-2077
Fax: (866) 856-1878
E-mail: debbie@phoenix
    careergroup.com
www.phoenixcareergroup.com

Dr. David G. Phreaner, CWDP
Second Start/Working Futures
Rochester, N.H.
Phone: (603) 335-6847
Fax: (603) 335-6852
E-mail: dphreaner@second-start.org

Haley Richardson, CPRW, JCTC
Résumés Done Right
Riverview, Fla.
E-mail: resumesdoneright@
    rocketmail.com
www.resumesdoneright.com

Jane Roqueplot, CWDP, CECC
JaneCo's Sensible Solutions
Sharon, Pa.
Toll-free: (888) 526-3267
E-mail: info@janecos.com
www.janecos.com

Barbara Safani, CERW, NCRW,
CPRW, CCM
Career Solvers
New York, N.Y.
Toll-Free: (866) 333-1800
Phone: (212) 579-7230
E-mail: info@careersolvers.com
www.careersolvers.com

Billie R. Sucher, JCTC, CCM
Urbandale, Iowa
Phone: (515) 276-0061
Fax: (515) 334-8076
E-mail: billie@billiesucher.com
www.billiesucher.com

Linda Tancs
Career/Workplace Coach and Branding
    Strategist
Hillsborough, N.J.
Phone: (888) 582-4072
E-mail: info@lindatancs.com
www.latancs.com

Tanya Taylor, CHRP, MCRS
TNT Human Resources Management
Toronto, Ontario, Canada
Phone: (416) 887-5819
E-mail: Info@tntresumewriter.com
www.tntresumewriter.com

Edward Turilli, CPRW
AccuWriter Resume Service
North Kingstown, R.I.
Phone: (401) 268-3020
Bonita Springs, Fla.
Phone: (239) 298-9514
E-mail: edtur@cox.net
www.resumes4-u.com

Joellyn Wittenstein Schwerdlin CCMC,
JCTC, CPRW
Career-Success-Coach.com
Worcester, Mass.
Phone: (508) 459-2854
Fax: (508) 459-2856
E-Mail: joellyn@career-success-
    coach.com
www.career-success-coach.com

A Glossary of Professional Certifications

Ever wonder what the letters behind someone's name mean? Initials behind the sample writers' names designate certifications each has voluntarily earned. Designations are awarded by a professional organization. They are awarded based on a candidate's professional evaluation, usually measured by formal testing, of the candidate's level of expertise in a specific skill area.

The certification examination process generally requires time-consuming study and may include both experience-based knowledge acquired in the field, and curriculum-based knowledge gained by study of assigned learning texts.

Certification is an indication that the certified professional is a player in a field's large body of knowledge and that the professional meets documented standards and achievement requirements.

Many — but not all — of the certifications accorded to this book's sample writers were awarded by one of the professional organizations listed in the following section.

Certification evaluations are voluntary for professional writers. For their own reasons, not all of those whose excellent work appears in these pages have sought credentialing.

If you do not find the initials behind a sample writer's name on the following list, the initials may refer to membership in one of the professional organizations in the next section.

ACCC — Associate Certified Career Coach

CARW — Certified Advanced Resume Writer

CC — Career Coach

CCC — Certified Career Coach

CCM — Credentialed Career Manager

CCMC — Certified Career Management Coach

CECC — Certified Electronic Career Coach

CEIC — Certified Employment Interview Consultant

CEIP — Certified Employment Interview Professional

CERW — Certified Expert Resume Writer

CHRP — Certified Human Resources Professional

CIS — Certified Interview Strategist

CMP — Certified Career Management Practitioner

CPBS — Certified Personal Branding Strategist

CPCC — Certified Professional Career Coach

CPRW — Certified Professional Resume Writer

CRC — Certified Rehabilitation Counselor

CRS — Certified Resume Strategist

CWDP — Certified Workforce Development Professional

DCC — Distance Career Counselor

GCDF — Global Career Development Facilitator

IJCTC or **JCTC** — International Job Career & Transition Coach

MCRS — Master Certified Resume Strategist

MRW — Master Resume Writer

NCC — National Certified Counselors

NCCC — National Certified Career Counselor

NCRW — Nationally Certified Resume Writer

Professional Organizations

Professional writers of job letters belong to professional organizations to stay current with new ideas, continue professional development, and connect with other serious experts. The five professional organizations that follow are responsible for inviting their members to contribute their best work to this book. The certification designations awarded by each organization are noted.

Association of Online Resume and Career Professionals (AORCP)
Certifications Awarded:
Certified Master Resume Specialist (CMRS)
Web site: www.aorcp.com
Contact: Karen M. Silins, karen@aorcp.com

Career Directors International (CDI)
Certifications Awarded:
Certified Advanced Resume Writer (CARW)
Certified Expert Resume Writer (CERW)
Master Career Director (MCD)
Certified Employment Interview Consultant (CEIC)

Certified Career Research Expert (CCRE)
Corrections Career Transition Certified (CCTC)
Certified Military Resume Writer (CFRW)
Certified Federal Resume Writer (CFRW)
Certified Web Portfolio Practitioner (CWPP)
Certified Electronic Career Coach (CECC)
Web site: www.careerdirectors.com
Contact: Laura DeCarlo, laura@careerdirectors.com

Career Management Alliance
Certifications Awarded:
Master Resume Writer (MRW)
Credentialed Career Manager (CCM)
Web site: www.careermanagementalliance.com
Contact: Liz Sumner, liz@careermanagementalliance.com

The National Resume Writers' Association (NRWA)
Certifications Awarded:
Nationally Certified Resume Writer (NCRW)
Web site: www.nrwaweb.com
Contact: Robyn Feldberg, President; Yvette Campbell, Administrative
Manager, adminmanager@thenrwa.com

Professional Association of Resume Writers & Career Coaches (PARW/CC)
Certifications Awarded:
Certified Professional Resume Writer (CPRW)
Certified Employment Interview Professional (CEIP)
Certified Professional Career Coach (CPCC)
Web site: www.parw.com
Contact: Frank Fox, parwhq@aol.com

Index

BUSINESS, CAREERS & PERSONAL FINANCE

Accounting For Dummies, 4th Edition*
978-0-470-24600-9

Bookkeeping Workbook For Dummies†
978-0-470-16983-4

Commodities For Dummies
978-0-470-04928-0

Doing Business in China For Dummies
978-0-470-04929-7

E-Mail Marketing For Dummies
978-0-470-19087-6

Job Interviews For Dummies, 3rd Edition*†
978-0-470-17748-8

Personal Finance Workbook For Dummies*†
978-0-470-09933-9

Real Estate License Exams For Dummies
978-0-7645-7623-2

Six Sigma For Dummies
978-0-7645-6798-8

Small Business Kit For Dummies, 2nd Edition*†
978-0-7645-5984-6

Telephone Sales For Dummies
978-0-470-16836-3

BUSINESS PRODUCTIVITY & MICROSOFT OFFICE

Access 2007 For Dummies
978-0-470-03649-5

Excel 2007 For Dummies
978-0-470-03737-9

Office 2007 For Dummies
978-0-470-00923-9

Outlook 2007 For Dummies
978-0-470-03830-7

PowerPoint 2007 For Dummies
978-0-470-04059-1

Project 2007 For Dummies
978-0-470-03651-8

QuickBooks 2008 For Dummies
978-0-470-18470-7

Quicken 2008 For Dummies
978-0-470-17473-9

Salesforce.com For Dummies, 2nd Edition
978-0-470-04893-1

Word 2007 For Dummies
978-0-470-03658-7

EDUCATION, HISTORY, REFERENCE & TEST PREPARATION

African American History For Dummies
978-0-7645-5469-8

Algebra For Dummies
978-0-7645-5325-7

Algebra Workbook For Dummies
978-0-7645-8467-1

Art History For Dummies
978-0-470-09910-0

ASVAB For Dummies, 2nd Edition
978-0-470-10671-6

British Military History For Dummies
978-0-470-03213-8

Calculus For Dummies
978-0-7645-2498-1

Canadian History For Dummies, 2nd Edition
978-0-470-83656-9

Geometry Workbook For Dummies
978-0-471-79940-5

The SAT I For Dummies, 6th Edition
978-0-7645-7193-0

Series 7 Exam For Dummies
978-0-470-09932-2

World History For Dummies
978-0-7645-5242-7

FOOD, GARDEN, HOBBIES & HOME

Bridge For Dummies, 2nd Edition
978-0-471-92426-5

Coin Collecting For Dummies, 2nd Edition
978-0-470-22275-1

Cooking Basics For Dummies, 3rd Edition
978-0-7645-7206-7

Drawing For Dummies
978-0-7645-5476-6

Etiquette For Dummies, 2nd Edition
978-0-470-10672-3

Gardening Basics For Dummies*†
978-0-470-03749-2

Knitting Patterns For Dummies
978-0-470-04556-5

Living Gluten-Free For Dummies†
978-0-471-77383-2

Painting Do-It-Yourself For Dummies
978-0-470-17533-0

HEALTH, SELF HELP, PARENTING & PETS

Anger Management For Dummies
978-0-470-03715-7

Anxiety & Depression Workbook For Dummies
978-0-7645-9793-0

Dieting For Dummies, 2nd Edition
978-0-7645-4149-0

Dog Training For Dummies, 2nd Edition
978-0-7645-8418-3

Horseback Riding For Dummies
978-0-470-09719-9

Infertility For Dummies†
978-0-470-11518-3

Meditation For Dummies with CD-ROM, 2nd Edition
978-0-471-77774-8

Post-Traumatic Stress Disorder For Dummies
978-0-470-04922-8

Puppies For Dummies, 2nd Edition
978-0-470-03717-1

Thyroid For Dummies, 2nd Edition†
978-0-471-78755-6

Type 1 Diabetes For Dummies*†
978-0-470-17811-9

* Separate Canadian edition also available
† Separate U.K. edition also available

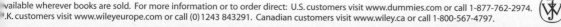
Available wherever books are sold. For more information or to order direct: U.S. customers visit www.dummies.com or call 1-877-762-2974. U.K. customers visit www.wileyeurope.com or call (0)1243 843291. Canadian customers visit www.wiley.ca or call 1-800-567-4797.

INTERNET & DIGITAL MEDIA

AdWords For Dummies
978-0-470-15252-2

Blogging For Dummies, 2nd Edition
978-0-470-23017-6

**Digital Photography All-in-One
Desk Reference For Dummies, 3rd Edition**
978-0-470-03743-0

Digital Photography For Dummies, 5th Edition
978-0-7645-9802-9

**Digital SLR Cameras & Photography
For Dummies, 2nd Edition**
978-0-470-14927-0

**eBay Business All-in-One Desk Reference
For Dummies**
978-0-7645-8438-1

eBay For Dummies, 5th Edition*
978-0-470-04529-9

eBay Listings That Sell For Dummies
978-0-471-78912-3

Facebook For Dummies
978-0-470-26273-3

The Internet For Dummies, 11th Edition
978-0-470-12174-0

Investing Online For Dummies, 5th Edition
978-0-7645-8456-5

iPod & iTunes For Dummies, 5th Edition
978-0-470-17474-6

MySpace For Dummies
978-0-470-09529-4

Podcasting For Dummies
978-0-471-74898-4

**Search Engine Optimization
For Dummies, 2nd Edition**
978-0-471-97998-2

Second Life For Dummies
978-0-470-18025-9

**Starting an eBay Business For Dummies
3rd Edition†**
978-0-470-14924-9

GRAPHICS, DESIGN & WEB DEVELOPMENT

**Adobe Creative Suite 3 Design Premium
All-in-One Desk Reference For Dummies**
978-0-470-11724-8

**Adobe Web Suite CS3 All-in-One Desk
Reference For Dummies**
978-0-470-12099-6

AutoCAD 2008 For Dummies
978-0-470-11650-0

**Building a Web Site For Dummies,
3rd Edition**
978-0-470-14928-7

**Creating Web Pages All-in-One Desk
Reference For Dummies, 3rd Edition**
978-0-470-09629-1

**Creating Web Pages For Dummies,
8th Edition**
978-0-470-08030-6

Dreamweaver CS3 For Dummies
978-0-470-11490-2

Flash CS3 For Dummies
978-0-470-12100-9

Google SketchUp For Dummies
978-0-470-13744-4

InDesign CS3 For Dummies
978-0-470-11865-8

**Photoshop CS3 All-in-One
Desk Reference For Dummies**
978-0-470-11195-6

Photoshop CS3 For Dummies
978-0-470-11193-2

Photoshop Elements 5 For Dummies
978-0-470-09810-3

SolidWorks For Dummies
978-0-7645-9555-4

Visio 2007 For Dummies
978-0-470-08983-5

Web Design For Dummies, 2nd Editio
978-0-471-78117-2

Web Sites Do-It-Yourself For Dummie
978-0-470-16903-2

Web Stores Do-It-Yourself For Dummie
978-0-470-17443-2

LANGUAGES, RELIGION & SPIRITUALITY

Arabic For Dummies
978-0-471-77270-5

Chinese For Dummies, Audio Set
978-0-470-12766-7

French For Dummies
978-0-7645-5193-2

German For Dummies
978-0-7645-5195-6

Hebrew For Dummies
978-0-7645-5489-6

Ingles Para Dummies
978-0-7645-5427-8

Italian For Dummies, Audio Set
978-0-470-09586-7

Italian Verbs For Dummies
978-0-471-77389-4

Japanese For Dummies
978-0-7645-5429-2

Latin For Dummies
978-0-7645-5431-5

Portuguese For Dummies
978-0-471-78738-9

Russian For Dummies
978-0-471-78001-4

Spanish Phrases For Dummies
978-0-7645-7204-3

Spanish For Dummies
978-0-7645-5194-9

Spanish For Dummies, Audio Set
978-0-470-09585-0

The Bible For Dummies
978-0-7645-5296-0

Catholicism For Dummies
978-0-7645-5391-2

The Historical Jesus For Dummies
978-0-470-16785-4

Islam For Dummies
978-0-7645-5503-9

**Spirituality For Dummies,
2nd Edition**
978-0-470-19142-2

NETWORKING AND PROGRAMMING

ASP.NET 3.5 For Dummies
978-0-470-19592-5

C# 2008 For Dummies
978-0-470-19109-5

Hacking For Dummies, 2nd Edition
978-0-470-05235-8

Home Networking For Dummies, 4th Edition
978-0-470-11806-1

Java For Dummies, 4th Edition
978-0-470-08716-9

**Microsoft® SQL Server™ 2008 All-in-One
Desk Reference For Dummies**
978-0-470-17954-3

**Networking All-in-One Desk Reference
For Dummies, 2nd Edition**
978-0-7645-9939-2

**Networking For Dummies,
8th Edition**
978-0-470-05620-2

SharePoint 2007 For Dummies
978-0-470-09941-4

**Wireless Home Networking
For Dummies, 2nd Edition**
978-0-471-74940-0

OPERATING SYSTEMS & COMPUTER BASICS

Mac For Dummies, 5th Edition
978-0-7645-8458-9

Laptops For Dummies, 2nd Edition
978-0-470-05432-1

Linux For Dummies, 8th Edition
978-0-470-11649-4

MacBook For Dummies
978-0-470-04859-7

**Mac OS X Leopard All-in-One
Desk Reference For Dummies**
978-0-470-05434-5

Mac OS X Leopard For Dummies
978-0-470-05433-8

Macs For Dummies, 9th Edition
978-0-470-04849-8

PCs For Dummies, 11th Edition
978-0-470-13728-4

Windows® Home Server For Dummies
978-0-470-18592-6

Windows Server 2008 For Dummies
978-0-470-18043-3

**Windows Vista All-in-One
Desk Reference For Dummies**
978-0-471-74941-7

Windows Vista For Dummies
978-0-471-75421-3

Windows Vista Security For Dummies
978-0-470-11805-4

SPORTS, FITNESS & MUSIC

Coaching Hockey For Dummies
978-0-470-83685-9

Coaching Soccer For Dummies
978-0-471-77381-8

Fitness For Dummies, 3rd Edition
978-0-7645-7851-9

Football For Dummies, 3rd Edition
978-0-470-12536-6

GarageBand For Dummies
978-0-7645-7323-1

Golf For Dummies, 3rd Edition
978-0-471-76871-5

Guitar For Dummies, 2nd Edition
978-0-7645-9904-0

**Home Recording For Musicians
For Dummies, 2nd Edition**
978-0-7645-8884-6

**iPod & iTunes For Dummies,
5th Edition**
978-0-470-17474-6

Music Theory For Dummies
978-0-7645-7838-0

Stretching For Dummies
978-0-470-06741-3

Get smart @ dummies.com®

- **Find a full list of Dummies titles**
- **Look into loads of FREE on-site articles**
- **Sign up for FREE eTips e-mailed to you weekly**
- **See what other products carry the Dummies name**
- **Shop directly from the Dummies bookstore**
- **Enter to win new prizes every month!**

Separate Canadian edition also available
Separate U.K. edition also available

Available wherever books are sold. For more information or to order direct: U.S. customers visit www.dummies.com or call 1-877-762-2974. U.K. customers visit www.wileyeurope.com or call (0) 1243 843291. Canadian customers visit www.wiley.ca or call 1-800-567-4797.